SMART DESIGN SERIES

350 NARROW-LOT HOME PLANS

Designs & Ideas for Homes up to 50 feet wide

Published by Hanley Wood
One Thomas Circle, NW, Suite 600
Washington, DC 20005

Distribution Center
29333 Lorie Lane
Wixom, Michigan 48393

Group Vice President, General Manager, Andrew Schultz
Associate Publisher, Editorial Development, Jennifer Pearce
Managing Editor, Hannah McCann
Senior Editor, Nate Ewell
Associate Editor, Simon Hyoun
Senior Plan Merchandiser, Morenci C. Clark
Plan Merchandiser, Nicole Phipps
Proofreader/Copywriter, Dyana Weis
Graphic Artist, Joong Min
Plan Data Team Leader, Susan Jasmin
Production Manager, Brenda McClary

Vice President, Retail Sales, Scott Hill
National Sales Manager, Bruce Holmes
Director, Plan Products, Matt Higgins

Most Hanley Wood titles are available at quantity discounts with bulk purchases for educational,
business, or sales promotional use. For information, please contact Bruce Holmes at bholmes@hanleywood.com.

BIG DESIGNS, INC.
President, Creative Director, Anthony D'Elia
Vice President, Business Manager, Megan D'Elia
Vice President, Design Director, Chris Bonavita
Editorial Director, John Roach
Assistant Editor, Patricia Starkey
Senior Art Director, Stephen Reinfurt
Production Director, David Barbella
Photo Editor, Christine DiVuolo
Graphic Designer, Frank Augugliaro
Graphic Designer, Billy Doremus
Graphic Designer, Jacque Young
Assistant Production Manager, Rich Fuentes

SPECIAL CONTRIBUTORS
Bishop Publishing
Editorial Director, Morin Bishop
Design Director, Barbara Chilenskas

PHOTO CREDITS
Front Cover and Page 1: Courtesy of Drummond Designs, Inc. See page 265 for details.
Back Cover Left: Courtesy of Drummond Designs, Inc. See page 8 for details.
Back Cover Right: Courtesy of Jannis Vann & Associates, Inc. See page 197 for details.
Facing Page Top Right: Courtesy of Studer Residential Designs, Inc.
Facing Page Top Left: Courtesy of Jannis Vann & Associates, Inc.
Facing Page Middle: Courtesy of Drummond Designs, Inc.

10 9 8 7 6 5 4 3 2 1

Printed in the United States of America

Library of Congress Control Number: 2005927714

ISBN-13: 978-1-93113-143-8
ISBN-10: 1-931131-43-0

SMART DESIGN SERIES

350 NARROW-LOT HOME PLANS

hanley▲wood

Contents

ONLINE EXTRA!

Hanley Wood Passageway

The Hanley Wood Passageway is an online search tool for your home plan needs! Discover even more useful information about building your new home, search additional new home plans, access online ordering, and more at www.hanleywood books.com/narrowlothomeplans

hanley▲wood

This home's charming cottage appeal would fit in any neighborhood. See page 75 for more details.

WILLIAM E. POOLE DESIGNS, INC., ISLANDS OF BEAUFORT, BEAUFORT, SC

Narrow Lots, Wide Selection
There's no shortage of gorgeous homes within these pages

The dwindling availability of land for new homes means that many of today's buildable lots are limited in size, especially width. That presents a challenge to architects and homeowners alike to create the home they want on a smaller footprint.

The designers and architects presented in these pages have certainly risen to that challenge. Working exclusively with plans under 50 feet wide, these homes show clearly that a narrow lot doesn't need to limit your choices when it comes to a new home.

Narrow lots do require proper planning and a careful eye for detail. There's no room to waste space in a narrow lot home, and the plans featured here make the most of every inch. That attention to detail is just one of several themes you'll find highlighted throughout this book. Among the others:

Attractive exteriors

Your first impression of a home begins at the curb, and a narrow exterior does nothing to limit the beauty of the homes featured here. The designers have captured some of the most time-tested, beautiful home styles—designs that are sure to provide curb appeal and offer possible solutions for any neighborhood.

Open floor plan design

One way to maximize available space in a narrow-lot home is to limit wasted space, designing floor plans that are light on unnecessary walls and hallways. Open floor plans provide not only a perfect solution for a narrow lot, but also more livable interiors. Open designs recognize that the kitchen is at the center of most families' lives—the rest of the home's living spaces extend out naturally from there. It's smart, space-saving architecture that also meshes perfectly with the way we live.

Outdoor access

A small home can feel that much larger when its living spaces open to new possibilities outdoors. You'll find this theme carried out throughout this book, as kitchens and family rooms connect easily to decks, patios, or porches. Considering outdoor living spaces now—before the building stage—will help you maximize your enjoyment of your home.

Perfect personal spaces

Part of the attention to detail that's carried through in this book is an understanding of the importance of personal space. As much as homeowners appreciate a well-crafted open floor plan that creates an informal living space, there remains a need for that one spot you can call your own. Every home in this book features a fantastic master suite that provides a personal escape—the perfect place to start and end your day. Other personal touches include studies or home offices that offer privacy, whether it's for work or just to get away with a good book.

No limit to luxury

The designers featured in these pages have created narrow homes that fit within 50-foot-wide lots, but they have placed no restraints on luxury. As more and more homeowners look to simplify their lives, they turn to smaller homes—much like these narrow designs. Instead of spending money on sprawling square footage, they take care to fill these smaller homes with the finest materials and products they can afford. Just as the designers exhibited attention to detail in creating each home's blueprints, homeowners can add their own unique touch by paying attention to every detail inside. ∎

Below: A distinctive wraparound porch gives this home (page 368) the appearance of a design much wider than its 45 feet would suggest.

Square front porch columns give this home (page 26) a distinct Craftsman appeal.

Homes For American Neighborhoods

A traditional American style can help give your narrow-lot home curb appeal

Just the fact that your narrow-lot home has, by definition, a relatively small facade doesn't limit your opportunity to create a striking and inviting exterior. In fact, with the right planning, a narrow-lot home can have all the charm and curb appeal of its larger counterparts.

It begins with making an informed decision about the architectural style you prefer. Some simply won't translate to a narrow lot—a Georgian home, for example, is traditionally much wider than it is deep. It's symmetrical.

Your search won't be too limited, however, as you'll see in this section. We've gathered a beautiful collection of "Homes for American Neighborhoods"—time-tested styles that will fit in new and established communities across the country. Many of these styles developed in cities and towns where narrow lots were common.

A broad range of styles will fit well in narrow sites, from the Greek Revival homes that were dominant in North American architecture in the first half of the 19th Century to the Craftsman homes that were popular 100 years later.

Craftsman homes, for example, first appeared in Southern California around 1903. They gained popularity quickly across the country over the next 20 years, especially in larger towns where you will still find streets lined with their square columns supporting quaint front porches.

Other styles, from Cape Cods to Victorians to Contemporary plans, present narrow-lot options as well.

Perfect Porches

Adding a front porch to your home has long been considered the perfect way to extend a friendly greeting to neighbors and passersby.

Front porches are also a fantastic opportunity to add depth to the facade of a smaller home, making it appear that much larger while providing additional living space.

Country homes have perfected this appeal of the front porch. A farmhouse or Victorian home, especially one with even a slight wraparound porch, can clearly demonstrate how this charming addition to the front of your house can make it more visually appealing.

Garage Considerations

Since so many of these architectural styles, like the first Craftsman homes, were developed before the widespread arrival of the automobile, they have been tweaked over the years to incorporate garages. Space for a garage can be especially challenging on a

Right: Arch-topped garage doors decorate the facade of this home, found on page 82.

narrow lot—many will have to face the street, and can often overwhelm the facade.

There are a number of options to consider if you would like to avoid a front-facing garage. A side-loading garage, if there is room on your lot, is often preferred. Some designs will even place a side-loading garage at the back of the house, a plan which may only require the width of the driveway to extend alongside your home.

Another possibility is a side-loading garage at the front of the home, extending toward the street. A number of plans available in this book present this option, which preserves the view of the house from the street and provides a convenient location for your garage.

Materials and More

Details can make the facade of a narrow-lot home truly spectacular. Give careful consideration not only to the architectural details while you search for a plan, but also the materials you select during the building process.

Small doesn't have to mean Spartan, and keen attention to detail in smaller homes is a growing trend in home building. More and more couples and families are choosing to live in beautiful homes that may not be the biggest on the block. The money they save by opting for a smaller square footage can be redirected towards higher-quality materials – meaning you can make a statement with your home whatever its size.

When creating curb appeal for your narrow-lot home, consider the materials you plan to use for siding, the front door, windows, and more. In some cases you may even consider using higher-quality materials on the front of your home than you do on the sides and back, to maximize your curb appeal. ∎

YOUR CARRIAGE AWAITS

Because narrow lots often force a home's garage to face the street, it can be a design challenge to prevent two large garage doors from overwhelming a home's curb appeal. Recent trends from garage door companies have offered solutions, however, in the form of "carriage house" doors with classic looks at affordable prices—and standard overhead openings like those you are accustomed to with six-panel doors. What's more, they come in a range of styles and price levels, from custom wood doors to more affordable steel options that look like wood from the street.

Simple Pleasure

A perfect starter home, this design combines comfort and practicality

This home's clean, modern lines create an open, airy feel.

This home, at just 35 feet wide and with a classic American exterior, is the perfect example of a narrow-lot home that will fit comfortably into any neighborhood. Its understated yet distinctive styling creates significant curb appeal, as its three overlapping gables in the front give the home an added sense of depth.

Inside, the homeowners have let their modern taste shine through the traditional exterior, but in a way that doesn't feel out of place. Bright colors mix with dark wood finishes to establish the style, while open spaces connecting with each other give the entire home a roomy feel.

SMART DESIGN SERIES

Left: This home features classic good looks, and can be adapted to fit on a sloping lot. Above Left: Colorful walls brighten the living spaces. Above Right: Open design enhances the family room.

The family room, dining area, and kitchen all flow together seamlessly, with a glorious sunroom located just off the kitchen for an easy transition to the outdoors. Yellow and orange walls, plus large windows, welcome light throughout the first floor. In addition, most of the family room features a two-story ceiling, giving it an even more wide-open feel. A fireplace warms the family room, while doors on either side welcome light in and invite guests out to the backyard.

The kitchen features a dining booth—a smart use of space—along with a work island and plenty of built-in storage. A bedroom—which could be used as either the master or a guest room—is also on the first floor, along with a full bath and a laundry room.

A see-through, commercial-style stairway adds to the modern look of the home, and contributes to its spacious appeal. Since most narrow-lot homes include a second floor, incorporating this type of stairway is a great way to add visual space if it will work with your decor.

The dining area opens to a sunroom, creating a greater sense of space and bringing natural light indoors.

The modern theme carries through in the dining room furniture and lighting choices. Right: The kitchen includes a mix of wood and frosted glass cabinets.

PLAN: HPK1300001

STYLE: CAPE COD

FIRST FLOOR: 958 SQ. FT.

SECOND FLOOR: 510 SQ. FT.

TOTAL: 1,468 SQ. FT.

BEDROOMS: 3

BATHROOMS: 2

WIDTH: 35' - 0"

DEPTH: 29' - 8"

FOUNDATION: UNFINISHED BASEMENT

Upstairs a hallway overlooks the family room, and two bedrooms share a full bath. The larger of the two was designed in this home with semi-transparent walls, allowing light to pass through while maintaining privacy. It's yet another design element that adds a sense of space to this smaller home.

While designed with an unfinished basement, this model was built on a hillside lot, allowing for a walkout basement and even more living space below ground. ■

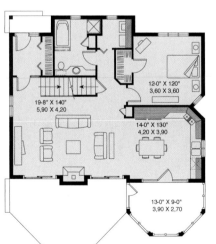

first floor

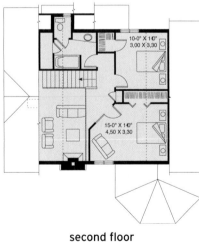

second floor

PLAN: HPK1300002

STYLE: CRAFTSMAN

FIRST FLOOR: 1,371 SQ. FT.

SECOND FLOOR: 916 SQ. FT.

TOTAL: 2,287 SQ. FT.

BEDROOMS: 3

BATHROOMS: 2½

WIDTH: 43' - 0"

DEPTH: 69' - 0"

FOUNDATION: CRAWLSPACE

■ The decorative pillars and the wraparound porch are just the beginning of this comfortable home. Inside, an angled U-shaped stairway leads to the second-floor sleeping zone. On the first floor, French doors lead to a bay-windowed den that shares a see-through fireplace with the two-story family room. The large island kitchen includes a writing desk, a corner sink, a breakfast nook, and access to the laundry room, the powder room, and the two-car garage. Upstairs, the master suite is a real treat with its French-door access, vaulted ceiling, and luxurious bath. Two other bedrooms and a full bath complete the second floor.

first floor

second floor

PLAN: HPK1300003

STYLE: CRAFTSMAN

FIRST FLOOR: 1,478 SQ. FT.

SECOND FLOOR: 629 SQ. FT.

TOTAL: 2,107 SQ. FT.

BEDROOMS: 3

BATHROOMS: 2½

WIDTH: 32' - 0"

DEPTH: 59' - 0"

FOUNDATION: CRAWLSPACE

■ With its shingle siding and decorative front porch, this Craftsman delight will shine in any neighborhood. The spacious dining room is accessed by the well-equipped kitchen via the butler's pantry. In the rear, the more private and casual breakfast nook and gathering room create an open space for intimate entertaining. The master suite on the right offers a luxurious bath, twin walk-in closets, and a bumped-out window. Two secondary bedrooms share a full bath on the second floor.

first floor

second floor

PLAN: HPK1300004

STYLE: CRAFTSMAN

FIRST FLOOR: 1,060 SQ. FT.

SECOND FLOOR: 914 SQ. FT.

TOTAL: 1,974 SQ. FT.

BEDROOMS: 3

BATHROOMS: 3

WIDTH: 32' - 0"

DEPTH: 35' - 0"

FOUNDATION: CRAWLSPACE

■ This charming Craftsman design offers a second-story master bedroom with four windows under the gabled dormer. The covered front porch displays column and pier supports. The hearth-warmed gathering room opens to the dining room on the right, where the adjoining kitchen offers enough space for an optional breakfast booth. A home office/guest suite is found in the rear. The second floor holds the lavish master suite and a second bedroom suite with its own private bath.

GARAGE
20'-0" x 22'-0"

COVERED PORCH

HOME OFFICE / GUEST SUITE
13'-2" x 13'-10"

W.I.C.

PANT.

KITCHEN
12'-0" x 15'-8"

OPT. BUILT-IN BREAKFAST BOOTH

BATH

OPT. 2ND SINK

UP

OPT. CABINETS

GATHERING ROOM
18'-6" x 14'-4"

DINING ROOM
12'-0" x 14'-4"

COVERED PORCH

first floor

LIN.

MASTER BATH

DN

SUITE 2
12'-2" x 13'-4"

W.I.C.

LAUN.

BATH

ATTIC STOR.

MASTER SUITE
14'-0" x 15'-8"

W.I.C.

ATTIC STOR.

second floor

PLAN: HPK1300323

STYLE: CRAFTSMAN

FIRST FLOOR: 1,440 SQ. FT.

SECOND FLOOR: 1,514 SQ. FT.

TOTAL: 2,954 SQ. FT.

BEDROOMS: 4

BATHROOMS: 3½

WIDTH: 30' - 0"

DEPTH: 68' - 0"

FOUNDATION: FINISHED BASEMENT

■ A stylish Craftsman at just under 3,000 square feet, this home features an open layout ideal for entertaining. Rooms are distinguished by columns, eliminating the use of unnecessary walls. At the rear of the home, the expansive family room, warmed by a fireplace, faces the adjoining breakfast area and kitchen. Access to the sundeck makes alfresco meals an option. A walk-in pantry is an added bonus. The second floor houses the family bedrooms, including the lavish master suite, two bedrooms separated by a Jack-and-Jill bath, and a fourth bedroom with a private, full bath. The second floor laundry room is smart and convenient. A centrally located, optional computer station is perfect for a family computer. A sizable recreation room on the basement level completes this plan.

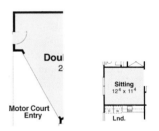

optional layouts

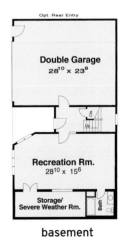

basement

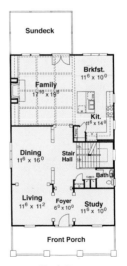

first floor

second floor

PLAN: HPK1300005

STYLE: TRADITIONAL

FIRST FLOOR: 1,282 SQ. FT.

SECOND FLOOR: 541 SQ. FT.

TOTAL: 1,823 SQ. FT.

BEDROOMS: 3

BATHROOMS: 2½

WIDTH: 32' - 0"

DEPTH: 49' - 8"

FOUNDATION: CRAWLSPACE

■ This intriguing Northeastern-style home celebrates unique angles, beautiful details, and a fresh look for a home like no other. Enter from a columned porch to the airy gathering room, warmed by a cozy corner hearth. An open floor plan places the dining room to the left with a clear view of the fireplace. An arched hall leads past a powder room to the wide galley kitchen and sunny breakfast nook. The master suite is located nearby, complete with a box-bay sitting area, massive walk-in closet, and a lavish private bath. A staircase at the front of the home wraps around an open area and presents two generous bedrooms that share a Jack-and-Jill bath. A two-car garage at the rear of the home provides plenty of room for the family fleet, without blocking the home's enchanting facade.

first floor

second floor

PLAN: HPK1300006

STYLE: CRAFTSMAN
FIRST FLOOR: 1,392 SQ. FT.
SECOND FLOOR: 708 SQ. FT.
TOTAL: 2,100 SQ. FT.
BEDROOMS: 3
BATHROOMS: 2½
WIDTH: 32' - 0"
DEPTH: 55' - 0"
FOUNDATION: CRAWLSPACE

■ Craftsman stylings grace this two-story traditional home, designed for a narrow lot. Shingles and siding present a warm welcome; the front porch opens to the dining room and the gathering room, allowing great entertainment options. The kitchen connects to the living areas with a snack bar and works hard with an island and lots of counter space. The master suite is on this level and delights in a very private bath. Two bedrooms on the upper level have private vanities and a shared bath. Extra storage or bonus space is available for future development.

first floor

second floor

PLAN: HPK1300007

STYLE: TRADITIONAL

SQUARE FOOTAGE: 1,161

BONUS SPACE: 891 SQ. FT.

BEDROOMS: 3

BATHROOMS: 1½

WIDTH: 38' - 0"

DEPTH: 42' - 5"

FOUNDATION: UNFINISHED BASEMENT

■ This spacious split-level home is well suited to a medium-to-narrow-frontage lot. Steps lead up to a covered front porch at the entry with a single door into the foyer and double doors into the living room. The living room and dining room are part of one large open area, warmed by a fireplace. The kitchen is L-shaped and saves room for a breakfast table. The kitchen can be isolated by pocket doors at each entrance. A few steps up take you to the upper-level sleeping quarters. The master bedroom sits to the back and features a walk-in closet and half-bath. Family bedrooms sit to the front and share a full bath. Unfinished space in the basement provides 891 square feet for future development that might include a family room with fireplace and an additional bedroom with half-bath. The two-car garage offers storage and work-bench space.

first floor

din
9'5 X 9'5

k
10'6 X 12'4

brk

mbr
10'10 X 12'4

WALK-IN CLOSET

12'4 X 16'
liv

VERANDAH

9' X 11'5
br3

10' X 10'5
br2

GARAGE WALL LINE BELOW

basement

UNFINISHED

UNFINISHED

UNFINISHED

F

W D

STOR. BENCH

20'7 X 20'6
two-car garage

BRICK PLANTER

PLAN: HPK1300008

STYLE: TRADITIONAL

FIRST FLOOR: 1,266 SQ. FT.

SECOND FLOOR: 856 SQ. FT.

TOTAL: 2,122 SQ. FT.

BONUS SPACE: 301 SQ. FT.

BEDROOMS: 4

BATHROOMS: 2½

WIDTH: 40' - 0"

DEPTH: 52' - 10"

FOUNDATION: UNFINISHED WALKOUT BASEMENT

■ This bright and airy home will surely make your time at home the best part of your day. Light streams into the living and dining rooms through a wall of three tall windows. A fireplace offers cheery nights, and a rear door opens to a porch. The family room, host to a second fireplace, and the multiwindowed breakfast area work well as a unit. A den—or make it a spare bedroom—and a sunny bonus room round out the main level. Sure to bring pleasure, the luxurious master suite enjoys a front-facing box bay with three big windows. Two other bedrooms share a bath with a skylight; one of the rooms boasts corner windows. The plan comes with a two-car garage.

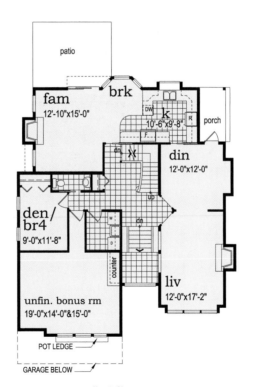

first floor

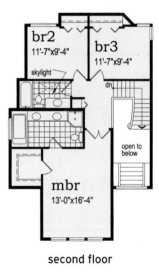

second floor

PLAN: HPK1300009

STYLE: CAPE COD

FIRST FLOOR: 1,387 SQ. FT.

SECOND FLOOR: 929 SQ. FT.

TOTAL: 2,316 SQ. FT.

BEDROOMS: 4

BATHROOMS: 3

WIDTH: 30' - 0"

DEPTH: 51' - 8"

FOUNDATION: CRAWLSPACE

THIS HOME, AS SHOWN IN THE PHOTOGRAPH, MAY DIFFER FROM THE ACTUAL BLUEPRINTS. FOR MORE DETAILED INFORMATION, PLEASE CHECK THE FLOOR PLANS CAREFULLY.
ANDREW LAUTMAN, LAUTMAN PHOTOGRAPHY

rear exterior

■ Perfect for a narrow lot, this shingle-and-stone Nantucket Cape home caters to the casual lifestyle. The side entrance gives direct access to the wonderfully open living areas: gathering room with fireplace and an abundance of windows; island kitchen with angled, pass-through snack bar; and dining area with sliding glass doors to a covered eating area. Note also the large deck that further extends the living potential. Also on this floor is the large master suite with a compartmented bath, private dressing room, and walk-in closet. Upstairs, you'll find the three family bedrooms. Of the two bedrooms that share a bath, one features a private balcony.

first floor

second floor

PLAN: HPK1300010

STYLE: CRAFTSMAN

FIRST FLOOR: 1,302 SQ. FT.

SECOND FLOOR: 960 SQ. FT.

TOTAL: 2,262 SQ. FT.

BEDROOMS: 3

BATHROOMS: 2^1/$_2$

WIDTH: 40' - 0"

DEPTH: 40' - 0"

FOUNDATION: CRAWLSPACE

■ This vacation home is certain to be a family favorite. The two-story great room boasts a built-in media center, access to a front deck, and a two-sided fireplace, shared by the adjacent den. The spacious island kitchen is ideal for entertaining. The second floor houses the master suite, two additional family bedrooms, and a full bath. A workshop and extra storage space in the garage are added bonuses.

garage

first floor

second floor

PLAN: HPK1300011

STYLE:	CRAFTSMAN
FIRST FLOOR:	1,109 SQ. FT.
SECOND FLOOR:	970 SQ. FT.
TOTAL:	2,079 SQ. FT.
BEDROOMS:	3
BATHROOMS:	2½
WIDTH:	45' - 0"
DEPTH:	52' - 0"
FOUNDATION:	CRAWLSPACE

■ Two-story homes truly maximize usable space on a lot—essentially, you get twice as much home with the same amount of lot space as a one-story home. But that's not the only—or even best reason—to build this one. This home has an enchanting exterior, and an expertly executed floor plan. An angled entry opens to a foyer that contains a half-bath, coat closet, and stairway to the upper level. A home office with window seat is at the front of the plan; the vaulted great room and dining area is at the back. A fireplace keeps gatherings cozy in the great room; a covered porch off the dining area inspires al fresco meals. The master suite is on the upper level, along with two family bedrooms.

first floor

DINING
14/0 X 12/0
(9' CLG.)

PORCH
12/6 X 7/6

VAULTED
GREAT RM.
18/0 X 15/0

14/0 X 10/8 +/-
(9' CLG.)

PAN

REF

GARAGE
11/0 X 19/0

UP

STOR

OFFICE
12/6 X 10/0 +
(9' CLG.)

GARAGE
19/0 X 21/0

WINDOW SEAT

© by Designer, All Rights Reserved

second floor

VAULTED
MASTER
14/0 X 17/6

SPA

DN.

SHELVES

LINEN

BR. 2
11/2 X 10/4

PLANT
SHELF

BR. 3
11/10 X 10/2

PLAN: HPK1300012

STYLE: COUNTRY COTTAGE

FIRST FLOOR: 1,171 SQ. FT.

SECOND FLOOR: 993 SQ. FT.

TOTAL: 2,164 SQ. FT.

BEDROOMS: 3

BATHROOMS: 2½

WIDTH: 45' - 0"

DEPTH: 49' - 0"

FOUNDATION: CRAWLSPACE

■ Faux sash glazing and shutters on the windows, a stone facade, and tiered gables give this exterior an old-fashioned appeal. Inside, a tiered hallway with a half bath leads to the great room, with vaulted ceiling and fireplace. This room features great outdoor viewing and access to a rear porch. The dining area forms a large room with the kitchen, centering around a contoured prep island and snack bar. The dining room also offers exit to the outside. A handy desk is built into the kitchen next to the refrigerator. An office to the right of the entry and a garage with 11' x 16' shop round out the main floor. All three bedrooms are found upstairs, as is a balcony area to the first floor and closets galore. The master bedroom contains a vaulted ceiling and luxury spa for true luxury. Also note the designated attic/storage space.

first floor

second floor

PLAN: HPK1300013

STYLE: CRAFTSMAN
FIRST FLOOR: 1,216 SQ. FT.
SECOND FLOOR: 1,390 SQ. FT.
TOTAL: 2,606 SQ. FT.
BEDROOMS: 4
BATHROOMS: $2\frac{1}{2}$
WIDTH: 50' - 0"
DEPTH: 42' - 0"
FOUNDATION: CRAWLSPACE

■ Little things mean a lot—and here, the details add up to a marvelous plan. Exterior elements lend curb appeal to the two-story layout. Stone accents, lap siding, and a dormer window highlight the attention in the exterior planning. Both formal and casual dining spaces are included, and flank an open kitchen that overlooks the great room. At the back of the plan, near a service entry to the double garage, are a laundry room and half bath. Sleeping quarters are upstairs, and include three family bedrooms and a master suite. A spa tub, separate shower, dual sinks, and a walk-in closet highlight the master bath. Family bedrooms share a full bath with double sinks.

first floor

second floor

PLAN: HPK1300014

STYLE: TRADITIONAL

FIRST FLOOR: 1,142 SQ. FT.

SECOND FLOOR: 1,463 SQ. FT.

TOTAL: 2,605 SQ. FT.

BEDROOMS: 3

BATHROOMS: 2½

WIDTH: 50' - 0"

DEPTH: 42' - 0"

FOUNDATION: CRAWLSPACE

■ A touch of European styling dresses the facade of this comfortable two-story home. Stone detailing at the main level and around the entryway complements board-and-batten siding above. Beyond the foyer lies open living space with a great room, dining room, and kitchen. Decorative columns define the areas, and help to visually separate them, while still providing a sense of space. The great room rises a full two stories, and is graced by a hearth and media center. The dining room features a wall of windows on one side, and sliding glass doors (to the rear yard) on the other. A tucked-away nook at the back of the plan serves well as a home office or den. On the upper level is a vaulted master suite with bath. Bedroom 3 shares a full bath with Bedroom 2. Shop space in the two-car garage will appeal to the family handyperson.

first floor

second floor

PLAN: HPK1300015

STYLE: TRADITIONAL

FIRST FLOOR: 1,207 SQ. FT.

SECOND FLOOR: 1,147 SQ. FT.

TOTAL: 2,354 SQ. FT.

BEDROOMS: 4

BATHROOMS: 3½

WIDTH: 48' - 0"

DEPTH: 49' - 0"

■ Stone and siding lend a rustic look to this two-story home. Columns define the formal dining room and family room where a fireplace is centered between two windows. The U-shaped, island kitchen adjoins the sunny morning nook. The living room/study resides to the left of the foyer. The mudroom does double-duty as a utility room. The second floor houses the sleeping quarters, including the master suite and three additional bedrooms that share a full bath.

first floor

second floor

PLAN: HPK1300016

STYLE: COUNTRY COTTAGE

FIRST FLOOR: 1,198 SQ. FT.

SECOND FLOOR: 668 SQ. FT.

TOTAL: 1,866 SQ. FT.

BEDROOMS: 4

BATHROOMS: 2½

WIDTH: 40' - 0"

DEPTH: 47' - 0"

FOUNDATION: CRAWLSPACE

■ A fine example of a Craftsman bungalow, this four-bedroom home will be a delight to own. The efficient kitchen offers a serving island to the dining area, while the glow from the corner fireplace in the great room adds cheer to the entire area. Located on the first floor for privacy, the vaulted master bedroom features a walk-in closet, a private bath with a dual-bowl vanity, and access to the rear yard. Upstairs, three secondary bedrooms share a full hall bath and a large linen closet. The two-car garage will easily shelter the family fleet.

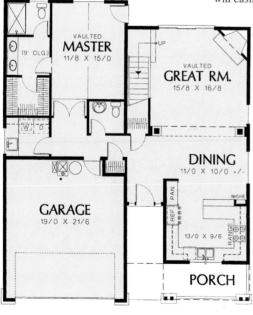

first floor

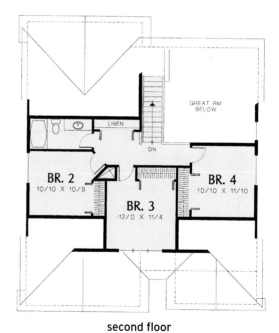

second floor

PLAN: HPK1300017

STYLE: TRADITIONAL
FIRST FLOOR: 716 SQ. FT.
SECOND FLOOR: 784 SQ. FT.
TOTAL: 1,500 SQ. FT.
BATHROOMS: 2½
WIDTH: 36' - 0"
DEPTH: 44' - 0"
FOUNDATION: CRAWLSPACE

■ A traditional neighborhood look is accented by stone and decorative arches on this stylish new design. Simplicity is the hallmark of this plan, giving the interior great flow and openness. The foyer, with a coat closet, leads directly into the two-story great room with abundant natural light and a warming fireplace. The island kitchen and dining area are to the left and enjoy rear-porch access. Upstairs, a vaulted master suite with a private bath joins two additional bedrooms to complete the plan.

second floor

first floor

PLAN: HPK1300018

STYLE: CRAFTSMAN

FIRST FLOOR: 1,118 SQ. FT.

SECOND FLOOR: 1,335 SQ. FT.

TOTAL: 2,453 SQ. FT.

BEDROOMS: 4

BATHROOMS: 2$\frac{1}{2}$

WIDTH: 48' - 0"

DEPTH: 40' - 0"

FOUNDATION: CRAWLSPACE

■ Ideal for a corner lot, the combination of wood siding and stone complements a carriage-style garage door and cedar shingle detailing on the outside of this home. The interior opens through an angled front entry, with den on the left and a half-bath on the right. The back of the main level is lined with an open living/dining area. The dining area adjoins an island kitchen, complete with a roomy pantry and built-in desk. Bedrooms are on the upper level. They include a vaulted master suite with spa bath, walk-in closet with window seat, and separate tub and shower. The second floor laundry room is an added convenience.

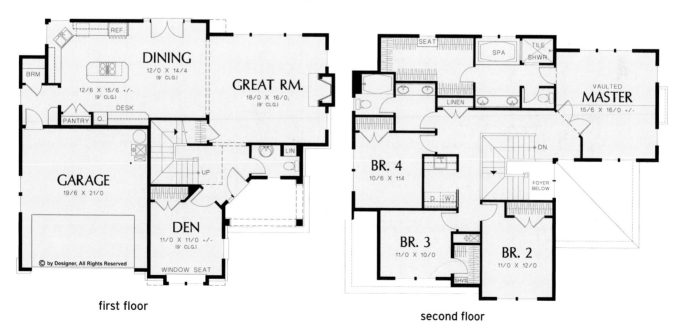

first floor

second floor

PLAN: HPK1300019

STYLE: TRADITIONAL
FIRST FLOOR: 968 SQ. FT.
SECOND FLOOR: 977 SQ. FT.
TOTAL: 1,945 SQ. FT.
BEDROOMS: 4
BATHROOMS: $2\frac{1}{2}$
WIDTH: 40' - 0"
DEPTH: 46' - 0"
FOUNDATION: CRAWLSPACE

■ This traditional home offers lovely formal rooms for entertaining. The living room has a centered fireplace and access to the front covered porch. A gourmet kitchen with a cooktop island serves the dining room. French doors open the morning nook to the outdoors; a second fireplace warms the family room. Upstairs, the master suite has a corner walk-in closet and an oversized shower. Three secondary bedrooms are connected by a stair hall.

first floor

second floor

PLAN: HPK1300020

STYLE: CRAFTSMAN

FIRST FLOOR: 970 SQ. FT.

SECOND FLOOR: 988 SQ. FT.

TOTAL: 1,958 SQ. FT.

BEDROOMS: 3

BATHROOMS: 2½

WIDTH: 40' - 0"

DEPTH: 43' - 0"

FOUNDATION: CRAWLSPACE

■ A sensible floor plan, with living spaces on the first floor and bedrooms on the second floor, is the highlight of this Craftsman home. Elegance reigns in the formal living room, with a vaulted ceiling and columned entry; this room is open to the dining room, which is brightened by natural light from two tall windows. Ideal for informal gatherings, the family room boasts a fireplace flanked by built-in shelves. The efficient kitchen includes a central island and double sink, and the nearby nook features easy access to the outdoors through sliding glass doors. The master suite includes a lavish bath with a corner spa tub and compartmented toilet; two additional bedrooms, one with a walk-in closet, share a full bath.

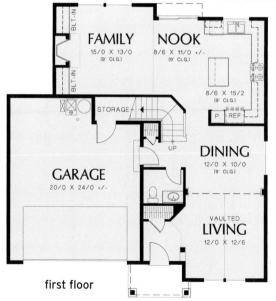

first floor

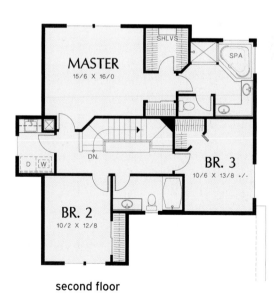

second floor

PLAN: HPK1300021

STYLE: CRAFTSMAN

FIRST FLOOR: 1,561 SQ. FT.

SECOND FLOOR: 578 SQ. FT.

TOTAL: 2,139 SQ. FT.

BONUS SPACE: 238 SQ. FT.

BEDROOMS: 3

BATHROOMS: $2\frac{1}{2}$

WIDTH: 50' - 0"

DEPTH: 56' - 6"

FOUNDATION: CRAWLSPACE, UNFINISHED WALKOUT BASEMENT, SLAB

■ Come home to this delightful bungalow, created with you in mind. From the covered front porch, the foyer opens to the dining room on the left and vaulted family room ahead. An elongated island in the well-planned kitchen makes meal preparation a joy. A sunny breakfast nook is perfect for casual pursuits. Tucked to the rear, the master suite enjoys ultimate privacy and a luxurious break from the world with a vaulted bath and garden tub. Secondary bedrooms share a full bath upstairs; a bonus room is ready to expand as your needs change.

first floor

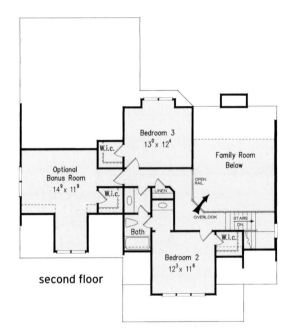

second floor

PLAN: HPK1300022

STYLE: TRADITIONAL

FIRST FLOOR: 919 SQ. FT.

SECOND FLOOR: 927 SQ. FT.

TOTAL: 1,846 SQ. FT.

BATHROOMS: 2½

WIDTH: 44' - 0"

DEPTH: 40' - 0"

QUOTE ONE®

■ This wonderful design begins with the wraparound porch. Explore further and find a two-story entry with a coat closet and plant shelf above and a strategically placed staircase alongside. The island kitchen with a boxed window over the sink is adjacent to a large bay-windowed dinette. The great room includes many windows and a fireplace. A powder room and laundry room are both conveniently placed on the first floor. Upstairs, the large master suite contains His and Hers walk-in closets, corner windows, and a bath area featuring a double vanity and whirlpool tub. Two pleasant secondary bedrooms have interesting angles, and a third bedroom in the front features a volume ceiling and an arched window.

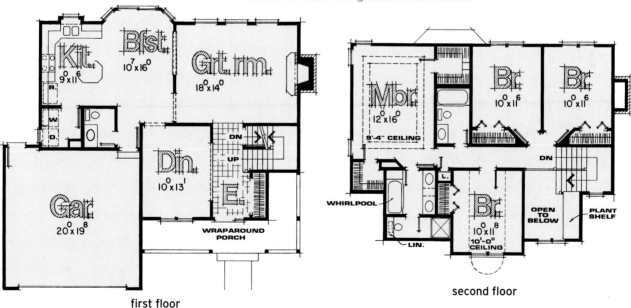

first floor

second floor

PLAN: HPK1300023

STYLE: CRAFTSMAN

FIRST FLOOR: 1,283 SQ. FT.

SECOND FLOOR: 1,010 SQ. FT.

TOTAL: 2,293 SQ. FT.

BEDROOMS: 4

BATHROOMS: 3½

WIDTH: 38' - 0"

DEPTH: 59' - 0"

FOUNDATION: UNFINISHED WALKOUT BASEMENT

■ A stone-and-siding facade, and availability of alternate elevations provide a unique design for this traditional Craftsman. A columned front porch transitions to a curved entry, which steps into the living room's two-story clearance. The dining and kitchen area combine to create one spacious room. The kitchen features a center island, snack bar, and L-shaped counter space. A bayed window in the dining area provides peaceful views of the rear, as does an exit to the porch. The master bedroom also offers private access to the porch. Upstairs are three more bedrooms with two additional baths, and a study with built-in cabinets and desks. A balcony provides views to the first floor.

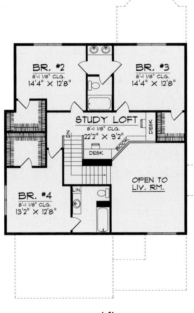

first floor

second floor

PLAN: HPK1300024

STYLE: TRADITIONAL

FIRST FLOOR: 1,369 SQ. FT.

SECOND FLOOR: 1,336 SQ. FT.

TOTAL: 2,705 SQ. FT.

BEDROOMS: 4

BATHROOMS: 2½

WIDTH: 49' - 0"

DEPTH: 46' - 4"

■ This spacious four-bedroom home offers a Craftsman-style facade with shingled gables and column and pier porch supports. A convenient butler's pantry is situated between the dining room and the hearth room. In the far left corner of the first floor, the family room offers a see-through fireplace and a built-in entertainment center. The master suite, three additional bedrooms, and a full bath join a computer loft on the second floor.

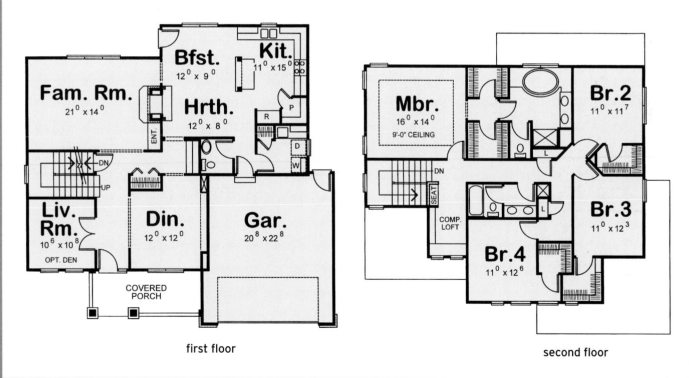

first floor

second floor

PLAN: HPK1300025

STYLE: COUNTRY COTTAGE

FIRST FLOOR: 916 SQ. FT.

SECOND FLOOR: 895 SQ. FT.

TOTAL: 1,811 SQ. FT.

BONUS SPACE: 262 SQ. FT.

BEDROOMS: 3

BATHROOMS: 2½

WIDTH: 44' - 0"

DEPTH: 38' - 0"

FOUNDATION: SLAB,
UNFINISHED WALKOUT
BASEMENT, CRAWLSPACE

■ Gables at varying heights, a traditional front porch, and shuttered windows give a small-town look to this family home. The two-story foyer leads to the dining room on the left or to the family room, which is straight ahead past the powder room, coat closet, and entrance to the garage. The family room is open to the kitchen, which boasts a work island, corner window sink, and access to the laundry room. The second floor contains a master suite with two walk-in closets, two family bedrooms that share a bath but have private walk-in closets, an overlook to the foyer below, and an optional bonus room

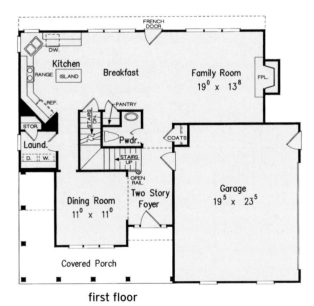

first floor

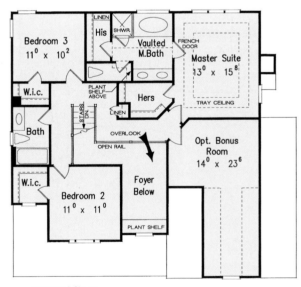

second floor

PLAN: HPK1300026

STYLE: CRAFTSMAN

FIRST FLOOR: 1,496 SQ. FT.

SECOND FLOOR: 615 SQ. FT.

TOTAL: 2,111 SQ. FT.

BONUS SPACE: 277 SQ. FT.

BEDROOMS: 3

BATHROOMS: 2½

WIDTH: 40' - 4"

DEPTH: 70' - 0"

© 2002 Donald A. Gardner, Inc.

■ Stone, siding, and jack-arch details create a traditional Craftsman plan you will love to come home to. Thoughtful details, including built-in cabinets, a fireplace, and a snack bar to the kitchen, will make the great room a family favorite. Porches off the great room and breakfast nook, one screened and one open, invite outdoor living. The master suite is located at the rear of the plan for quiet and privacy. Here, His and Hers closets and a lavish bath are sure to delight. Two upstairs bedrooms and a bonus room round out this home.

second floor

first floor

Houses For American Neighborhoods

PLAN: HPK1300027

STYLE: SOUTHERN COLONIAL

FIRST FLOOR: 1,645 SQ. FT.

SECOND FLOOR: 563 SQ. FT.

TOTAL: 2,208 SQ. FT.

BONUS SPACE: 255 SQ. FT.

BEDROOMS: 3

BATHROOMS: 2½

WIDTH: 50' - 0"

DEPTH: 54' - 0"

FOUNDATION: CRAWLSPACE, UNFINISHED WALKOUT BASEMENT, SLAB

■ This Southern Country home will charm you from the curb, but don't stop there! Inside, a wonderful floor plan offers natural light, spacious rooms, and options to expand. The two-story foyer opens on the right to an elegant dining room. Continue past an art niche to the vaulted family room, lit by radius windows that frame a fireplace. The island kitchen is conveniently located near the breakfast nook and large laundry room. A keeping room offers a cozy place to relax. The master suite claims the entire left side of the home, with a lavish spa bath and abundant closet space. Two bedrooms on the second floor share a full bath and access optional bonus space.

first floor

second floor

PLAN: HPK1300028

STYLE: COUNTRY COTTAGE

FIRST FLOOR: 1,862 SQ. FT.

SECOND FLOOR: 661 SQ. FT.

TOTAL: 2,523 SQ. FT.

BONUS SPACE: 315 SQ. FT.

BEDROOMS: 3

BATHROOMS: 2½

WIDTH: 56' - 0"

DEPTH: 56' - 6"

FOUNDATION: UNFINISHED WALKOUT BASEMENT, CRAWLSPACE

■ Fabulous amenities and breathtaking heights are exciting features of this traditional design. The huge vaulted family room with fireplace dominates the center of the plan, separating the master suite and dining/cooking areas. Upstairs, an overlook loft provides utility space as well as design interest for the upstairs bedrooms. An optional bonus room is an inspiring blank canvas for the owners to express their lifestyle; turn the space into a study, exercise room, home office, media room, studio, or fourth bedroom. Pleasing dormers and a gabled entry beautify the exterior.

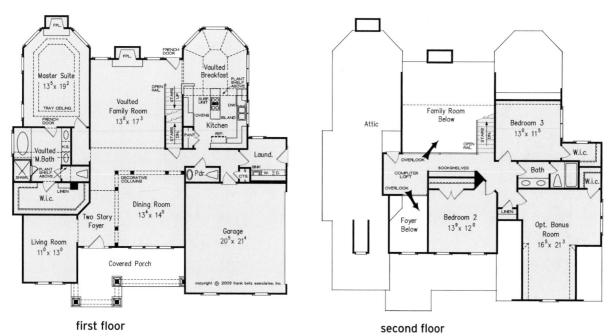

first floor

second floor

PLAN: HPK1300029

STYLE: COUNTRY COTTAGE

FIRST FLOOR: 1,405 SQ. FT.

SECOND FLOOR: 1,226 SQ. FT.

TOTAL: 2,631 SQ. FT.

BEDROOMS: 5

BATHROOMS: 3

WIDTH: 49' - 0"

DEPTH: 49' - 0"

FOUNDATION: CRAWLSPACE

■ A wealth of windows in the front of this two-story country home creates ample natural light throughout. Once inside, the formal living room and dining room flank the foyer. A short hallway leads to the family room. A fireplace on the rear wall warms the U-shaped kitchen and breakfast area to the left. A serving bar allows casual dining in both areas. A family bedroom/office and full bath complete the first floor. The second floor houses the master suite, enhanced by a tray-ceiling, and boasting a walk-in closet, roomy bath with dual-sink vanities, separate shower and tub, and a private toilet. Three additional family bedrooms on this floor share a full bath.

PLAN: HPK1300030

STYLE: COUNTRY COTTAGE
FIRST FLOOR: 1,716 SQ. FT.
SECOND FLOOR: 618 SQ. FT.
TOTAL: 2,334 SQ. FT.
BEDROOMS: 3
BATHROOMS: 3
WIDTH: 47' - 0"
DEPTH: 50' - 0"
FOUNDATION: CRAWLSPACE

■ This country farmhouse enjoys special features such as gables, dormers, plenty of windows, and a covered front porch. Columns adorn the home throughout for an extra touch of elegance. The formal dining room enjoys a tray ceiling and is open to the kitchen, which enjoys access to either a utility room or the breakfast nook with a bay window. The massive great room enjoys a vaulted ceiling, a cozy fireplace, and built-ins—French doors tie this room to a vaulted rear porch. On the left of this home is a study/office along with the sumptuous master suite. The second floor holds two family bedrooms—both with walk-in closets and built-in desks—sharing a full bath.

first floor

second floor

PLAN: HPK1300031

STYLE: FARMHOUSE
FIRST FLOOR: 1,710 SQ. FT.
SECOND FLOOR: 618 SQ. FT.
TOTAL: 2,328 SQ. FT.
BEDROOMS: 3
BATHROOMS: 3
WIDTH: 47' - 0"
DEPTH: 50' - 0"
FOUNDATION: CRAWLSPACE

■ Decorative details complement this home's country facade, and pedimented arches and a covered porch add sophistication. The foyer leads to the vaulted great room where a fireplace awaits. Both the magnificent master suite and the great room showcase French doors to the rear vaulted porch. The breakfast bay sheds sunlight onto the spacious kitchen. An elegant coffered ceiling and three-window bay dress up the front study (or make it into an office). Two bedrooms, both with walk-in closets, share the second level with a bath and an equipment room.

first floor

second floor

PLAN: HPK1300032

STYLE: FARMHOUSE
FIRST FLOOR: 1,710 SQ. FT.
SECOND FLOOR: 618 SQ. FT.
TOTAL: 2,328 SQ. FT.
BEDROOMS: 3
BATHROOMS: 3
WIDTH: 47' - 0"
DEPTH: 50' - 0"
FOUNDATION: CRAWLSPACE

■ Here's a new American farmhouse that's just right for any neighborhood—in town or far away. A perfect interior starts with an open foyer and interior vistas through a fabulous great room. A fireplace anchors the living space while a beamed, vaulted ceiling adds volume. Decorative columns open the central interior to the gourmet kitchen and breakfast area, which boasts a bay window. The master wing includes a study that easily converts to a home office. Upstairs, the secondary bedrooms feature built-in desks and walk-in closets.

first floor

second floor

PLAN: HPK1300033

STYLE: CRAFTSMAN
FIRST FLOOR: 1,322 SQ. FT.
SECOND FLOOR: 1,262 SQ. FT.
TOTAL: 2,584 SQ. FT.
BEDROOMS: 4
BATHROOMS: 3
WIDTH: 48' - 0"
DEPTH: 50' - 0"
FOUNDATION: CRAWLSPACE,
UNFINISHED WALKOUT
BASEMENT, SLAB

■ With Craftsman detail and traditional charm, this four-bedroom home captures the comfort and style you've been searching for. From a wrapping porch, enter the two-story foyer with a decorative niche that displays special photos or treasures to all your guests. Continue to a beautiful family room, graced with a two-story ceiling and second-floor radius windows. The kitchen is open and spacious, leading to a breakfast area, hearth-warmed keeping room, and elegant dining room. A bedroom on this level also serves as an ideal den or home office. Upstairs, two secondary bedrooms share a full bath. The master suite is ready for relaxation with a sunny sitting room and soothing vaulted bath. A laundry room on this level makes wash day a breeze.

first floor

second floor

PLAN: HPK1300034

STYLE: COUNTRY COTTAGE

FIRST FLOOR: 1,290 SQ. FT.

SECOND FLOOR: 985 SQ. FT.

TOTAL: 2,275 SQ. FT.

BONUS SPACE: 186 SQ. FT.

BEDROOMS: 4

BATHROOMS: 3

WIDTH: 45' - 0"

DEPTH: 43' - 4"

FOUNDATION: CRAWLSPACE,
UNFINISHED WALKOUT
BASEMENT, SLAB

■ This casually elegant European Country-style home offers more than just a slice of everything you've always wanted: it is designed with room to grow. Formal living and dining rooms are defined by decorative columns and open from a two-story foyer, which leads to open family space. A two-story family room offers a fireplace and shares a French door to the rear property with the breakfast room. A gallery hall with a balcony overlook connects two sleeping wings upstairs. The master suite boasts a vaulted bath, and the family hall leads to bonus space.

first floor

second floor

■ A brick one-story garage with a flowerbox window lends this two-story home a cottage feel. Inside, efficient use of space and flexibility adds to the appeal. A formal dining room opens from the two-story foyer, and leads to a cleverly designed kitchen. A serving bar connects the kitchen and breakfast nook. The hearth-warmed family room is just steps away. Four bedrooms—three family bedrooms and a roomy master suite—fill the second level. Note the option of turning Bedroom 4 into a sitting area for the master suite.

PLAN: HPK1300035

STYLE: COUNTRY COTTAGE

FIRST FLOOR: 947 SQ. FT.

SECOND FLOOR: 981 SQ. FT.

TOTAL: 1,928 SQ. FT.

BEDROOMS: 4

BATHROOMS: 2½

WIDTH: 41' - 0"

DEPTH: 39' - 4"

FOUNDATION: CRAWLSPACE, UNFINISHED WALKOUT BASEMENT

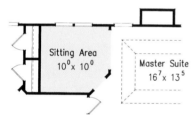

Sitting Area 10⁰ x 10⁰

Master Suite 16⁷ x 13⁵

optional layout

first floor

second floor

PLAN: HPK1300036

STYLE: COUNTRY COTTAGE

FIRST FLOOR: 990 SQ. FT.

SECOND FLOOR: 912 SQ. FT.

TOTAL: 1,902 SQ. FT.

BONUS SPACE: 116 SQ. FT.

BEDROOMS: 4

BATHROOMS: 3

WIDTH: 47' - 0"

DEPTH: 37' - 4"

FOUNDATION: UNFINISHED WALKOUT BASEMENT, CRAWLSPACE

■ This traditional country cottage boasts a household filled with amenities. Beyond the covered front porch, the foyer welcomes you to a dining room. The kitchen overlooks the breakfast room with a pantry. The two-story grand room offers a fireplace, a French door to the rear, and an open-rail staircase to the second floor. The fourth bedroom can be converted to a home office. Upstairs, the master suite features a vaulted bath, walk-in closet, and optional sitting room. Two family bedrooms and a full bath complete the plan.

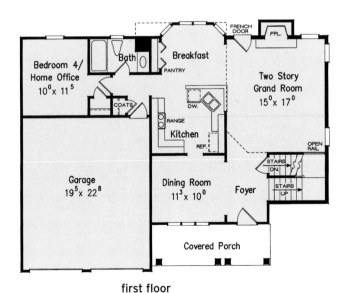

first floor

second floor

PLAN: HPK1300037

STYLE: COUNTRY COTTAGE

SQUARE FOOTAGE: 1,509

BEDROOMS: 3

BATHROOMS: 2

WIDTH: 49' - 0"

DEPTH: 34' - 4"

FOUNDATION: UNFINISHED
WALKOUT BASEMENT

■ Inside this well-planned traditional home, an elegant sunlit foyer leads up a short flight of stairs to an immense vaulted great room with a fireplace. Arched openings lead to the open bayed breakfast area and kitchen. The master suite is tucked to one side with plenty of amenities—entrance to a private covered porch, plenty of storage, and decorative built-in plant shelves. Two family bedrooms occupy the opposite side of the home and share a full bath and more closet space. An unfinished basement provides for future lifestyle needs.

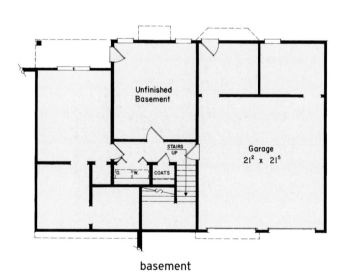

basement

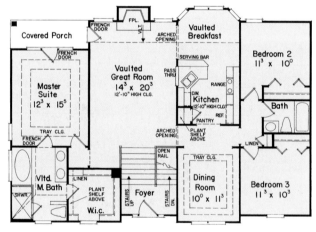

first floor

PLAN: HPK1300038

STYLE: TRADITIONAL

SQUARE FOOTAGE: 1,363

BEDROOMS: 3

BATHROOMS: 2

WIDTH: 44' - 0"

DEPTH: 43' - 0"

FOUNDATION: UNFINISHED BASEMENT

■ A columned, covered entry charms the exterior of this three-bedroom, split-entry home. Inside, a one-and-a-half-story foyer boasts a dual staircase—one up to the main-floor living area and the other down to the basement. The living area includes a gas fireplace and windows on all walls, ensuring natural light. The adjacent dining room with a buffet alcove exits through a sliding glass door to the rear patio. The roomy kitchen has a raised snack bar, built-in pantry, and access to a bayed eating area surrounded by windows. A skylight brightens the hall to the three bedrooms. Look for His and Hers closets and a private bath in the master suite. Future expansion is reserved for space on the lower level.

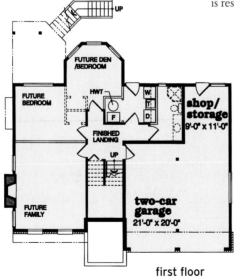

first floor

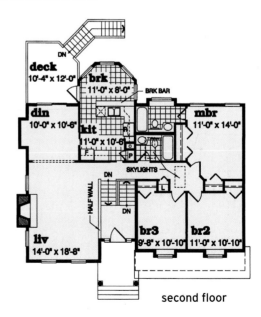

second floor

PLAN: HPK1300039

STYLE: TRADITIONAL

MAIN LEVEL: 1,392 SQ. FT.

LOWER LEVEL: 560 SQ. FT.

TOTAL: 1,952 SQ. FT.

BEDROOMS: 3

BATHROOMS: 2

WIDTH: 46' - 0"

DEPTH: 30' - 10"

FOUNDATION: FINISHED
WALKOUT BASEMENT

■ By entering this home between two levels, the foyer distributes the traffic to either the main areas of the home or the garage and future areas on the lower level. A huge archtop window in the living room is a focal point and bathes the room in sunlight. Adjacent is a formal dining room, perfect for entertaining. The large kitchen has a flair of its own, including angled cabinets and a bayed breakfast area leading to the rear sun deck. Three bedrooms complete this level of the home. Two family bedrooms on the front share a hall bath. The master bedroom includes an octagonal tray ceiling which adds to the elegance of the large room. A vaulted garden bath and large walk-in closet complete the suite. The lower level of the plan has abundant bonus space to extend the living space of the upper level.

main level

lower level

PLAN: HPK1300040

STYLE: COUNTRY COTTAGE

MAIN LEVEL: 1,249 SQ. FT.

LOWER LEVEL: 46 SQ. FT.

TOTAL: 1,295 SQ. FT.

BEDROOMS: 3

BATHROOMS: 2

WIDTH: 45' - 0"

DEPTH: 31' - 4"

FOUNDATION: UNFINISHED WALKOUT BASEMENT

■ With a double garage and unfinished basement space on the lower level, this design lives like a one-story home, but has the space of two levels. A vaulted great room features a fireplace flanked by windows. The U-shaped kitchen features a large dining area and a corner window sink. Bedrooms are split for privacy, with the master suite to the right of the great room and family bedrooms to the left. Note the many pampering amenities in the master suite.

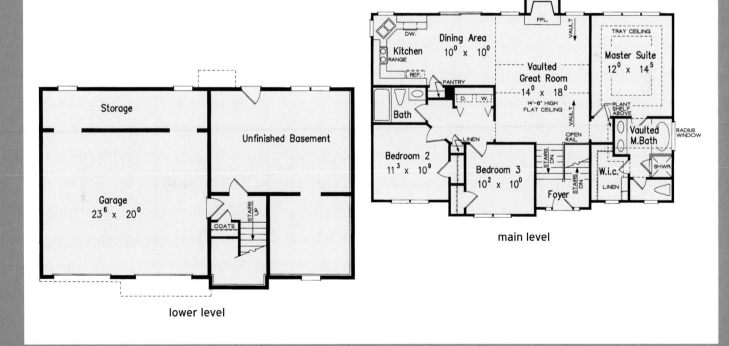

lower level

main level

PLAN: HPK1300041

STYLE: TRADITIONAL

FIRST FLOOR: 1,092 SQ. FT.

SECOND FLOOR: 1,059 SQ. FT.

TOTAL: 2,151 SQ. FT.

BEDROOMS: 3

BATHROOMS: 2½

WIDTH: 48' - 0"

DEPTH: 38' - 4"

FOUNDATION: CRAWLSPACE, UNFINISHED WALKOUT BASEMENT

■ Volume ceilings play a part in this design: both the family room and the foyer are two-story areas with overlooks from above. A powder room and a coat closet are directly off the foyer, which opens on the left to the living room and dining room and directly ahead to the kitchen and breakfast area. Upstairs, the master suite features a sitting room and, through French doors, a luxurious bath and walk-in closet. Two family bedrooms—one with a walk-in closet—share a bath that has a double-bowl vanity.

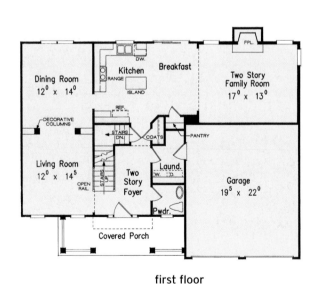

first floor

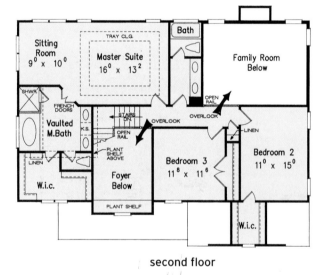

second floor

PLAN: HPK1300042

STYLE: COUNTRY COTTAGE

FIRST FLOOR: 1,351 SQ. FT.

SECOND FLOOR: 1,312 SQ. FT.

TOTAL: 2,663 SQ. FT.

BEDROOMS: 4

BATHROOMS: 3

WIDTH: 50' - 0"

DEPTH: 41' - 4"

FOUNDATION: CRAWLSPACE, UNFINISHED WALKOUT BASEMENT

■ Brick, siding, and bright windows embellish this Colonial-influenced home. Flexibility is the bedrock of this plan, with options to fit your lifestyle. The upper-level master suite can be transformed to include a private sitting room. This exquisite suite has unique diamond-shaped bath with separate vanities and a tub with a built-in shelf above. Downstairs, employ a guest room or opt for a home office. The two-story family room allows for versatility of interior design.

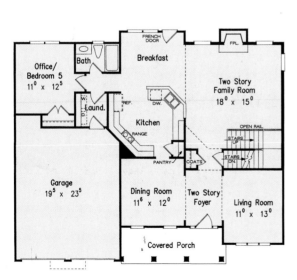

first floor

second floor

PLAN: HPK1300043

STYLE: CRAFTSMAN

FIRST FLOOR: 889 SQ. FT.

SECOND FLOOR: 865 SQ. FT.

TOTAL: 1,754 SQ. FT.

BEDROOMS: 3

BATHROOMS: $2^{1}/_{2}$

WIDTH: 50' - 0"

DEPTH: 40' - 10"

FOUNDATION: UNFINISHED BASEMENT

■ A three-bedroom, two-story home with distinctive design elements that add value and lasting beauty to a home make this a choice for any neighborhood. A large foyer with an exciting turned staircase and rich wood railing reminds one of an earlier era. The foyer combined with a grand opening to the great room and fireplace wall presents an attractive first impression. Numerous windows allow an abundance of light to brighten the great room and dining area and continue into the kitchen. An open counter with seating separates the dining area and provides for quick meals and conversation. A second-floor master bedroom suite with spacious walk-in closet and garden bath creates a pleasurable retreat. The large upstairs hall with built-in desk and shelf area provides for a shared computer or study area. Two additional bedrooms—each with walk-in closets—creates a home designed for individual comfort and convenience.

second floor

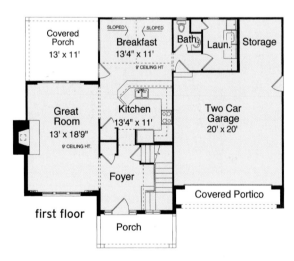

first floor

PLAN: HPK1300044

STYLE: CRAFTSMAN

FIRST FLOOR: 1,130 SQ. FT.

SECOND FLOOR: 1,070 SQ. FT.

TOTAL: 2,200 SQ. FT.

BEDROOMS: 4

BATHROOMS: 2½

WIDTH: 49' - 0"

DEPTH: 40' - 0"

■ A sophisticated stone-and-siding facade goes well with the windows that align this home. The covered entry opens to the sunny living room which is in turn connected to the dining room. The adjoining island kitchen serves both the dining room and the breakfast nook with ease and efficiency. The family room enjoys a hearth and a beautiful view. Three family bedrooms and a master suite are located upstairs.

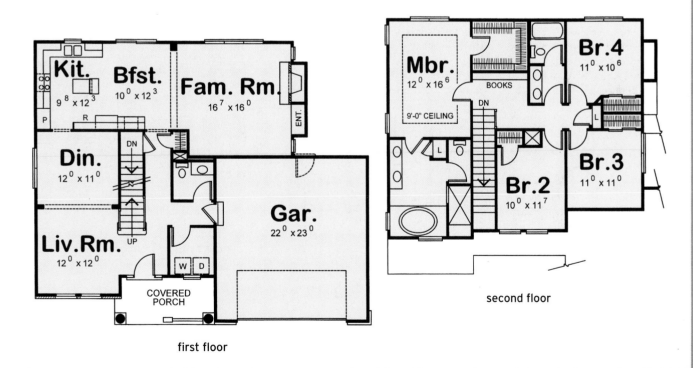

first floor

second floor

PLAN: HPK1300045

STYLE: TRADITIONAL

FIRST FLOOR: 915 SQ. FT.

SECOND FLOOR: 994 SQ. FT.

TOTAL: 1,909 SQ. FT.

BEDROOMS: 3

BATHROOMS: 2½

WIDTH: 38' - 0"

DEPTH: 38' - 0"

FOUNDATION: UNFINISHED BASEMENT

3,60 X 2,50
12'-0" X 8'-4"

4,20 X 3,70
14'-0" X 12'-4"

5,50 X 4,20
18'-4" X 14'-0"

4,00 X 6,10
13'-4" X 20'-4"

2,20 X 2,40
7'-4" X 8'-0"

first floor

4,40 X 3,60
14'-8" X 12'-0"

3,10 X 4,20
10'-4" X 14'-0"

3,60 X 3,90
12'-0" X 13'-0"

second floor

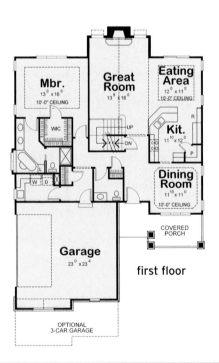

Mbr.
13'0 x 16'6
10'-0" CEILING

WIC

Great Room
13'8 x 18'0

Eating Area
12'0 x 11'0
10'-0" CEILING

Kit.
11'10 x 12'0

Dining Room
11'10 x 11'0
10'-0" CEILING

Garage
23'0 x 23'4

COVERED PORCH

OPTIONAL 3-CAR GARAGE

first floor

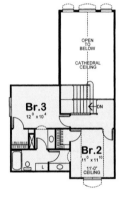

OPEN TO BELOW

CATHEDRAL CEILING

Br.3
12'0 x 10'4

Br.2
11'0 x 11'10
11'-0" CEILING

second floor

PLAN: HPK1300046

STYLE: TRADITIONAL

FIRST FLOOR: 1,503 SQ. FT.

SECOND FLOOR: 516 SQ. FT.

TOTAL: 2,019 SQ. FT.

BEDROOMS: 3

BATHROOMS: 2 ½

WIDTH: 43' - 4"

DEPTH: 60' - 8"

PLAN: HPK1300047

STYLE: TRADITIONAL
FIRST FLOOR: 1,830 SQ. FT.
SECOND FLOOR: 925 SQ. FT.
TOTAL: 2,755 SQ. FT.
BEDROOMS: 4
BATHROOMS: 2½
WIDTH: 50' - 0"
DEPTH: 63' - 0"

■ Arched windows and decorative shutters lend a country feel to this traditional design. Inside, a two-story foyer opens on the right to a vaulted study and on the left to the dining room. Arches invite all to enter the living room, where an 18-foot vault and corner fireplace create a pleasant ambiance. Beyond the gourmet kitchen and sunny nook, the master suite is tucked away with a tray ceiling and French doors to the extravagant bath. Three upper-level bedrooms share a full bath and game room with plenty of space to kick back and relax. The plan is completed by a three-car garage.

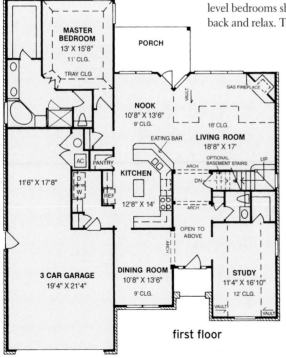

first floor

second floor

PLAN: HPK1300048

STYLE:	TRADITIONAL
FIRST FLOOR:	1,650 SQ. FT.
SECOND FLOOR:	1,038 SQ. FT.
TOTAL:	2,688 SQ. FT.
BEDROOMS:	4
BATHROOMS:	$3\frac{1}{2}$
WIDTH:	50' - 0"
DEPTH:	60' - 0"

■ Charming highlights abound in this quaint family manor. A petite covered porch welcomes you to the foyer; inside, the dining room/optional study is open to the immense living room with a corner fireplace. The kitchen features an island, pantry, and an eating bar which overlooks the bayed breakfast nook. The three-car garage accommodates everyone in the family. The master suite resides on the first floor for privacy and offers a private bath and walk-in closet. Upstairs, three family bedrooms and a playroom complete the home.

first floor

second floor

PLAN: HPK1300049

STYLE: TRADITIONAL

SQUARE FOOTAGE: 1,595

BONUS SPACE: 312 SQ. FT.

BEDROOMS: 3

BATHROOMS: 2

WIDTH: 49' - 0"

DEPTH: 60' - 0"

■ Varying rooflines and strong brick columns leading to the entrance provide bold first impressions to visitors of this home. Come inside to find a practical and inviting floor plan filled with thoughtful touches. Secluded to the far left of the plan are two bedrooms which share a full bath; the master suite is tucked away in the back right corner of the plan with an enormous walk-in closet and master bath. Living spaces are open to each other, with the kitchen easily serving the nook and living room—adorned with a lovely plant ledge—and a dining room nearby. Venture upstairs to the optional game room and finish it at your leisure.

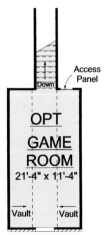

Access Panel

Down

OPT GAME ROOM
21'-4" x 11'-4"

Vault   Vault

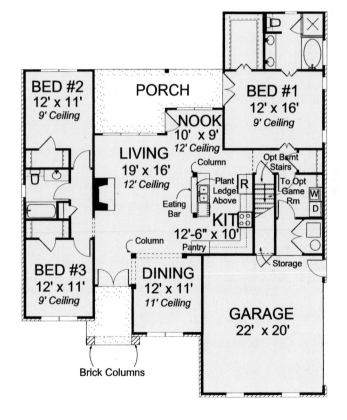

BED #2
12' x 11'
9' Ceiling

PORCH

BED #1
12' x 16'
9' Ceiling

NOOK
10' x 9'
12' Ceiling

LIVING
19' x 16'
12' Ceiling

Column

Opt Bsmt Stairs

Plant Ledge Above

R

To Opt Game Rm

W   D

Eating Bar

KIT
12'-6" x 10'

BED #3
12' x 11'
9' Ceiling

Column

Pantry

Storage

DINING
12' x 11'
11' Ceiling

GARAGE
22' x 20'

Brick Columns

PLAN: HPK1300050

STYLE: COUNTRY COTTAGE
SQUARE FOOTAGE: 1,768
BEDROOMS: 3
BATHROOMS: 2
WIDTH: 49' - 0"
DEPTH: 66' - 0"

■ "Neat and tidy" sums up this French cottage design. Front-facing roof gables, an arched front porch, and a bay window on the dining room offer a welcome to all. From the foyer, arches work to combine the cavernous living area, dining room, and kitchen. A corner fireplace frames the living room and an expansive view through the screened porch to the rear property. A modern and convenient kitchen offers a raised eating bar, preparation island, and a pantry. A view to the side porch is available from the nook. The kitchen lets off to family bedrooms on the right-hand side of this plan, with a separate bath from the rest of the house, and lots of individual closet space. The master suite on the left side has private access to the study. Double doors open to the bath, which contains a corner, Roman-style tub, enormous walk-in closet with built-in shelving, compartmented toilet and shower, and dual vanities.

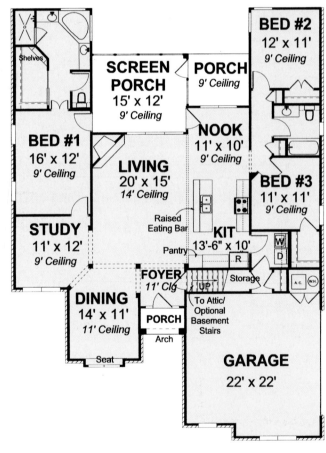

PLAN: HPK1300051

STYLE: TRADITIONAL

SQUARE FOOTAGE: 1,694

BEDROOMS: 4

BATHROOMS: 2

WIDTH: 50' - 0"

DEPTH: 53' - 0"

■ A rustic front porch and shed dormer lend Craftsman flavor to this traditional one-story home. The foyer opens to the dining room, which leads into the well-planned kitchen. Ahead, an open arrangement makes the living room and morning nook appear more spacious, enhanced by a vaulted ceiling and porch access. The master suite is situated for privacy and delights in a private bath. Three bedrooms complete the plan on the opposite side of the home; one may be turned into a study, accessed from the foyer through French doors.

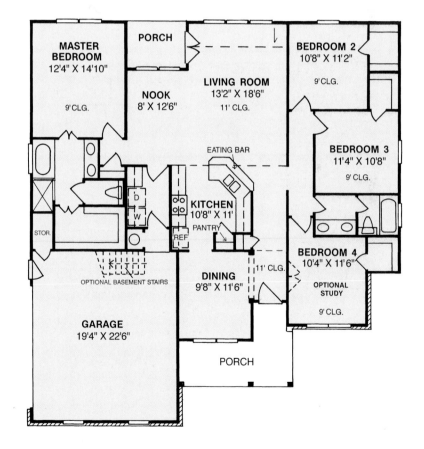

PLAN: HPK1300052

STYLE: TRADITIONAL
FIRST FLOOR: 1,568 SQ. FT.
SECOND FLOOR: 680 SQ. FT.
TOTAL: 2,248 SQ. FT.
BEDROOMS: 4
BATHROOMS: 2½
WIDTH: 50' - 0"
DEPTH: 48' - 0"

■ Dramatic gables and a vintage frame shape the exterior of this family design. Formal rooms flank the foyer; ahead, the vaulted family room is warmed by a corner fireplace. The kitchen is thoughtfully placed between the dining room and casual breakfast nook. The master suite is a pampering retreat with a walk-in closet and private bath with a whirlpool tub. Upstairs, three additional bedrooms—all with walk-in closets—share a full bath.

first floor

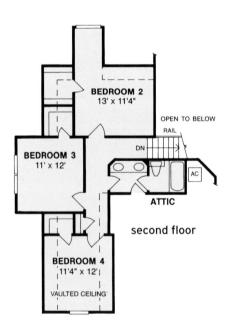

second floor

PLAN: HPK1300053

STYLE: TRADITIONAL

SQUARE FOOTAGE: 1,606

BONUS SPACE: 338 SQ. FT.

BEDROOMS: 3

BATHROOMS: 2

WIDTH: 50' - 0"

DEPTH: 54' - 0"

■ This smart, traditional plan packs a lot of living space into its modest square footage. A stately columned porch leads to the foyer, which boasts a convenient coat closet to its left. Just ahead, the great room's cathedral ceiling amplifies elegance; its cozy hearth offers the warmth of home. The kitchen features ample counter space and is book-ended by a formal dining room and a sunny breakfast nook. The rear deck will provide many seasons of fun and relaxation. Two bedrooms—one that could be converted to a study—share a full bath on the left of the plan. A divine master suite is secluded behind the garage, with a vaulted ceiling, stunning master bath, and walk-in closet. The utility room is convenient to both the kitchen and the garage. Bonus space awaits expansion upstairs.

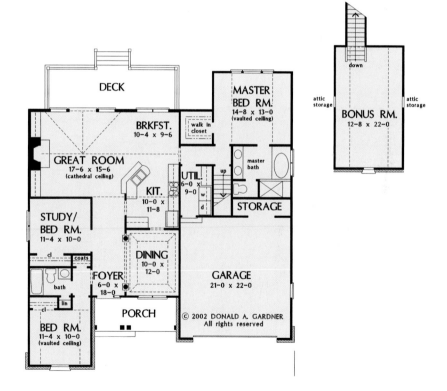

© 2002 Donald A. Gardner, Inc.

PLAN: HPK1300054

STYLE: CRAFTSMAN

SQUARE FOOTAGE: 1,952

BONUS SPACE: 339 SQ. FT.

BEDROOMS: 4

BATHROOMS: 3

WIDTH: 50' - 0"

DEPTH: 60' - 0"

■ As at home in a development as it is in an orchard, this design combines country charm with Craftsman appeal. A Palladian-style window fills the study/bedroom with light, and a stone wall and cozy front porch recall times past. A sole column and tray ceiling distinguish the dining room that opens to a great room, which features French doors to the rear porch and a striking two-room fireplace. An angled counter separates the kitchen from the great room and breakfast nook. With a master bath, two full additional baths, an optional study/bedroom, and a bonus room, this home has plenty of space for growing families.

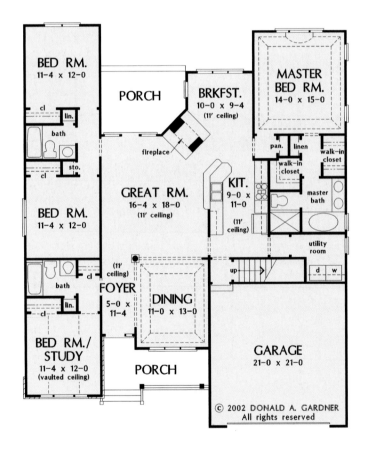

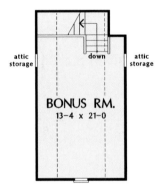

PLAN: HPK1300055

STYLE: TRADITIONAL

SQUARE FOOTAGE: 1,700

BONUS SPACE: 333 SQ. FT.

BEDROOMS: 3

BATHROOMS: 2

WIDTH: 49' - 0"

DEPTH: 65' - 4"

■ This homespun traditional plan has a porch that goes on and on—and that's accessible from nearly every room in the house. Columns and fanlight windows dress up the facade; the interior offers a unique layout that's perfect for family living. The hearth-warmed great room is amplified by a cathedral ceiling, and it views the porch at the side and rear. The spacious kitchen, complete with pantry, opens to a bay-windowed breakfast nook that has a door to the porch. Three bedrooms make up the right wing's sleeping quarters, including two that share a full bath and access to the utility room. The deluxe master suite at the rear boasts a picture window, walk-in closet, elegant bath, and porch access. Upstairs, bonus space can become whatever kind of room you wish.

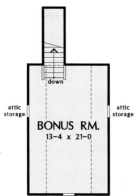

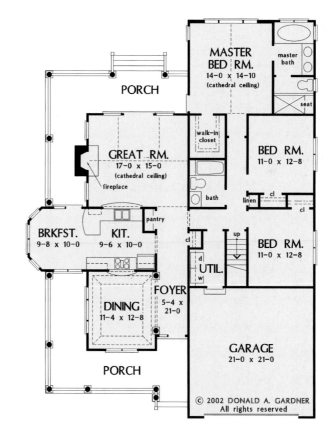

© 2001 Donald A. Gardner, Inc.

PLAN: HPK1300056

STYLE: CRAFTSMAN
FIRST FLOOR: 1,707 SQ. FT.
SECOND FLOOR: 514 SQ. FT.
TOTAL: 2,221 SQ. FT.
BONUS SPACE: 211 SQ. FT.
BEDROOMS: 4
BATHROOMS: 2½
WIDTH: 50' - 0"
DEPTH: 71' - 8"

■ Stone and horizontal siding give a definite country flavor to this two-story home. The front study makes an ideal guest room with the adjoining powder room. The formal dining room is accented with decorative columns that define its perimeter. The great room boasts a fireplace, built-ins, and a magnificent view of the backyard beyond one of two rear porches. The master suite boasts two walk-in closets and a private bath. Two bedrooms share a full bath on the second floor.

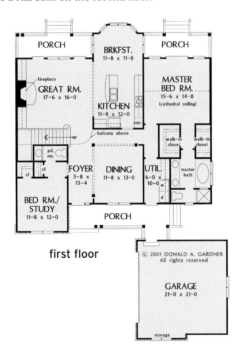

first floor

© 2001 DONALD A. GARDNER
All rights reserved

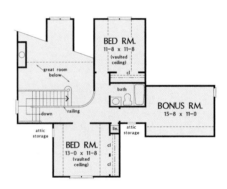

second floor

PLAN: HPK1300057

PLAN: HPK1300057

STYLE: CRAFTSMAN

FIRST FLOOR: 1,608 SQ. FT.

SECOND FLOOR: 581 SQ. FT.

TOTAL: 2,189 SQ. FT.

BEDROOMS: 3

BATHROOMS: 2½

WIDTH: 46' - 0"

DEPTH: 63' - 0"

■ Arched lintels and a stone pediment add European flair to this design, while a wide porch support and matchstick detailing add a Craftsman flavor. The expansive great room, just to the left of the foyer, boasts a vaulted ceiling, a fireplace, and built-in bookshelves; elegant columns define the adjacent dining room. The kitchen showcases a central island cooktop and opens to a cozy porch. The master suite, conveniently close to the laundry area, also features a vaulted ceiling as well as a walk-in closet. On the second floor, two family bedrooms include walk-in closets and share a full bath.

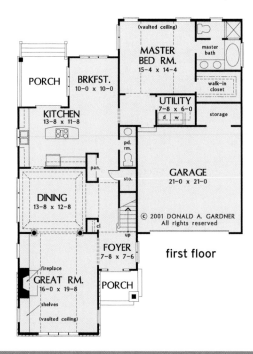

first floor

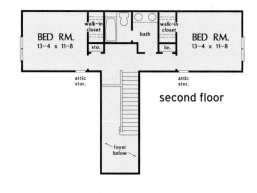

second floor

© William E. Poole Designs, Inc.

PLAN: HPK1300058

STYLE: COUNTRY COTTAGE
FIRST FLOOR: 1,627 SQ. FT.
SECOND FLOOR: 783 SQ. FT.
TOTAL: 2,410 SQ. FT.
BONUS SPACE: 418 SQ. FT.
BEDROOMS: 4
BATHROOMS: 2½
WIDTH: 46' - 0"
DEPTH: 58' - 6"
FOUNDATION: CRAWLSPACE

■ This "little jewel" of a home emanates a warmth and joy not soon forgotten. The two-story foyer leads to the formal living room, defined by graceful columns. A formal dining room opens off from the living room, making entertaining a breeze. A family room at the back features a fireplace and works well with the kitchen and breakfast areas. A lavish master suite is secluded on the first floor; three family bedrooms reside upstairs.

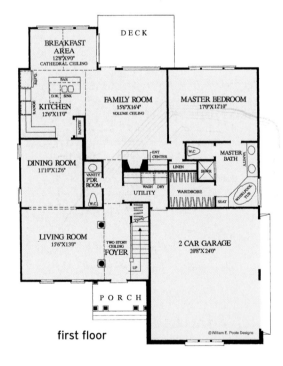

first floor

second floor

PLAN: HPK1300059

STYLE: COUNTRY COTTAGE

FIRST FLOOR: 1,001 SQ. FT.

SECOND FLOOR: 466 SQ. FT.

TOTAL: 1,467 SQ. FT.

BONUS SPACE: 292 SQ. FT.

BEDROOMS: 3

BATHROOMS: 2½

WIDTH: 42' - 0"

DEPTH: 42' - 0"

FOUNDATION: CRAWLSPACE, UNFINISHED WALKOUT BASEMENT, SLAB

■ Arched transoms set off by keystones add the final details to the traditional exterior of this home. The foyer opens to a vaulted family room, which enjoys a warm fireplace and leads to a two-story dining area with built-in plant shelves and to a U-shaped kitchen with an angled countertop and spacious pantry. Down the hall, the abundant master suite boasts a tray ceiling and can be found in its own secluded area. Upstairs, two additional bedrooms are found sharing a full bath—note both bedrooms enjoy French doors. An optional bonus room with a walk-in closet is included in this plan.

first floor

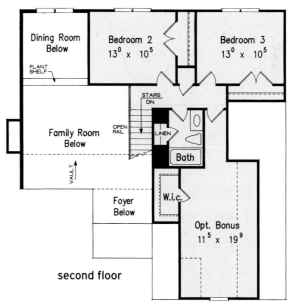

second floor

PLAN: HPK1300060

STYLE:	COUNTRY COTTAGE
SQUARE FOOTAGE:	1,627
BEDROOMS:	3
BATHROOMS:	2
WIDTH:	37' - 0"
DEPTH:	66' - 0"
FOUNDATION:	SLAB

■ This easy-living design offers plenty of open spaces and height without sacrificing function. A laundry/utility room placed near the kitchen ensures quiet enjoyment for those in the bedroom, as well as easy entry to the kitchen. The continuous breakfast nook and family room form the heart of the plan and allow privacy in the master suite. A tray ceiling, large walk-in closet, compartmented toilet, and whirlpool tub make this suite a quiet retreat. Two more bedrooms and a full bath complete the plan.

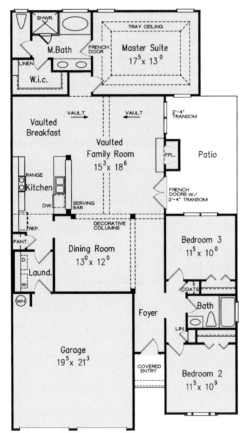

PLAN: HPK1300061

STYLE: SOUTHERN COLONIAL

SQUARE FOOTAGE: 1,671

BEDROOMS: 3

BATHROOMS: 2

WIDTH: 50' - 0"

DEPTH: 51' - 0"

FOUNDATION: SLAB,
CRAWLSPACE, UNFINISHED
WALKOUT BASEMENT

■ Asymmetrical gables, a columned porch, and an abundance of windows brighten the exterior of this compact home. An efficient kitchen boasts a pantry and a serving bar that it shares with the formal dining room and the vaulted family room. A sunny breakfast room and nearby laundry room complete the living zone. Be sure to notice extras such as the focal-point fireplace in the family room and a plant shelf in the laundry room. The sumptuous master suite offers a door to the backyard, a vaulted sitting area, and a pampering bath. Two family bedrooms share a hall bath.

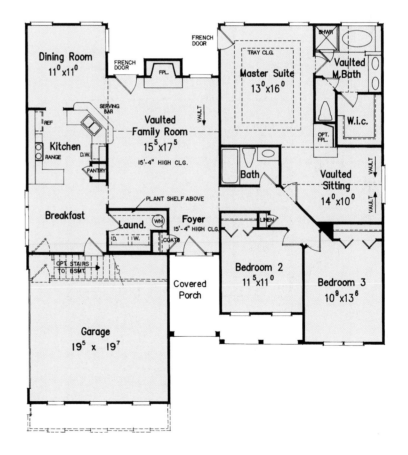

PLAN: HPK1300062

STYLE: COUNTRY COTTAGE

SQUARE FOOTAGE: 1,506

BEDROOMS: 3

BATHROOMS: 2

WIDTH: 40' - 0"

DEPTH: 52' - 0"

FOUNDATION: SLAB, UNFINISHED WALKOUT BASEMENT, CRAWLSPACE

■ Stunning brick facade is highlighted by elegant arched accents on entry and garage, a copper-topped bow window, and a single gable. A petite floor plan offers all the comforts of a much larger home without wasting space or functionality. Two family bedrooms sit to the front of the design and share a full hall bath. The master suite enjoys a rear view, tray ceiling, walk-in closet, and private bath. Vaulted ceilings add height and elegance to the family room, featuring a fireplace, and the dining room. The unique shape of the kitchen maintains efficient planning and still provides space for more casual meals in the breakfast space.

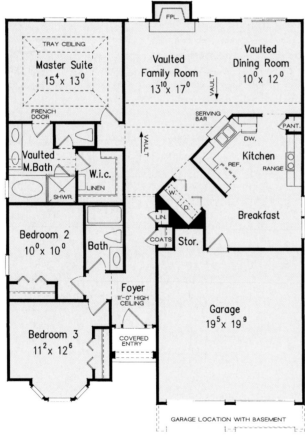

PLAN: HPK1300063

STYLE: CRAFTSMAN

SQUARE FOOTAGE: 1,544

BEDROOMS: 2

BATHROOMS: 2

WIDTH: 40' - 0"

DEPTH: 60' - 0"

FOUNDATION: FINISHED

WALKOUT BASEMENT

■ This Cape Cod design is enhanced with shingles, stone detailing, and muntin windows. The entry is flanked on the left by a bedroom/den, perfect for overnight guests or a cozy place to relax. The hearth-warmed great room enjoys expansive views of the rear deck area. The dining room is nestled next to the island kitchen, which boasts plenty of counter space. The master bedroom is positioned at the rear of the home for privacy and accesses a private bath. Two family bedrooms and a spacious games room complete the finished basement.

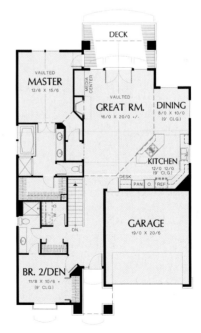

PLAN: HPK1300064

STYLE: TRANSITIONAL
FIRST FLOOR: 1,814 SQ. FT.
SECOND FLOOR: 923 SQ. FT.
TOTAL: 2,737 SQ. FT.
BEDROOMS: 4
BATHROOMS: 2½
WIDTH: 50' - 0"
DEPTH: 54' - 0"
FOUNDATION: CRAWLSPACE

■ The foyer of this modern stucco home is flanked by a den and formal dining room and leads directly to the dramatic two-story great room. The angled kitchen adjoins the sunny breakfast nook and serves the formal dining room with ease. The master suite boasts a tray ceiling and private bath with a corner tub, separate shower, walk-in closet and dual sinks. Upstairs, three additional family bedrooms share one full bath.

first floor

second floor

PLAN: HPK1300065

STYLE: COUNTRY COTTAGE

FIRST FLOOR: 1,704 SQ. FT.

SECOND FLOOR: 734 SQ. FT.

TOTAL: 2,438 SQ. FT.

BONUS SPACE: 479 SQ. FT.

BEDROOMS: 3

BATHROOMS: 3½

WIDTH: 50' - 0"

DEPTH: 82' - 6"

FOUNDATION: CRAWLSPACE

■ Elegant country—that's one way to describe this attractive three-bedroom home. Inside, comfort is evidently the theme, with the formal dining room flowing into the U-shaped kitchen and casual dining taking place in the sunny breakfast area. The spacious, vaulted great room offers a fireplace and built-ins. The first-floor master suite is complete with a walk-in closet, a whirlpool tub, and a separate shower. Upstairs, the sleeping quarters include two family bedrooms with private baths and walk-in closets.

first floor

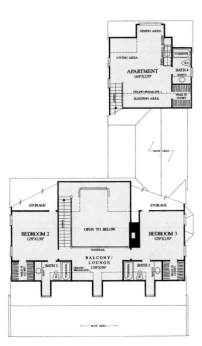

second floor

PLAN: HPK1300066

STYLE: TRADITIONAL

SQUARE FOOTAGE: 1,879

FUTURE SPACE: 965 SQ. FT.

BEDROOMS: 3

BATHROOMS: 2

WIDTH: 45' - 0"

DEPTH: 62' - 0"

FOUNDATION: SLAB,
UNFINISHED BASEMENT,
CRAWLSPACE

■ A sunburst over the entry door, columns supporting the covered porch, three dormers, and shutters give this home a comforting air. Inside, the living room contains a warming fireplace framed by windows. Sunshine or moonlight fills the formal dining room through bay windows—making any meal a glowing experience. The kitchen adjoins the dining room with a snack bar and shares the natural lighting of both the sunroom and the dining area. Nearby, the master suite has a private bath with a walk-in closet, separate shower, large oval tub, and two-sink vanity. Two bedrooms share a full bath accessed via the living room.

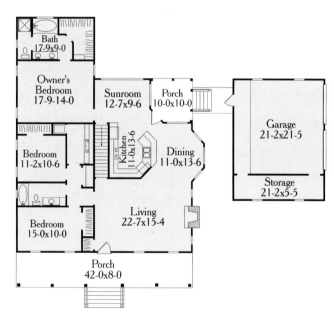

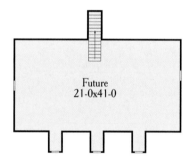

PLAN: HPK1300067

STYLE: CAPE COD

FIRST FLOOR: 1,016 SQ. FT.

SECOND FLOOR: 766 SQ. FT.

TOTAL: 1,782 SQ. FT.

BEDROOMS: 3

BATHROOMS: 2½

WIDTH: 33' - 0"

DEPTH: 30' - 0"

FOUNDATION: UNFINISHED BASEMENT

■ Here's an expandable Colonial with a full measure of Cape Cod charm. Salt-box shapes and modular structures popular in Early America enjoyed a revival at the turn of the century and have come to life again—this time with added square footage and some very comfortable amenities. Upstairs, a spacious master suite shares a gallery hall which leads to two family bedrooms and sizable storage space. The expanded version of the basic plan adds a study wing to the left of the foyer as well as an attached garage with a service entrance to the kitchen.

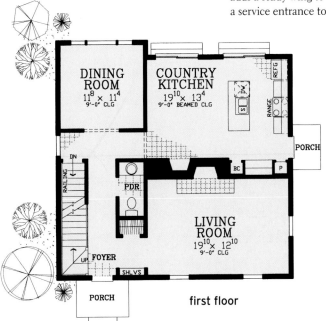

first floor

second floor

PLAN: HPK1300068

STYLE: TRADITIONAL

SQUARE FOOTAGE: 1,501

BEDROOMS: 3

BATHROOMS: 2

WIDTH: 48' - 0"

DEPTH: 57' - 4"

FOUNDATION: CRAWLSPACE, SLAB, UNFINISHED BASEMENT

■ This ranch-style home provides an inviting front covered porch with rustic accents. Inside, the family room provides a lovely fireplace and is open to a kitchen/dining area that accesses a rear covered porch. Nearby, a utility room leads into the two-car garage. The master bedroom provides spacious views of the rear property and privately accesses the rear covered porch. This bedroom also features a walk-in closet and a full bath with linen storage. Bedrooms 2 and 3 share a full hall bath.

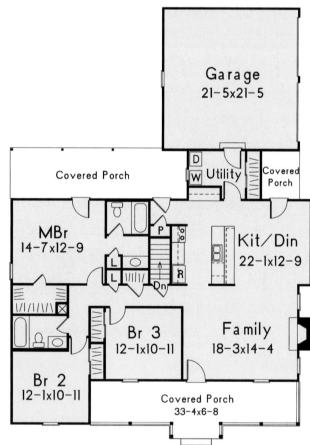

PLAN: HPK1300069

STYLE: TRADITIONAL

SQUARE FOOTAGE: 1,479

BEDROOMS: 2

BATHROOMS: 2

WIDTH: 48' - 0"

DEPTH: 50' - 0"

■ A covered porch and interesting window treatments add charisma to this cheerful ranch home. The entry opens to a sunny great room with a center fireplace framed by transom windows. Nearby, an efficient kitchen is highlighted by an island snack bar, a corner sink flanked with windows, and access to the backyard. The spacious master suite features a walk-in closet and a pampering master bath with a whirlpool tub and a compartmented toilet and shower area. Two secondary bedrooms—one an optional den designed with French doors—share a full hall bath.

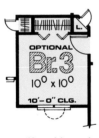

optional layout

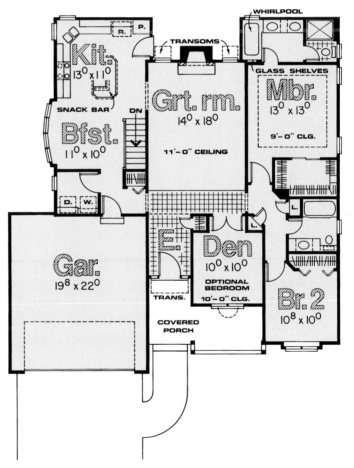

Houses For American Neighborhoods

PLAN: HPK1300324

STYLE: CRAFTSMAN
FIRST FLOOR: 1,622 SQ. FT.
SECOND FLOOR: 1,131 SQ. FT.
TOTAL: 2,753 SQ. FT.
BONUS SPACE: 444 SQ. FT.
BEDROOMS: 4
BATHROOMS: 3½
WIDTH: 39' - 6"
DEPTH: 76' - 0"
FOUNDATION: CRAWLSPACE

■ With an eye to the future, this home offers room to expand or space to be creative. With a first-floor master, the homeowners are afforded a private retreat from the other family bedrooms. A sundeck off of the breakfast nook extends the living space outdoors. The second floor offers a wealth of opportunity with a large bonus space and bedrooms that can be converted to an office or a guest room. Extra storage space is an added bonus. The central loft/study area is ideal for a family computer. Upgraded ceiling treatments can be found throughout.

first floor

second floor

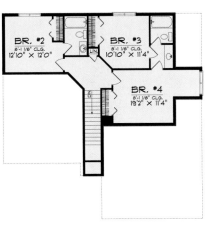

second floor

first floor

PLAN: HPK1300070

STYLE: BUNGALOW

FIRST FLOOR: 1,202 SQ. FT.

SECOND FLOOR: 731 SQ. FT.

TOTAL: 1,933 SQ. FT.

BEDROOMS: 4

BATHROOMS: 3½

WIDTH: 44' - 0"

DEPTH: 44' - 0"

FOUNDATION: UNFINISHED BASEMENT

PLAN: HPK1300071

STYLE: BUNGALOW

FIRST FLOOR: 1,248 SQ. FT.

SECOND FLOOR: 866 SQ. FT.

TOTAL: 2,114 SQ. FT.

BEDROOMS: 4

BATHROOMS: 3½

WIDTH: 42' - 0"

DEPTH: 51' - 0"

FOUNDATION: UNFINISHED BASEMENT

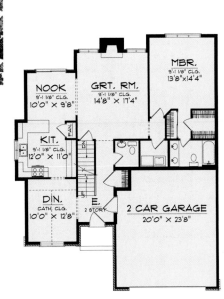

second floor

first floor

PLAN: HPK1300072

STYLE: COUNTRY COTTAGE

SQUARE FOOTAGE: 1,580

BEDROOMS: 3

BATHROOMS: 2½

WIDTH: 50' - 0"

DEPTH: 48' - 0"

FOUNDATION: CRAWLSPACE

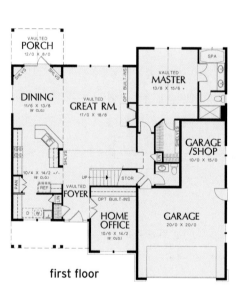

first floor

second floor

PLAN: HPK1300073

STYLE: CRAFTSMAN

FIRST FLOOR: 1,603 SQ. FT.

SECOND FLOOR: 471 SQ. FT.

TOTAL: 2,074 SQ. FT.

BEDROOMS: 3

BATHROOMS: 2½

WIDTH: 50' - 0"

DEPTH: 56' - 0"

FOUNDATION: CRAWLSPACE

PLAN: HPK1300074

STYLE: CRAFTSMAN

FIRST FLOOR: 636 SQ. FT.

SECOND FLOOR: 830 SQ. FT.

TOTAL: 1,466 SQ. FT.

BEDROOMS: 3

BATHROOMS: 2½

WIDTH: 28' - 0"

DEPTH: 43' - 6"

FOUNDATION: CRAWLSPACE

■ Traditional and Craftsman elements shape the exterior of this lovely family home. The two-story foyer leads down the hall to a great room with a warming fireplace. The U-shaped kitchen includes a window sink and is open to the breakfast nook. A powder room is located near the garage. Upstairs, the master suite provides a private bath and walk-in closet. The two family bedrooms share a full hall bath across from the second-floor laundry room. Linen closets are available in the hall and inside the full hall bath.

first floor

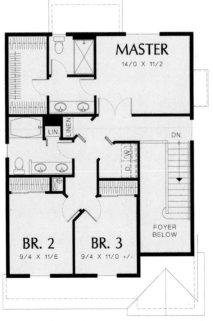

second floor

PLAN: HPK1300075

STYLE: COUNTRY COTTAGE

FIRST FLOOR: 1,315 SQ. FT.

SECOND FLOOR: 1,380 SQ. FT.

TOTAL: 2,695 SQ. FT.

BEDROOMS: 5

BATHROOMS: 3

WIDTH: 50' - 0"

DEPTH: 44' - 0"

FOUNDATION: UNFINISHED
WALKOUT BASEMENT

■ This plan says "welcome home," as Craftsman details make a warm entry. The view from the front door to the family room's two-story fireplace wall is amazing. The garage entry brings you past a home office, which can easily be used as a guest bedroom. The expansive kitchen/breakfast area also features a command center—perfect for the family computer. A staircase leads to the second-floor balcony where three bedrooms share a bath. The master suite features a window seat on the back wall, dramatized by a stepped ceiling and large windows overlooking the back yard. An oversized master closet even has extra storage space that could be cedar-lined for those out-of-season clothes. The second-floor laundry and computer desk complete this well-appointed design.

first floor

second floor

PLAN: HPK1300076

STYLE: TRADITIONAL

SQUARE FOOTAGE: 1,416

BEDROOMS: 3

BATHROOMS: 2

WIDTH: 49' - 0"

DEPTH: 58' - 0"

■ A front walk leads to the porch, alongside the front-loading garage (with workshop area), in this great first-time home. Enter through an arched ceiling into the formal living room, where a cozy fireplace beneath a sloped-ceiling awaits. The kitchen and dining room are just to the left; the kitchen features a curving snack bar, suitable for accommodating hungry neighborhood pals. To the right of the main entry lies the master suite, with mammoth walk-in closet (large enough for its own window!) and dual vanities. The living room also lets off onto a rear screened porch—which, in turn, offers access to the exterior. The dining room offers views to the porch, living room and kitchen, creating an expansive effect. The kitchen accesses the pantry and laundry room, simplifying housework. Bedrooms 2 and 3 exist to the left of the plan, through the dining room, with shared bath and separate closets.

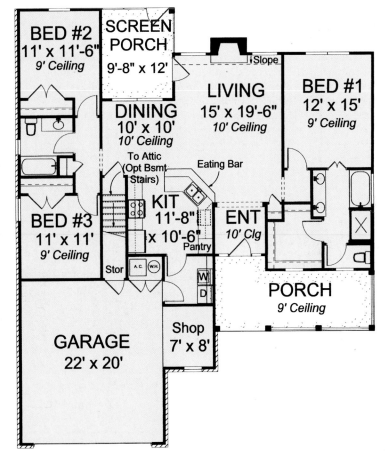

PLAN: HPK1300077

STYLE: COUNTRY COTTAGE

SQUARE FOOTAGE: 1,390

BEDROOMS: 3

BATHROOMS: 2

WIDTH: 50' - 0"

DEPTH: 55' - 8"

FOUNDATION: UNFINISHED

WALKOUT BASEMENT

■ Stone and siding, a front porch, and multiple gables decorate the exterior of this charming one-floor plan. An open design creates a feeling of spaciousness throughout, allowing for the enjoyment of formal and casual spaces. Defined by decorative columns, each room is separate, yet accessible to the others. Traffic flows easily from room to room. Guests are comfortably accommodated in two additional rooms on the second floor. Other options include a kitchen that can accommodate a small dining area, or designed to offer more cabinets and a larger great room. The gas fireplace can be located in the corner or on the rear wall. The master bedroom enjoys a raised-center ceiling and a private bath. This delightful home is designed with an unfinished walk-out basement that can be decorated to provide additional living space.

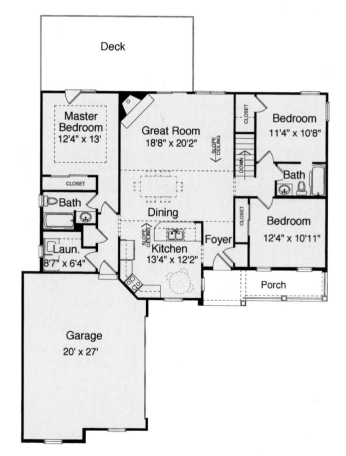

PLAN: HPK1300078

STYLE: TRADITIONAL

SQUARE FOOTAGE: 1,812

BONUS SPACE: 210 SQ. FT.

BEDROOMS: 3

BATHROOMS: 2

WIDTH: 46' - 0"

DEPTH: 65' - 0"

■ This traditional's exterior design is hall-marked by matching gridwork. A columned front porch and brick facade complete this tasteful, yet modest, touch. Inside, your house has been carefully designed to hold all of your needs on one floor. The first two bedrooms, along with a shared bath, are accessible from the foyer. Here, you also pass an optional staircase which can lead toward a game room or basement. The sloping living and dining rooms each provides 11 feet of vertical clearance. A pantry and kitchen (with island) are tucked away on your left. There is still plenty of space for a master suite with double vanity, spa tub, and ample closet. A good-sized garage affords room for two vehicles or for excess storage.

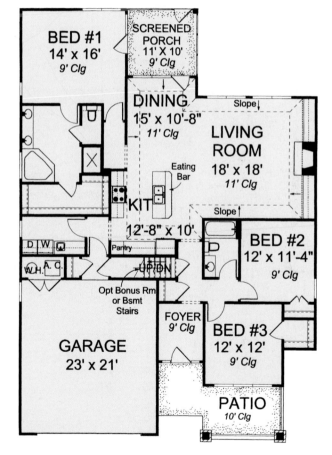

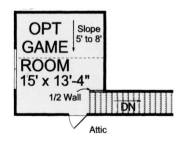

PLAN: HPK1300079

STYLE: TRADITIONAL

SQUARE FOOTAGE: 1,560

BEDROOMS: 4

BATHROOMS: 2

WIDTH: 44' - 0"

DEPTH: 58' - 0"

■ This home boasts a charming exterior and an efficient interior. A covered porch leads to a foyer with access to the living room on the right, or to the other half of the house on the left. Proceed through the living room—with fireplace and vaulted ceilings—to the kitchen, dining room, and pantry area, to the first bedroom, with private double vanity bath, and rear porch access. Three other bedrooms are housed on the other side of the floor plan, along with the garage and optional basement area.

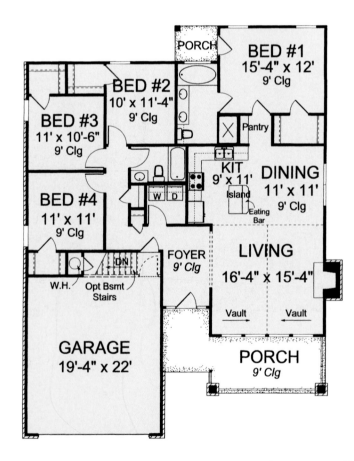

PLAN: HPK1300080

STYLE: COUNTRY COTTAGE

MAIN LEVEL: 1,230 SQ. FT.

LOWER LEVEL: 769 SQ. FT.

TOTAL: 1,999 SQ. FT.

BEDROOMS: 3

BATHROOMS: $2\frac{1}{2}$

WIDTH: 40' - 0"

DEPTH: 52' - 6"

FOUNDATION: FINISHED
WALKOUT BASEMENT

■ This petite country cottage design is enhanced with all the modern amenities. Inside, through a pair of double doors, the family den is illuminated by large window. The kitchen, which features efficient pantry space, opens to the living/dining area. This spacious room is highlighted by a scissor vaulted ceiling, and features a warming fireplace and nook space. The living/dining room also overlooks a large rear deck, which is accessed through a back door. Secluded on the ground level for extra privacy, the vaulted master bedroom includes a private full bath and a walk-in closet. A laundry room, two-car garage, and powder room all complete this floor. Downstairs, two additional family bedrooms share a hall bath. The recreation room is an added bonus. Extra storage space is also available on this floor.

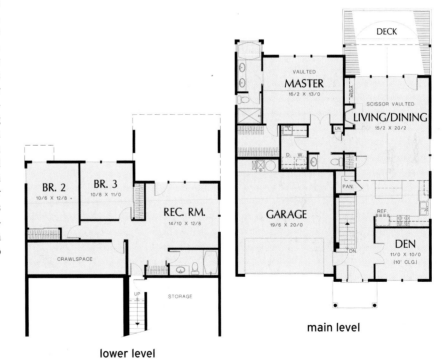

lower level

main level

PLAN: HPK1300325

STYLE: COUNTRY COTTAGE
FIRST FLOOR: 1,285 SQ. FT.
SECOND FLOOR: 1,726 SQ. FT.
TOTAL: 3,011 SQ. FT.
BEDROOMS: 4
BATHROOMS: 3½
WIDTH: 44' - 0"
DEPTH: 50' - 0"
FOUNDATION: UNFINISHED BASEMENT

■ A picture-perfect addition to any neighborhood, this Craftsman home is brimming with curb appeal. Inside, the imaginative design is abound with amenities. Highlights include intricate ceiling treatments, built-in bookcases and desks, and plant shelves. The island kitchen is open to the family room enabling constant interaction. Access to a rear patio invites the option of alfresco meals. The second floor houses four bedrooms, including the master suite. The fourth bedroom can be used as an office or a guest suite. Extra storage space in the two-car garage is an added bonus.

rear exterior

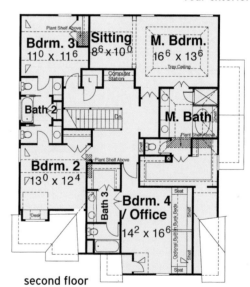

first floor

second floor

PLAN: HPK1300081

STYLE: COUNTRY COTTAGE

SQUARE FOOTAGE: 1,467

BEDROOMS: 3

BATHROOMS: 2

WIDTH: 49' - 0"

DEPTH: 43' - 0"

FOUNDATION: CRAWLSPACE

■ This charming traditional design boasts a cozy, compact floor plan. Vaulted ceilings add spaciousness to the dining area, living room, and master bedroom. The kitchen is open to the dining room and includes an island cooktop and corner sink. A service entry leads to the two-car garage and holds the laundry alcove and a storage closet. The master suite is as gracious as those found in much larger homes, with a walk-in closet and a bath with a spa tub, separate shower, and double sinks.

PLAN: HPK1300082

STYLE: COUNTRY COTTAGE

SQUARE FOOTAGE: 1,365

BEDROOMS: 3

BATHROOMS: 2

WIDTH: 37' - 0"

DEPTH: 53' - 0"

FOUNDATION: UNFINISHED
BASEMENT, SLAB

■ Simple country cottage charm is expressed with carriage-style garage doors on this narrow-lot design. The foyer opens to a living room with a full vaulted ceiling, rising to soaring heights for a feeling of expanded space. The dining area is elegantly defined by columns and a ceiling-height plant shelf. The country-style kitchen features wide windows facing the front property. Bedrooms are designed for privacy; the master suite hosts a dramatic vaulted ceiling and a private spa bath. Not to be missed: a rear patio that is perfect for summer barbecues.

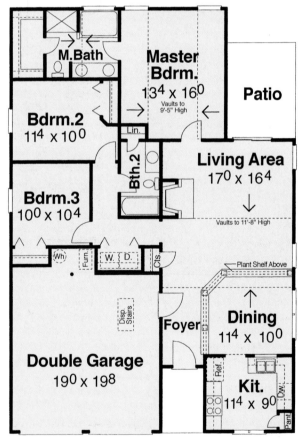

PLAN: HPK1300083

STYLE: CRAFTSMAN

SQUARE FOOTAGE: 1,195

BEDROOMS: 3

BATHROOMS: 2

WIDTH: 40' - 0"

DEPTH: 48' - 8"

■ Welcome home to a petite cottage that is economical to build and has plenty to offer. Enter from the covered porch to a family room with great views and a warming fireplace. The sunny dining area is adjacent and can be as formal or casual as you wish. The kitchen is planned for efficiency and hosts a serving bar and rear-porch access, perfect for outdoor dining. Three family bedrooms include a master suite with a private bath and two additional bedrooms that share a full bath.

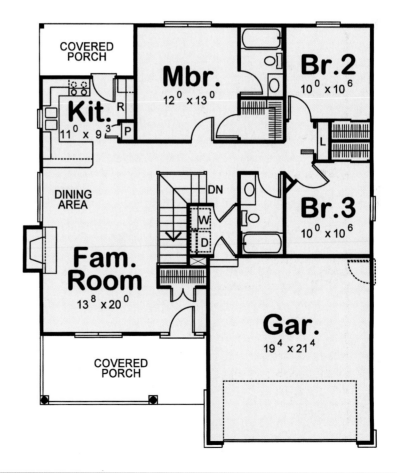

PHOTO COURTESY OF: DESIGN BASICS
THIS HOME, AS SHOWN IN THE PHOTOGRAPH, MAY DIFFER FROM THE ACTUAL BLUEPRINTS. FOR MORE DETAILED INFORMATION, PLEASE CHECK THE FLOOR PLANS CAREFULLY.

PLAN: HPK1300084

STYLE: TRADITIONAL	
FIRST FLOOR: 1,046 SQ. FT.	
SECOND FLOOR: 983 SQ. FT.	
TOTAL: 2,029 SQ. FT.	
BEDROOMS: 4	
BATHROOMS: 2½	
WIDTH: 48' - 0"	
DEPTH: 40' - 0"	

■ You can't get more traditional than this! The covered front porch leads to the foyer and the living room. The massive family room enjoys a fireplace and access to the breakfast nook and kitchen with its snack bar. All four bedrooms are snuggled upstairs, including the master bedroom and its private bath. Three additional family bedrooms, a bonus room, and a full bath complete the second floor.

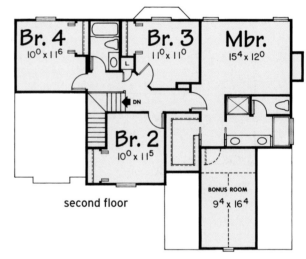

second floor

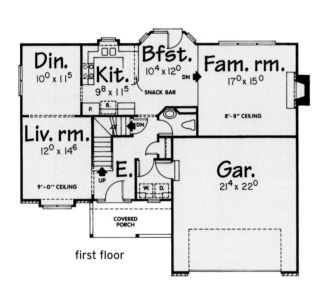

first floor

PLAN: HPK1300085

STYLE: TRADITIONAL

FIRST FLOOR: 1,230 SQ. FT.

SECOND FLOOR: 477 SQ. FT.

TOTAL: 1,707 SQ. FT.

BONUS SPACE: 195 SQ. FT.

BEDROOMS: 3

BATHROOMS: 2½

WIDTH: 40' - 0"

DEPTH: 52' - 10"

FOUNDATION: CRAWLSPACE

■ With sunny windows throughout and a wonderfully open living space, this plan appears larger than its modest square footage. The great room is highlighted with a corner window, fireplace, and soaring ceiling. The dining room continues the open feeling and is easily served from the kitchen. A bayed nook complements the island kitchen that also has a stylish wrap-around counter. The master bedroom suite has a lofty vaulted ceiling. Upstairs, two family bedrooms share a full hall bath; a bonus room can be developed as needed.

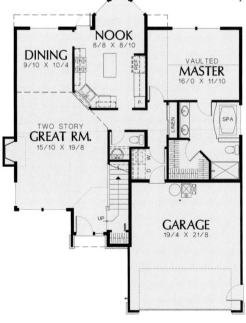

first floor

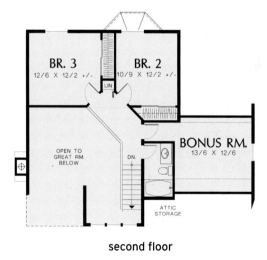

second floor

PLAN: HPK1300086

STYLE: TRADITIONAL

FIRST FLOOR: 802 SQ. FT.

SECOND FLOOR: 773 SQ. FT.

TOTAL: 1,575 SQ. FT.

BEDROOMS: 3

BATHROOMS: 2½

WIDTH: 36' - 0"

DEPTH: 46' - 8"

FOUNDATION: UNFINISHED BASEMENT

■ Brick and siding add character to this traditional design. A simple and functional floor plan keeps the casual living space open on the first floor and family quarters private upstairs. An island kitchen offers plenty of counter and storage space, a nearby laundry room, pantry, and adjoining breakfast nook work in unison for a flawless use of space. The master suite enjoys a vaulted ceiling, walk-in closet, and full bath. Two secondary bedrooms share a hall bath.

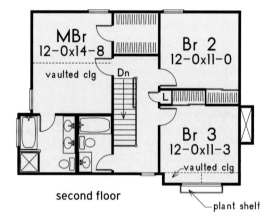

first floor

second floor

PLAN: HPK1300087

STYLE: TRADITIONAL

FIRST FLOOR: 1,395 SQ. FT.

SECOND FLOOR: 1,210 SQ. FT.

TOTAL: 2,605 SQ. FT.

BONUS SPACE: 225 SQ. FT.

BEDROOMS: 3

BATHROOMS: 2½

WIDTH: 47' - 0"

DEPTH: 49' - 6"

FOUNDATION: UNFINISHED BASEMENT

■ The well-balanced use of stucco and stone combined with box-bay window treatments and a covered entry make this English Country home especially inviting. The two-story foyer opens on the right to formal living and dining rooms, bright with natural light. A spacious U-shaped kitchen adjoins a breakfast nook with views of the outdoors. This area flows nicely into the two-story great room, which offers a through-fireplace to the media room. A plush retreat awaits the homeowner upstairs with a master suite that offers a quiet, windowed sitting area with views to the rear grounds. Two family bedrooms share a full bath and a balcony hall that has a dramatic view of the great room below.

first floor

second floor

PHOTO BY DAVE DAWSON
THIS HOME, AS SHOWN IN THE PHOTOGRAPH, MAY DIFFER FROM THE ACTUAL BLUEPRINTS. FOR MORE DETAILED INFORMATION, PLEASE CHECK THE FLOOR PLANS CAREFULLY.

PLAN: HPK1300088

STYLE: TRADITIONAL

FIRST FLOOR: 1,580 SQ. FT.

SECOND FLOOR: 595 SQ. FT.

TOTAL: 2,175 SQ. FT.

BEDROOMS: 3

BATHROOMS: 2½

WIDTH: 50' - 2"

DEPTH: 70' - 11"

FOUNDATION: WALKOUT BASEMENT

■ This home is a true Southern original. Inside, the spacious foyer leads directly to a large vaulted great room with its handsome fireplace. The dining room, just off the foyer, features a dramatic vaulted ceiling. The spacious kitchen offers both storage and large work areas opening up to the breakfast room. At the rear of the home you will find the master suite with its garden bath, His and Hers vanities, and an oversize closet. The second floor provides two additional bedrooms with a shared bath and a balcony overlook to the foyer below.

QUOTE ONE®

first floor

second floor

THIS HOME, AS SHOWN IN THE PHOTOGRAPH, MAY DIFFER FROM THE ACTUAL BLUEPRINTS. FOR MORE DETAILED INFORMATION, PLEASE CHECK THE FLOOR PLANS CAREFULLY. PHOTO COURTESY OF LIVING CONCEPTS

PLAN: HPK1300089

STYLE: TRADITIONAL

FIRST FLOOR: 1,056 SQ. FT.

SECOND FLOOR: 967 SQ. FT.

TOTAL: 2,023 SQ. FT.

BONUS SPACE: 291 SQ. FT.

BEDROOMS: 3

BATHROOMS: 2½

WIDTH: 45' - 0"

DEPTH: 40' - 0"

FOUNDATION: SLAB, CRAWLSPACE

QUOTE ONE®

■ This fashionable farmhouse shows off the height of style—but never at the expense of comfort. Inside, formal rooms flank the foyer and lead to casual living space. A family room with a fireplace opens to a breakfast area and gourmet kitchen. Upstairs, the lavish master suite offers twin vanities and a generous walk-in closet. Two additional bedrooms share a hall bath. A large bonus room includes a walk-in closet.

first floor

second floor

PLAN: HPK1300090

STYLE: TRADITIONAL

FIRST FLOOR: 1,563 SQ. FT.

SECOND FLOOR: 772 SQ. FT.

TOTAL: 2,335 SQ. FT.

BEDROOMS: 3

BATHROOMS: 2½

WIDTH: 45' - 0"

DEPTH: 55' - 8"

FOUNDATION: CRAWLSPACE

PHOTO BY ROBERT STARLING. THIS HOME, AS SHOWN IN THE PHOTOGRAPH, MAY DIFFER FROM THE ACTUAL BLUEPRINTS. FOR MORE DETAILED INFORMATION, PLEASE CHECK THE FLOOR PLANS CAREFULLY.

■ Graceful, elegant living takes place in this charming cottage, which showcases a stone-and-stucco facade. Inside, the formal dining room features a columned entrance and a tray ceiling; nearby, the kitchen boasts a central island and a bay window. The expansive gathering room includes a fireplace and opens to the covered rear veranda, which extends to a side deck. The master suite, also with a tray ceiling, offers a walk-in closet and lavish private bath. Upstairs, two family bedrooms—both with walk-in closets—share a full bath and the captain's quarters, which opens to a deck.

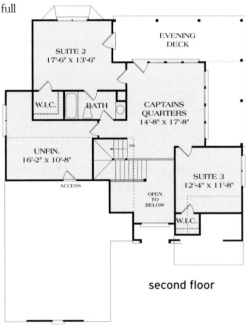

second floor

first floor

PLAN: HPK1300091

STYLE: TRADITIONAL

FIRST FLOOR: 1,185 SQ. FT.

SECOND FLOOR: 1,086 SQ. FT.

TOTAL: 2,271 SQ. FT.

BONUS SPACE: 193 SQ. FT.

BEDROOMS: 3

BATHROOMS: 2½

WIDTH: 50' - 0"

DEPTH: 43' - 10"

FOUNDATION: UNFINISHED BASEMENT

■ Bay windows on this brick two-story design offer symmetry and elegance to the first-floor living areas. The bay window in the living room adds just the right touch to this spacious room, which connects to the dining room and the kitchen beyond. The kitchen will please any gourmet with its abundant counter space, large pantry, and corner nook. A convenient utility room and a family room with an optional fireplace and backyard access are located nearby. Upstairs, two family bedrooms share a full hall bath, while the master suite features a private bath and a walk-in closet. A bonus room completes this level and offers future expansion room.

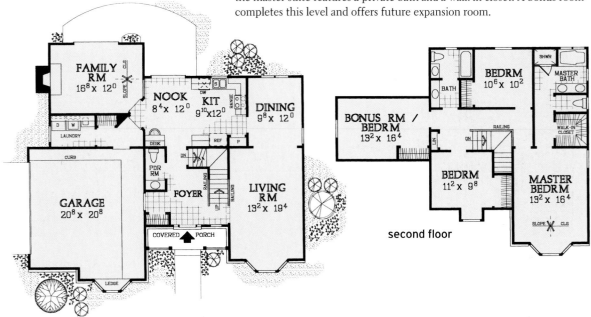

first floor

second floor

PLAN: HPK1300092

STYLE: TRANSITIONAL

FIRST FLOOR: 1,751 SQ. FT.

SECOND FLOOR: 1,143 SQ. FT.

TOTAL: 2,894 SQ. FT.

BONUS SPACE: 206 SQ. FT.

BEDROOMS: 4

BATHROOMS: 3½

WIDTH: 45' - 0"

DEPTH: 69' - 6"

FOUNDATION: CRAWLSPACE

■ Stately pilasters and a decorative balcony at a second-level window adorn this ornate four-bedroom design. Inside, columns define the formal dining room. Ahead is a great room with a fireplace, built-in bookshelves, and access to the rear deck. A breakfast nook nestles in a bay window and joins an efficient island kitchen. The master suite on the first level has a tray ceiling and a walk-in closet and garden tub in the bath. Upstairs, a versatile loft, three additional bedrooms, and two baths are connected by a hallway open to the great room below.

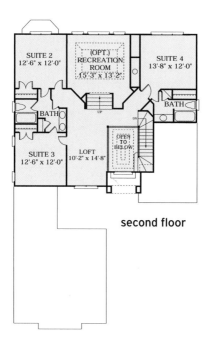

first floor

second floor

Three front-facing gables help this home (page 111) blend traditional and contemporary design.

Flexible Designs for Families

Smart use of interior space can expand living area in your narrow-lot home

An intelligent approach to the interior of your home can make any design—even those under 50 feet wide—feel spacious and provide plenty of room for a family. Part of that sense of space comes from interior design, but it begins with selecting a well-designed floor plan.

A few elements go into this selection process. As you flip through the pages of this book, use your imagination to make the floor plans come to life. Picture yourself in certain rooms, or the foyer, and consider the views through the house. Does the living room connect easily to the kitchen? How about the upstairs? These are ways designers can make a smaller space feel larger.

Measuring a room in your existing house or apartment may help you picture the space available in a floor plan. Most of us can imagine rooms more accurately in relation to another space, rather than simply interpreting dimensions from a floor plan.

All of this will help you narrow down your choices for the home plan that will fit you and your family perfectly.

Open Design

Early American homes featured small, box-like rooms that were designed that way, at least in part, because they were easy to heat. For years most new home design stuck to that approach.

More recently consumers have demanded more versatility and functionality in their floor plans, resulting in open, flowing spaces in the main living areas. The kitchen is often the centerpiece of these fresh designs, no longer closed off in a corner of the first floor. That gives families a sense of togetherness, even if they are engaging in different activities. Everyone can be within eye-shot, even with one person preparing dinner, one playing video games, one reading a book, and another working on a laptop. As busy as families can be these days, that bit of togetherness—even when everyone's doing his own thing—can mean a lot.

As much as these open floor plans fit with today's lifestyles, they also provide a perfect match for narrow-lot homes. By connecting rooms you take advantage of more space—less is wasted on hallways and walls—and a narrow-lot home doesn't feel so narrow.

Kitchen-Centric

Among the biggest demands for an open floor plan is that the design creates what some families call a "kitchen-centric" layout. That doesn't necessarily mean it will fall smack-dab in the middle of the first floor—but it does mean that the common living areas should fall just steps from the kitchen counter.

Most American families—or party hosts, for that matter—will tell you that everyone's activity flows through the kitchen. It follows that your new home should be designed to facilitate that activity. In the best plans, that means that the kitchen will include a snack bar and a small work desk, and will feature easy access to the living room (or great room, hearth room, or keeping room), the dining room, and an outdoor space (either a deck, patio, lanai, or porch).

Flexible Rooms

Another family-friendly feature you'll find in many new home plans is bonus space, which offers flexibility as your family grows. These areas can be left unfinished during the building process, saving money initially, but will be ready to finish off relatively easily if you find the need for an additional bedroom.

Alternatively, finish these areas when you build and use them for a kid's playroom, exercise room, or home office. They are typically perfect places for these types of rooms, offering privacy and convenience near the upstairs bedrooms. They can also keep the clutter—whether it's a child's toys or a parent's computer—out of the main living areas of the home. ■

SEPARATION ANXIETY

Left: Columns separate the open kitchen from the great room in this plan, found on page 134.

SCREEN PORCH
20'-10" X 11'-0"

2 CAR GARAGE
23'-6" X 21'-0"

STORAGE

GREAT ROOM
17'-0" X 19'-8"

© William E. Poole Designs

UP

D. UTILITY

BREAKFAST
17'-0" X 8'-8"

SEAT

BAR TOP
ISLAND

POWDER ROOM

SINK DW.

KITCHEN
19'-6" X 10'-0"

RANGE REFG.

PANTRY

ARCHED OPENING

DINING ROOM
14'-8" X 14'-0"

FOYER
7'-0" X 10'-4"

UP

STOOP

Some homeowners are wary of open floor plans, since they lack the definition from room to room of a traditional floor plan. But subtle design treatments can help distinguish your family room from your dining room, for example, while maintaining the spaciousness of an open floor plan.

These treatments can be as simple as an intelligent furniture arrangement, but they are more effective when designed as part of the home plan itself. Consider plans where the designer has included columns or an archway to separate two spaces. Even more subtle, some plans include different ceiling heights or ceiling treatments to separate two spaces.

Open Book

A bay-windowed library is the first of many treats this home has in store

The beautiful brick-and-stone exterior creates tremendous curb appeal.

The centrally located great room connects the entire house—even the loft upstairs.

Convenient built-ins create storage space alongside the fireplace.

A beautifully conceived open floor plan in this home means that nearly every space in the main living areas—from the front porch to the back porch—is within sight. But that doesn't mean you won't find some hidden gems at every turn.

Begin at the front of the home, where a well-appointed library occupies the room with the bay window to the left of the entrance. The addition of built-in shelves, like the ones these homeowners included, adds to the room's charm.

Around the corner, towards the garage, you'll find a handy walk-in closet as well as a spacious laundry room, which measures more than 50 square feet. Both of these spaces are well concealed from the living areas, but still conveniently located—just steps away from the kitchen and on the way to even more storage in the three-car garage.

Back inside, the ingenious layout makes each room flow easily into the next, creating a sense of space that hides the home's 50-foot width. The centerpiece is the great room, with its distinctive hearth flanked by built-in cabinets and shelves. It is separated from the dining room and foyer by columns,

and opens easily into the kitchen, breakfast area, and back porch.

The kitchen features an angled serving bar and a sink that's positioned to enjoy backyard views. A pantry and cabinets offer plenty of storage space.

Given privacy on the opposite side of the plan is the master suite. Its bedroom features a tray ceiling and access to the back porch. A private toilet, whirlpool tub, separate shower, and dual vanities create a luxurious bath, while the walk-in closet is spacious and lit from above by a skylight.

Above: The dining room enjoys a central location off the kitchen and great room. **Right:** A bay window provides terrific views in the library at the front of the home.

Taller ceilings throughout the first floor add to the sense of space.

White cabinets and stainless-steel appliances provide a contemporary look in the kitchen.

first floor

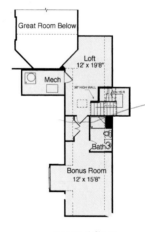

second floor

PLAN: HPK1300093

STYLE: EUROPEAN COTTAGE
FIRST FLOOR: 1,953 SQ. FT.
SECOND FLOOR: 652 SQ. FT.
TOTAL: 2,605 SQ. FT.
BEDROOMS: 2
BATHROOMS: 3
WIDTH: 50' - 0"
DEPTH: 75' - 0"
FOUNDATION: UNFINISHED BASEMENT, SLAB

Upstairs, a skylit loft overlooks the great room. It's the perfect spot for a semi-secluded home office or a children's play area. A bonus room, with full bath included, offers an ideal bedroom location, either for a child or a guest. ■

PLAN: HPK1300094

STYLE: TRANSITIONAL

FIRST FLOOR: 1,813 SQ. FT.

SECOND FLOOR: 921 SQ. FT.

TOTAL: 2,734 SQ. FT.

BEDROOMS: 3

BATHROOMS: 2½

WIDTH: 48' - 0"

DEPTH: 64' - 0"

FOUNDATION: CRAWLSPACE

■ The inviting facade gives way to an impressive, amenity-filled interior. Large rooms adjoin and create an open, spacious feel. The U-shaped kitchen easily serves the adjoining breakfast nook, dining room, and gathering room. The master suite dominates the right side of the plan, outfitted with tray ceilings, a dual-sink vanity, a garden tub with separate shower, a compartmented toilet, and a large walk-in closet. Upstairs, two additional family bedrooms share a full bath. A recreation room on this level accesses the rear veranda. Attic storage is an added bonus.

first floor

second floor

PLAN: HPK1300095

STYLE: NW CONTEMPORARY

FIRST FLOOR: 1,466 SQ. FT.

SECOND FLOOR: 1,369 SQ. FT.

TOTAL: 2,835 SQ. FT.

BEDROOMS: 4

BATHROOMS: 2½

WIDTH: 50' - 0"

DEPTH: 60' - 6"

FOUNDATION: CRAWLSPACE

■ Here's a contemporary home with a French Country spirit! Comfortably elegant formal rooms reside to the front of the plan, with a focal-point fireplace, a bay window, and decorative columns to help define the space. A central hall leads to the family area, which includes a gourmet kitchen with an island cooktop counter, a bayed breakfast nook, and a vaulted family room with an inglenook. Upstairs, a lavish master suite opens through French doors to a private deck, and a spacious bath boasts a windowed, tile-rimmed spa tub, twin vanities, and a generous walk-in closet. Three family bedrooms cluster around a central hall, which opens to a quiet den and enjoys a balcony overlook.

first floor

second floor

PLAN: HPK1300096

STYLE: TRADITIONAL

FIRST FLOOR: 1,200 SQ. FT.

SECOND FLOOR: 1,039 SQ. FT.

TOTAL: 2,239 SQ. FT.

BONUS SPACE: 309 SQ. FT.

BEDROOMS: 3

BATHROOMS: 2½

WIDTH: 50' - 0"

DEPTH: 40' - 5"

FOUNDATION: SLAB, CRAWLSPACE

■ A bay window accents the facade of this handsome, contemporary design. An angled staircase in the foyer leads to the second floor. A formal dining room is to the left of the foyer and the living room is to the right. A large family room features a fireplace and direct access to the rear deck. The U-shaped kitchen provides lots of room for a breakfast nook. The master suite on the second floor offers two walk-in closets and a separate sitting area.

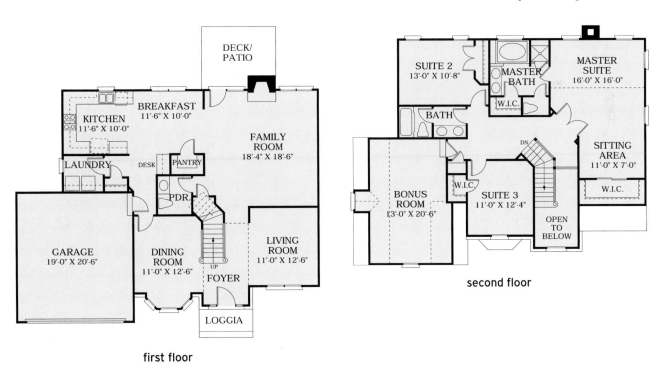

first floor

second floor

PLAN: HPK1300097

STYLE: TRANSITIONAL
FIRST FLOOR: 1,118 SQ. FT.
SECOND FLOOR: 1,144 SQ. FT.
TOTAL: 2,262 SQ. FT.
BEDROOMS: 4
BATHROOMS: $2\frac{1}{2}$
WIDTH: 46' - 0"
DEPTH: 40' - 0"
FOUNDATION: CRAWLSPACE

■ Tradition and classic lines combine with the delicate detail of Palladian windows for a timeless home with modern style. Upon entering from the covered stoop, the foyer opens to reveal a floor plan that flows easily from room to room, yet retains definition. Columns and an archway separate the living and dining rooms; a snack bar in the U-shaped kitchen makes it simple to serve the sunny breakfast nook. The gathering room is full of light and warmed by a cozy fireplace. Upstairs, the master suite relishes a private spa bath, as three secondary bedrooms share a full bath. Bonus space creates an ideal guest room, home office, or playroom.

first floor

second floor

PLAN: HPK1300098

STYLE: TRADITIONAL

FIRST FLOOR: 972 SQ. FT.

SECOND FLOOR: 843 SQ. FT.

TOTAL: 1,815 SQ. FT.

BONUS SPACE: 180 SQ. FT.

BEDROOMS: 3

BATHROOMS: 2½

WIDTH: 45' - 0"

DEPTH: 37' - 0"

FOUNDATION: CRAWLSPACE

■ A brick arch and a two-story bay window adorn the facade of this comfortable family home. Inside, the formal bayed living room and dining room combine to make entertaining a breeze. At the rear of the home, family life is easy with the open floor plan of the family room, breakfast nook, and efficient kitchen. A fireplace graces the family room, and sliding glass doors access the outdoors from the nook. A powder room is conveniently located in the entry hall. Upstairs, three bedrooms include the master suite with a pampering bath. A full hall bath with twin vanities is shared by the family bedrooms. A bonus room is available for future development as a study, library, or fourth bedroom.

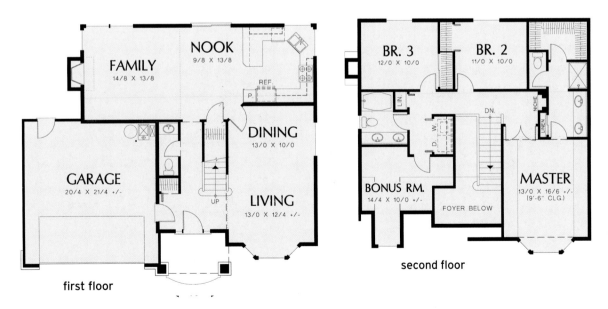

first floor

second floor

PLAN: HPK1300099

STYLE: CONTEMPORARY

FIRST FLOOR: 809 SQ. FT.

SECOND FLOOR: 815 SQ. FT.

TOTAL: 1,624 SQ. FT.

BONUS SPACE: 318 SQ. FT.

BEDROOMS: 3

BATHROOMS: 1½

WIDTH: 36' - 0"

DEPTH: 36' - 0"

FOUNDATION: UNFINISHED BASEMENT

■ With Old World charm on the outside and an easy-to-organize open floor plan inside, this home offers everything you've ever wanted...and more! The formal living and dining rooms flow together, but can be easily defined by well-placed furniture or a planter. The dining area is connected to the country-size kitchen by a snack bar. The kitchen opens to a cozy family dining and gathering area. Upstairs, a gorgeous bath with a huge corner tub and a shower serves three bedrooms. The larger master bedroom has sitting space and a huge walk-in wardrobe. A laundry conveniently rests on this floor, along with extra space for a fourth bedroom or a study.

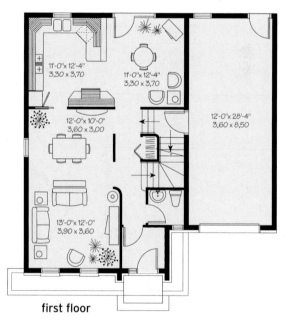

first floor

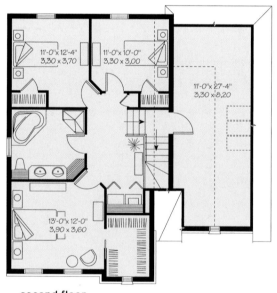

second floor

PLAN: HPK1300100

STYLE: TRADITIONAL

FIRST FLOOR: 766 SQ. FT.

SECOND FLOOR: 812 SQ. FT.

TOTAL: 1,578 SQ. FT.

BONUS SPACE: 291 SQ. FT.

BEDROOMS: 3

BATHROOMS: 2½

WIDTH: 34' - 0"

DEPTH: 38' - 0"

FOUNDATION: UNFINISHED BASEMENT

■ Snappy rooflines with stylish shuttered windows preview the family comforts offered inside this two-story contemporary home. A master bedroom with a private bath that enjoys a shower is separated from two other family bedrooms. All three rooms have hallway access to a swanky bath with a shower and a huge corner tub. The spacious island kitchen has plenty of room for more than one cook (the walk-in pantry is especially attractive) and easily serves the adjoining dining area. A laundry opens from the kitchen and a half-bath is located down the hall. The front living room can be entered through the foyer, which comes with a roomy coat closet.

first floor

second floor

PLAN: HPK1300101

STYLE: FARMHOUSE

FIRST FLOOR: 908 SQ. FT.

SECOND FLOOR: 967 SQ. FT.

TOTAL: 1,875 SQ. FT.

BONUS SPACE: 213 SQ. FT.

BEDROOMS: 3

BATHROOMS: 1½

WIDTH: 36' - 0"

DEPTH: 40' - 0"

FOUNDATION: UNFINISHED BASEMENT

■ On warm summer evenings, sit and talk on the covered front porch; when cold winter winds blow, curl up with your family in front of the living room fireplace. This is a two-story plan for comfort. Inside, the living room, dining area, and kitchen seamlessly fit together for maximum flexibility. An island snack bar in the kitchen makes serving quick meals a breeze. A study or home office with a nearby half-bath is a bonus that you will surely appreciate. The three upstairs bedrooms all have hallway access to the two bathrooms, another example of this home's versatility. The master bedroom with a mammoth walk-in closet is nearest the larger bath, which enjoys both a tub and shower. Additional space is available on this level for another bedroom, study, or playroom. A linen closet opens onto the hallway.

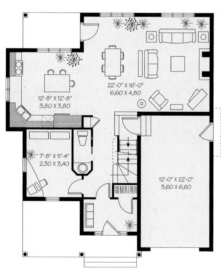

first floor

second floor

PLAN: HPK1300102

STYLE: FARMHOUSE

FIRST FLOOR: 971 SQ. FT.

SECOND FLOOR: 1,057 SQ. FT.

TOTAL: 2,028 SQ. FT.

BONUS SPACE: 305 SQ. FT.

BEDROOMS: 3

BATHROOMS: 2½

WIDTH: 46' - 0"

DEPTH: 40' - 0"

FOUNDATION: UNFINISHED BASEMENT

■ This two-story farmhouse-style plan is not only stunning on the outside, it is well-designed inside for the growing family. Upstairs, three bedrooms and two baths, with extra space for a fourth bedroom or playroom, highlight the possibilities offered by this home. A walk-in closet and lavish bath with a huge shower, tub, and dual-sink vanity make the master suite deluxe quality. The other bedrooms share a bath with a large double-basin vanity and access to a laundry. An open layout for the living room, dining area, and kitchen make it possible to arrange the space to best suit your familyís needs. A study or home office at the front also marks this plan's versatility.

first floor

second floor

PLAN: HPK1300103

STYLE: FARMHOUSE

FIRST FLOOR: 1,239 SQ. FT.

SECOND FLOOR: 1,137 SQ. FT.

TOTAL: 2,376 SQ. FT.

BONUS SPACE: 523 SQ. FT.

BEDROOMS: 4

BATHROOMS: 2½

WIDTH: 45' - 0"

DEPTH: 68' - 8"

FOUNDATION: UNFINISHED BASEMENT

■ Spacious, bright, and ready for busy family life, this elegant farmhouse brings a classic flavor to a modern home. Upon entry, the study is on the left and overlooks the front porch. The family room is great for casual relaxation or formal affairs. Quick snacks can be enjoyed at the kitchen's snack-bar island, and fine dining is available nearby. Utility rooms are on the right and open onto a quaint side porch. Completing this level is a two-car garage with special storage space for lawnmowers, motorcycles, or other equipment. Upstairs, the master suite delights with a unique curved-wall walk-in closet and a glamorous spa bath. Three additional bedrooms afford room for everyone, and bonus space is available to expand as your family grows.

second floor

first floor

PLAN: HPK1300104

STYLE: FARMHOUSE

FIRST FLOOR: 1,194 SQ. FT.

SECOND FLOOR: 1,085 SQ. FT.

TOTAL: 2,279 SQ. FT.

BONUS SPACE: 345 SQ. FT.

BEDROOMS: 4

BATHROOMS: 2½

WIDTH: 45' - 0"

DEPTH: 54' - 0"

FOUNDATION: UNFINISHED BASEMENT

■ Traditional and stately, this brick home will be a joy to own and a pleasure to come home to. The family room welcomes and warms with a corner hearth. A nearby study offers a quiet getaway. The kitchen is equipped with all the latest amenities and features an island snack bar. Enjoy alfresco dining on the rear porch, located just off the formal dining area. Bedrooms are located upstairs; the highlight is the master suite, resplendent with a walk-in closet and magnificent spa bath. Three additional bedrooms share a bath that allows privacy with a compartmented shower.

first floor

second floor

PLAN: HPK1300105

STYLE: FARMHOUSE

FIRST FLOOR: 1,383 SQ. FT.

SECOND FLOOR: 703 SQ. FT.

TOTAL: 2,086 SQ. FT.

BONUS SPACE: 342 SQ. FT.

BEDROOMS: 4

BATHROOMS: 3½

WIDTH: 49' - 0"

DEPTH: 50' - 0"

■ This enchanting farmhouse looks great in the country, on the water-front, or on your street! Inside, the foyer is accented by a barrel arch and opens on the right to a formal dining room. An 11-foot ceiling in the living room expands the space, as a warming fireplace makes it feel cozy. The step-saving kitchen easily serves the bayed breakfast nook. In the sumptuous master suite, a sitting area is bathed in natural light, and the walk-in closet is equipped with a built-in dresser. The luxurious bath features dual vanities and a spa tub. Three upstairs bedrooms, one with a private bath, access optional future space, designed to meet your family's needs.

second floor

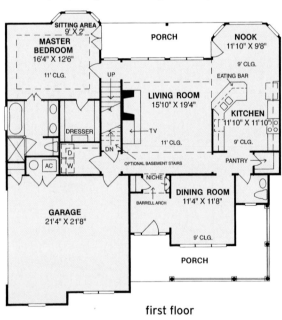

first floor

COVERED PORCH
8'-6" CLG.

DIN.
9'-1 1/8" CLG.
13'4" X 13'2"

FAM. RM.
9'-1 1/8" CLG.
13'0" X 16'4"

PAN.

KIT.
9'-1 1/8" CLG.
14'8" X 11'4"

DEN
9'-1 1/8" CLG.
10'6" X 10'4"

LIV. RM.
2 STORY CLG.
14'8" X 21'2"

2 CAR GARAGE
19'4" X 21'8"

first floor

BR. #2
9'-1 1/8" CLG.
11'0" X 11'0"

MBR.
TRAY CLG.
15'0" X 12'8"

STUDY LOFT
8'-1 1/8" CLG.
15'2" X 9'2"

BR. #3
8'-1 1/8" CLG.
14'2" X 11'0"

OPEN TO
LIV. RM.

second floor

PLAN: HPK1300106

STYLE: TRADITIONAL

FIRST FLOOR: 1,304 SQ. FT.

SECOND FLOOR: 1,045 SQ. FT.

TOTAL: 2,349 SQ. FT.

BEDROOMS: 3

BATHROOMS: 2$\frac{1}{2}$

WIDTH: 39' - 0"

DEPTH: 59' - 0"

FOUNDATION: UNFINISHED

WALKOUT BASEMENT

PLAN: HPK1300107

STYLE: COLONIAL

FIRST FLOOR: 870 SQ. FT.

SECOND FLOOR: 1,007 SQ. FT.

TOTAL: 1,877 SQ. FT.

BONUS SPACE: 263 SQ. FT.

BEDROOMS: 4

BATHROOMS: 2$\frac{1}{2}$

WIDTH: 40' - 0"

DEPTH: 49' - 0"

FOUNDATION: CRAWLSPACE

FAMILY
13/0 X 14/2
(9' CLG.)

NOOK
8/0 X 10/2
(9' CLG.)

PAN.

DINING
11/4 X 9/0
(9' CLG.)

GARAGE
19/6 X 27/0

LIVING
11/4 X 11/0
(9' CLG.)

UP

first floor

VAULTED
MASTER
13/8 X 12/2

BR. 4
11/10 X 10/0

BR. 2
11/8 X 10/0

BONUS
19/6 X 10/8

DN

BR. 3
11/8 X 10/0

second floor

PLAN: HPK1300108

STYLE: COUNTRY COTTAGE

FIRST FLOOR: 1,180 SQ. FT.

SECOND FLOOR: 1,024 SQ. FT.

TOTAL: 2,204 SQ. FT.

BONUS SPACE: 272 SQ. FT.

BEDROOMS: 3

BATHROOMS: 2½

WIDTH: 44' - 0"

DEPTH: 55' - 3"

FOUNDATION: CRAWLSPACE

first floor

second floor

PLAN: HPK1300109

STYLE: FRENCH

FIRST FLOOR: 1,158 SQ. FT.

SECOND FLOOR: 1,134 SQ. FT.

TOTAL: 2,292 SQ. FT.

BEDROOMS: 4

BATHROOMS: 2½

WIDTH: 46' - 0"

DEPTH: 47' - 10"

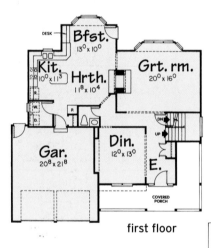

first floor

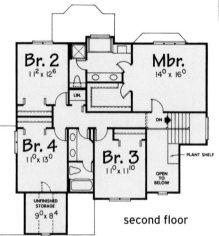

second floor

PLAN: HPK1300110

STYLE: EUROPEAN COTTAGE

FIRST FLOOR: 1,763 SQ. FT.

SECOND FLOOR: 947 SQ. FT.

TOTAL: 2,710 SQ. FT.

BEDROOMS: 3

BATHROOMS: 2½

WIDTH: 50' - 0"

DEPTH: 75' - 4"

FOUNDATION: WALKOUT
BASEMENT

■ A special feature of this classy home is the second-floor media room and adjoining exercise area. Convenient to two upstairs bedrooms and a full bath, the media room is a great place for family computers and a fax machine. On the main level, a gourmet kitchen provides a snack counter and a walk-in pantry. Double doors open to a gallery hall that leads to the formal dining room—an enchanting retreat for chandelier-lit evenings—that provides a breathtaking view of the front yard. A classic great room is warmed by a cozy fireplace and brightened by a wall of windows. The outdoor living area is spacious enough for grand events. The master suite is brightened by sweeping views of the backyard and a romantic fireplace just for two.

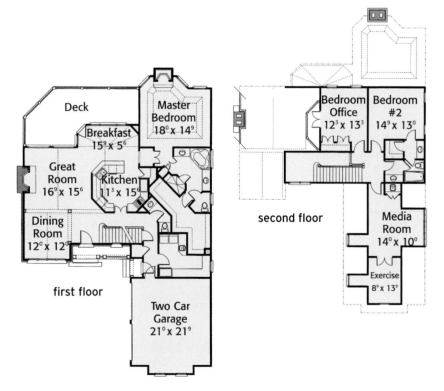

© William E. Poole Designs, Inc.

PLAN: HPK1300111

STYLE: CRAFTSMAN
FIRST FLOOR: 1,627 SQ. FT.
SECOND FLOOR: 783 SQ. FT.
TOTAL: 2,410 SQ. FT.
BONUS SPACE: 418 SQ. FT.
BEDROOMS: 4
BATHROOMS: 2½
WIDTH: 46' - 0"
DEPTH: 58' - 0"
FOUNDATION: CRAWLSPACE

■ Graceful rooflines and front-porch columns speak to the elegance this wonderful home offers, inside and out. A magnificent master suite with a gigantic walk-in closet and a private bath that includes a shower and whirlpool tub ensures relaxing comfort. Upstairs, three more bedrooms and space for a future recreation room can be found. The main living areas on the main level are organized for both casual comfort and formal get-togethers. The island counter in the kitchen conveniently houses a sink, the dishwasher, and a serving bar. The two-story family room enjoys a media center, fireplace, and entry to the rear terrace (or make it a deck).

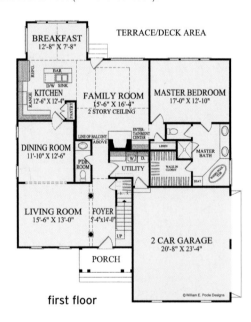

first floor

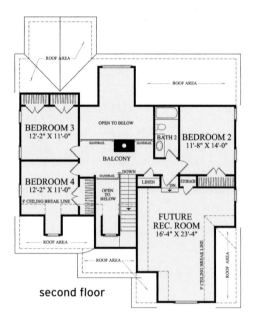

second floor

PLAN: HPK1300112

STYLE: TRADITIONAL

SQUARE FOOTAGE: 1,264

BONUS SPACE: 397 SQ. FT.

BEDROOMS: 3

BATHROOMS: 2

WIDTH: 47' - 0"

DEPTH: 40' - 4"

■ Two dormers balanced with a double gable and arch-top windows impart poise and charm to this efficient three-bedroom home. Relax on the front porch, or go inside to warm up by the fireplace in the great room. A cathedral ceiling and windows on two walls lend a bright and fresh feel to the great room. The dining room views the front yard through a beautiful arch-top picture window. The master suite enjoys a private bath, a walk-in closet, and a view of the backyard. This plan also allows for expansion into the second-floor bonus room.

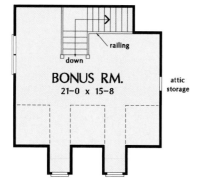

BONUS RM.
21-0 x 15-8

down   railing   attic storage

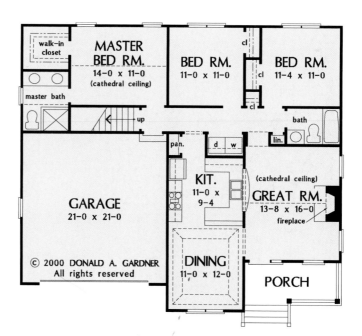

walk-in closet

MASTER BED RM.
14-0 x 11-0
(cathedral ceiling)

BED RM.
11-0 x 11-0

BED RM.
11-4 x 11-0

cl   cl   cl

master bath

up   bath

pan.   d w   lin.

GARAGE
21-0 x 21-0

KIT.
11-0 x 9-4

(cathedral ceiling)

GREAT RM.
13-8 x 16-0
fireplace

© 2000 DONALD A. GARDNER
All rights reserved

DINING
11-0 x 12-0

PORCH

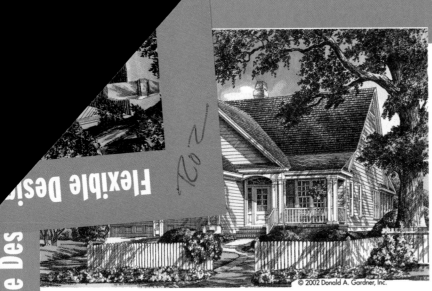

Flexible Des

PLAN: HPK1300113

STYLE: TRADITIONAL	
SQUARE FOOTAGE: 1,789	
BONUS SPACE: 312 SQ. FT.	
BEDROOMS: 3	
BATHROOMS: 2	
WIDTH: 39' - 0"	
DEPTH: 79' - 4"	

■ Here's a narrow-lot home with a convenient front-entry garage. Columns make a statement outside and inside the home. A rear dormer above a set of French doors fills the great room with light, and the screened porch is perfectly positioned for outdoor entertaining. The bonus room can be easily entered from the common living areas and would make a great home theater, gym, or playroom for the kids. A cathedral ceiling in the great room and vaulted ceilings in the master bedroom and dining room add visual space as well as beauty. An angled counter keeps the cook in the heart of conversation and allows the kitchen to remain open to the great room.

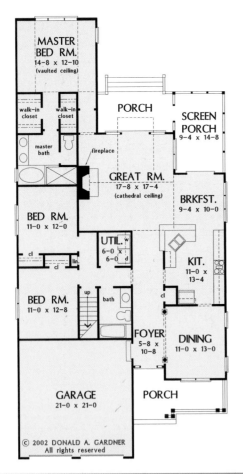

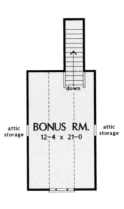

PLAN: HPK1300114

STYLE: TRADITIONAL

SQUARE FOOTAGE: 1,727

BONUS SPACE: 346 SQ. FT.

BEDROOMS: 3

BATHROOMS: 2

WIDTH: 46' - 0"

DEPTH: 66' - 4"

■ This home offers both the flexibility of an open floor plan and traditionally defined rooms. A bay window and French doors invite light inside, and a front porch and screened porch extend living space outdoors. With a breakfast counter, the kitchen is the heart of the home. A fireplace, flanked by high windows, enhances the great room, but can also be enjoyed from the kitchen. Tray ceilings crown the dining room, master bedroom, and study/bedroom; double doors, leading into the study/bedroom, add sophistication. The bonus room is perfectly positioned to create an additional bedroom, home gym, or playroom for the kids.

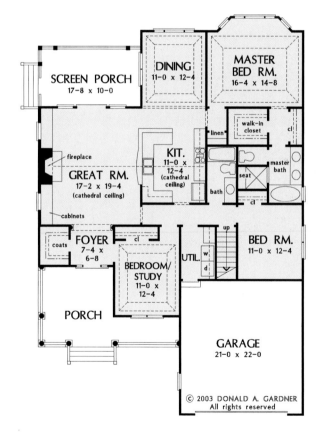

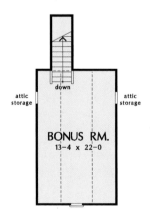

PLAN: HPK1300115

STYLE: COUNTRY COTTAGE

FIRST FLOOR: 1,289 SQ. FT.

SECOND FLOOR: 1,112 SQ. FT.

TOTAL: 2,401 SQ. FT.

BONUS SPACE: 184 SQ. FT.

BEDROOMS: 4

BATHROOMS: 3

WIDTH: 50' - 0"

DEPTH: 45' - 4"

FOUNDATION: CRAWLSPACE, UNFINISHED WALKOUT BASEMENT

■ Siding and subtle stone accents combine to give this country home a taste of European style. A wrapping, covered front porch invites family and friends; inside, a floor plan designed for family living makes a great impression. To the left of the two-story foyer, the living room flows into the dining room, separated only by elegant columns. An angled kitchen, with an island, opens to the sunny breakfast nook. A soaring family room is graced with an extended-hearth fireplace and lots of natural light. A bedroom to the right would make a quiet study or home office. The upper-level master suite revels in a bright sitting area, French doors, and a vaulted bath with a pampering tub. Two family bedrooms share a full bath and access a bonus space with storage, perfect for a playroom, computer room, or fifth bedroom.

first floor

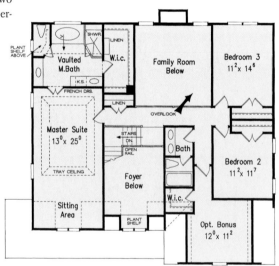

second floor

PLAN: HPK1300116

STYLE: EUROPEAN COTTAGE

FIRST FLOOR: 1,177 SQ. FT.

SECOND FLOOR: 457 SQ. FT.

TOTAL: 1,634 SQ. FT.

BONUS SPACE: 249 SQ. FT.

BEDROOMS: 3

BATHROOMS: 2½

WIDTH: 41' - 0"

DEPTH: 48' - 4"

FOUNDATION: CRAWLSPACE, UNFINISHED WALKOUT BASEMENT

■ Influenced by Early American architecture, this petite rendition offers all of the amenities you love in a space designed for small lots. A two-story foyer is lit by surrounding sidelights and a multipane dormer window. The dining room flows conveniently into the efficient kitchen, which opens to the breakfast nook, brightened by sliding glass doors. The vaulted family room is warmed by an extended-hearth fireplace. Past a well-concealed laundry room, the master suite pampers with a vaulted spa bath and immense walk-in closet. Two bedrooms upstairs access future bonus space.

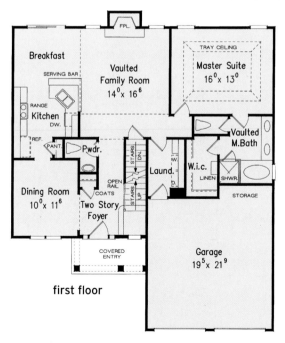

first floor

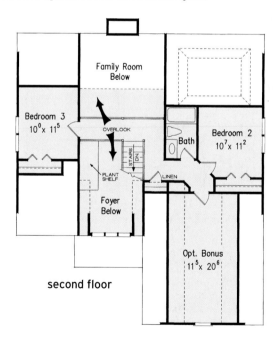

second floor

© William E. Poole Designs, Inc.

PLAN: HPK1300117

STYLE: COLONIAL

FIRST FLOOR: 1,634 SQ. FT.

SECOND FLOOR: 619 SQ. FT.

TOTAL: 2,253 SQ. FT.

BONUS SPACE: 229 SQ. FT.

BEDROOMS: 3

BATHROOMS: 2½

WIDTH: 46' - 0"

DEPTH: 54' - 5"

FOUNDATION: SLAB, CRAWLSPACE

■ A charming Colonial facade and a family-friendly layout distinguish this home plan. The serviceable island kitchen opens into the cozy breakfast nook and the family room, both with vaulted ceilings. Owners also benefit from the location of the master suite, tucked sensibly away from the high-traffic areas of the home. Additionally, the attending master bath provides the comfort of dual vanities, large walk-in closet, and a compartmented toilet. Upstairs, two bedrooms share a bath and a rec room awaits customization.

first floor

second floor

PLAN: HPK1300118

STYLE: TRADITIONAL
FIRST FLOOR: 1,803 SQ. FT.
SECOND FLOOR: 1,119 SQ. FT.
TOTAL: 2,922 SQ. FT.
BEDROOMS: 4
BATHROOMS: 3
WIDTH: 37' - 0"
DEPTH: 66' - 0"
FOUNDATION: CRAWLSPACE

■ This formidable exterior is a study in symmetry, highlighted by a steeply pitched roof and matching columns to garnish the entrance. Tall windows on the first floor and three dormers on top provide for plenty of sunlight inside. As you step through the foyer, you'll first want to glide down the long hallway to the combination morning/family room (with tray ceilings), where you can enjoy access to the veranda through separate sets of double doors. A dining room lies to your right, and a study to the left. Behind you lies the kitchen with prep island, butler's pantry, and straight through toward the dining room again. The left side of the main hallway houses the master suite, extra bathroom, laundry room, and garage. The study and master suite share a built-in bar. Upstairs are two family bedrooms with a shared bath and a game room, as well as linen closet and attic/storage area.

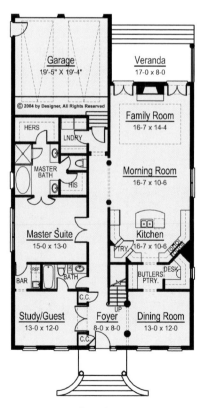

first floor

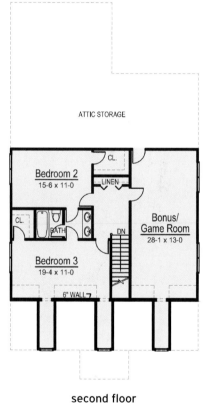

second floor

PLAN: HPK1300119

STYLE: GEORGIAN

FIRST FLOOR: 1,447 SQ. FT.

SECOND FLOOR: 1,169 SQ. FT.

TOTAL: 2,616 SQ. FT.

BONUS SPACE: 254 SQ. FT.

BEDROOMS: 3

BATHROOMS: 2½

WIDTH: 45' - 0"

DEPTH: 76' - 0"

FOUNDATION: SLAB

■ From the operable shutters to the authentic detail of the gable ends, this plan offers everything that makes this design timeless. Typical of Early American design are the large open spaces of the floor plan. Without walls to encumber the placement of furniture, the huge family living area is one tremendous space, with the island kitchen at the hub of activity. Arches lead to the dining room from the traditional foyer. All the family members enjoy the views from the second floor, while the master suite features not only views, but a generously-sized sleeping room with a unique split bath/closet design. Two front bedrooms share a split bath, making it versatile for the kids.

2 Car Garage

Covered Porch Utility

Family 25⁸ · 17⁴

Kitchen

Bath

Foyer

Dining 13⁰ · 15⁰

Entry

first floor

storage

Future Space 22² · 12⁰

down

W.I.C.

Master Bedroom 18² · 14⁰

Master Bath

Bath

down

W.I.C.

Bedroom 2 10⁵ · 14⁰

Bedroom 3 13⁰ · 15⁰

W.I.C.

Balcony

second floor

PLAN: HPK1300120

STYLE: COLONIAL

FIRST FLOOR: 1,376 SQ. FT.

SECOND FLOOR: 695 SQ. FT.

TOTAL: 2,071 SQ. FT.

BEDROOMS: 3

BATHROOMS: 2½

WIDTH: 47' - 0"

DEPTH: 49' - 8"

FOUNDATION: FINISHED
WALKOUT BASEMENT

■ The unique charm of this farmhouse begins with a flight of steps and a welcoming, covered front porch. Just inside, the foyer leads to the formal dining room on the left—with easy access to the kitchen—and straight ahead to the great room. Here, a warming fireplace and built-in entertainment center are balanced by access to the rear screened porch. The first-floor master suite provides plenty of privacy; upstairs, two family bedrooms share a full bath. The lower level offers space for a fourth bedroom, a recreation room, and a garage.

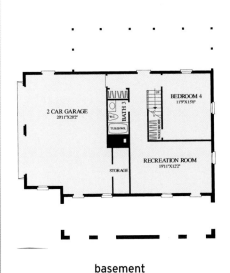

basement

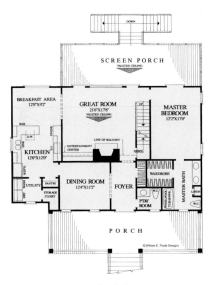

first floor

second floor

© William E. Poole Designs, Inc.

PLAN: HPK1300121

STYLE: COUNTRY COTTAGE

FIRST FLOOR: 1,291 SQ. FT.

SECOND FLOOR: 1,006 SQ. FT.

TOTAL: 2,297 SQ. FT.

BONUS SPACE: 351 SQ. FT.

BEDROOMS: 3

BATHROOMS: 2½

WIDTH: 45' - 0"

DEPTH: 64' - 3"

FOUNDATION: CRAWLSPACE

■ Bring the rustic charm of the country to the city with this narrow-lot home. A formal dining room is available when the occasion deems it necessary, but a large, open kichen will likely be the meal destination of choice. Columns distinguish the expansive great room on one side and French doors lead to a rear screen porch on the opposite side. The sleeping quarters are housed upstairs, including the master suite and two additional family bedrooms. The prospect of a future recreation room exists on this level as well.

second floor

first floor

PLAN: HPK1300326

STYLE: CRAFTSMAN

FIRST FLOOR: 1,659 SQ. FT.

SECOND FLOOR: 1,290 SQ. FT.

TOTAL: 2,949 SQ. FT.

BONUS SPACE: 463 SQ. FT.

BEDROOMS: 4

BATHROOMS: 3$\frac{1}{2}$

WIDTH: 43' - 4"

DEPTH: 82' - 0"

FOUNDATION: UNFINISHED BASEMENT

■ The stately brick facade evokes a timeless design. Once inside, formal living areas give way to the open floor plan, great for family interaction and entertaining. A side deck extends the living space outdoors. A rear staircase leads to a media room housed over the garage. A second stairwell accesses the remainder of the second floor, including the master suite and two family bedrooms separated by a Jack-and-Jill bath. Extra storage space in the garage is an added bonus.

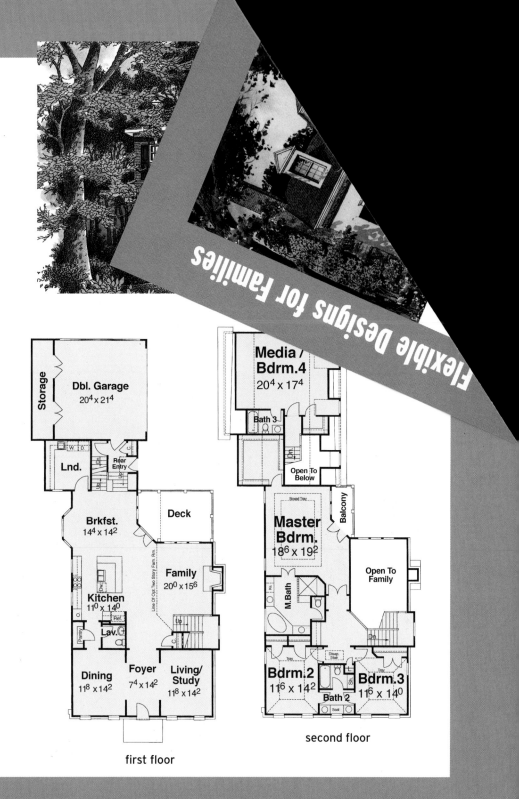

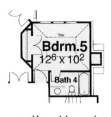

Bdrm.5
12⁶ x 10²

Bath 4

optional layout

first floor

second floor

PLAN: HPK1300122

STYLE: GEORGIAN
FIRST FLOOR: 1,447 SQ. FT.
SECOND FLOOR: 1,423 SQ. FT.
TOTAL: 2,870 SQ. FT.
BONUS SPACE: 264 SQ. FT.
BEDROOMS: 3
BATHROOMS: 2½
WIDTH: 45' - 0"
DEPTH: 80' - 0"
FOUNDATION: SLAB

■ This grand home delights with its beautiful Greek Revival facade. The magnificent portico offers a balcony that is accessible to Bedrooms 2 and 3. The foyer opens to the family room with its window wall and fireplace. The angled kitchen is sure to please with its proximity to the laundry room. Upstairs is the master suite, designed to pamper with a delightful private bath and walk-in closet. Bedrooms 2 and 3 share a full bath and balcony. Bonus space is available for future expansion above the two-car garage.

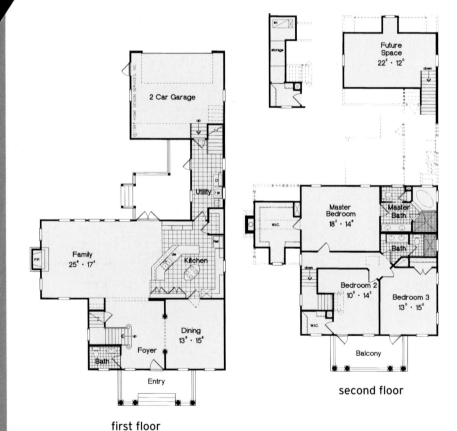

first floor

second floor

PLAN: HPK1300123

STYLE: FEDERAL

FIRST FLOOR: 900 SQ. FT.

SECOND FLOOR: 870 SQ. FT.

TOTAL: 1,770 SQ. FT.

BONUS SPACE: 198 SQ. FT.

BEDROOMS: 3

BATHROOMS: 2½

WIDTH: 45' - 0"

DEPTH: 36' - 11"

FOUNDATION: UNFINISHED BASEMENT

■ A pediment gable, ech... corners reveal the Georgian... mark the boundaries of the massive great room, where a triple wind... looks the rear deck and the kitchen and breakfast rooms. The second floor offers three bedrooms, including a master suite with a deluxe bath. Two family bedrooms share a full bath and adjoin a spacious bonus room.

Deck

Breakfast
10⁰ x 11⁰

Great Room
12⁰ x 17⁰

Laundry

Kitchen
8⁰ x 11³

Two Car Garage
20⁹ x 20⁹

Powder

Foyer

Dining Room
14⁰ x 11⁰

first floor

Master Bedroom
13⁰ x 13³

Master Bath

Bonus Room
16⁹ x 10⁹

Bedroom No. 3
9⁹ x 11⁰

Bedroom No. 2
13³ x 11⁰

second floor

PLAN: HPK1300124

PLAN:	HPK1300124
STYLE:	FARMHOUSE
FIRST FLOOR:	846 SQ. FT.
SECOND FLOOR:	804 SQ. FT.
TOTAL:	1,650 SQ. FT.
BONUS SPACE:	274 SQ. FT.
BEDROOMS:	3
BATHROOMS:	2½
WIDTH:	50' - 0"
DEPTH:	37' - 0"

■ Large multipane windows and steeply sloping rooflines lend a calming elegance to this two-story farmhouse. Inside, the great room features a warming fireplace and a bumped-out window. French doors access the three-season porch, a great place to escape to after a busy day. The U-shaped kitchen conveniently accesses a powder room to the left and the dining area to the right. Three bedrooms are nestled on the second floor—two family bedrooms sharing a full bath and a master suite with an over-sized whirlpool tub, separate shower, and twin vanity sinks. Laundry facilities sit on the second level for convenience. An unfinished storage area will protect all the family heirlooms.

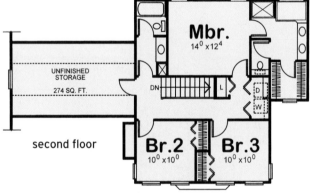

second floor

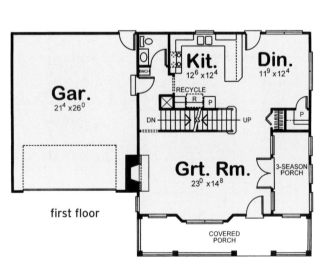

first floor

PLAN: HPK1300125

STYLE: TRADITIONAL

FIRST FLOOR: 1,286 SQ. FT.

SECOND FLOOR: 757 SQ. FT.

TOTAL: 2,043 SQ. FT.

BONUS SPACE: 638 SQ. FT.

BEDROOMS: 4

BATHROOMS: 3½

WIDTH: 49' - 0"

DEPTH: 48' - 0"

FOUNDATION: UNFINISHED BASEMENT

■ A home's facade can tell a lot about what lies inside. Fanlights, gables, and corner quoins add a touch of character that continues beyond the covered porch. The foyer leads to a breakfast nook and a U-shaped kitchen that continue on to a great room with a central fireplace and a separate dining area with access to the rear yard. The master bedroom, tucked away on the first floor, features a comfortable sitting area, a walk-in closet, and a private master bath. There is a special bedroom on the second floor with a walk-in closet and a private full bath with separate linen space. Two additional bedrooms share a full hall bath. Completing this amenity-filled plan is a bonus room that can be used for a variety of needs—an office, a computer room, or a games room.

first floor

second floor

PLAN: HPK1300126

STYLE: TRADITIONAL

FIRST FLOOR: 1,502 SQ. FT.

SECOND FLOOR: 535 SQ. FT.

TOTAL: 2,037 SQ. FT.

BONUS SPACE: 275 SQ. FT.

BEDROOMS: 3

BATHROOMS: 2½

WIDTH: 43' - 0"

DEPTH: 57' - 6"

■ This impressive home has an array of special features, yet it's cost-effective and easy to build for those on a limited budget. Tray ceilings elevate the bedroom/study, dining room, and master bedroom. Turret bays illuminate the formal dining room and study. The great room features a cathedral ceiling and a striking fireplace. A smart angled counter is all that separates the great room, kitchen, and bayed breakfast area. The master bedroom suite remains a private getaway from the rest of the home. Note the tub, large separate shower, and double vanity.

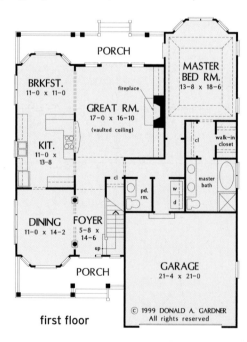

first floor

second floor

PLAN: HPK1300127

STYLE: COUNTRY COTTAGE

SQUARE FOOTAGE: 1,795

BONUS SPACE: 368 SQ. FT.

BEDROOMS: 3

BATHROOMS: 2

WIDTH: 45' - 0"

DEPTH: 72' - 4"

■ This lovely home incorporates style and practicality in an economical and charming package. A cathedral ceiling enhances the great room, which also displays a fireplace and built-ins. An optional loft/study above the kitchen overlooks the great room. The kitchen serves the breakfast bay, the dining room, and the great room. Sleeping arrangements include a delightful master suite, with two walk-in-closets, and two family bedrooms that share a hall bath. A bonus room over the garage offers room for future expansion.

© 1998 Donald A. Gardner, Inc.

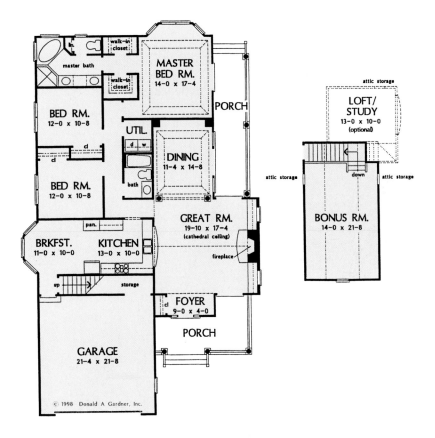

©1998 Donald A. Gardner, Inc.

PLAN: HPK1300128

STYLE: COUNTRY COTTAGE	
FIRST FLOOR: 1,336 SQ. FT.	
SECOND FLOOR: 523 SQ. FT.	
TOTAL: 1,859 SQ. FT.	
BONUS SPACE: 225 SQ. FT.	
BEDROOMS: 3	
BATHROOMS: 2½	
WIDTH: 45' - 0"	
DEPTH: 53' - 0"	

■ Gable treatments along with stone and horizontal siding give a definite country flavor to this two-story home. Inside, the foyer opens to a great room, which boasts a fireplace, built-ins, and a magnificent view of the backyard beyond an inviting rear porch. The kitchen is designed for high style with a column-defined cooktop island and serving-bar access to the dining area. The master suite finishes this level and includes two walk-in closets and a private bath. Two bedrooms share a full bath and bonus space on the second floor.

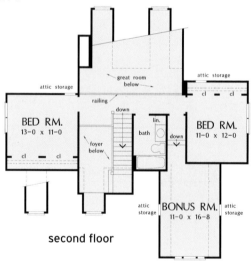

first floor

second floor

PLAN: HPK1300129

STYLE: TRADITIONAL

SQUARE FOOTAGE: 1,593

BONUS SPACE: 332 SQ. FT.

BEDROOMS: 3

BATHROOMS: 2

WIDTH: 50' - 0"

DEPTH: 54' - 0"

■ This two- (or three-) bedroom home offers a covered entry and a deck in the rear. The vaulted ceiling in the great room and tray ceiling in the dining room add richness to this charming, indulgent design. The great room, with fireplace and built-ins, features rear-deck access. The arch in the master bedroom's tray ceiling tops a triple window; note the shower seat in the master bath.

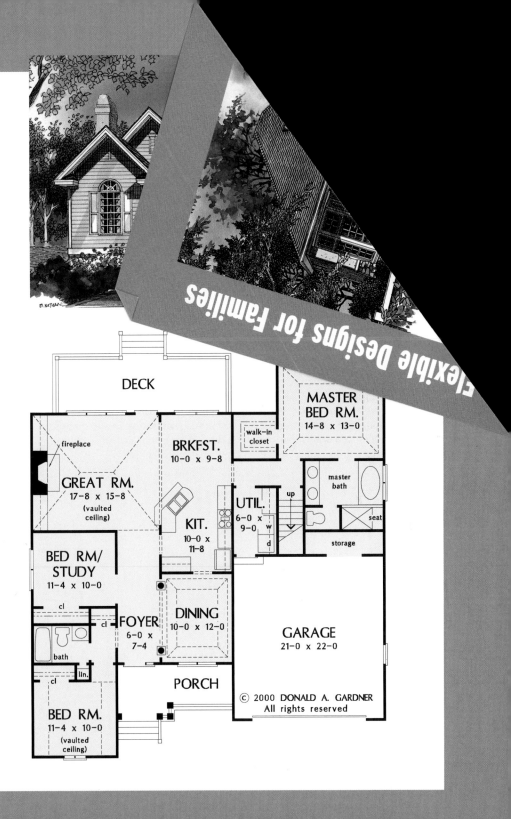

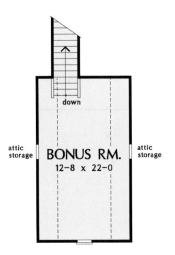

attic storage

BONUS RM.
12-8 x 22-0

attic storage

down

DECK

GREAT RM.
17-8 x 15-8
(vaulted ceiling)

fireplace

BRKFST.
10-0 x 9-8

walk-in closet

MASTER BED RM.
14-8 x 13-0

master bath

UTIL.
6-0 x 9-0

up

seat

storage

KIT.
10-0 x 11-8

BED RM/ STUDY
11-4 x 10-0

cl

cl

FOYER
6-0 x 7-4

DINING
10-0 x 12-0

GARAGE
21-0 x 22-0

bath

lin.

cl

BED RM.
11-4 x 10-0
(vaulted ceiling)

PORCH

PLAN: HPK1300130

STYLE: NW CONTEMPORARY

FIRST FLOOR: 1,786 SQ. FT.

SECOND FLOOR: 690 SQ. FT.

TOTAL: 2,476 SQ. FT.

BONUS SPACE: 204 SQ. FT.

BEDROOMS: 3

BATHROOMS: 2½

WIDTH: 50' - 0"

DEPTH: 52' - 0"

FOUNDATION: CRAWLSPACE

■ From the covered porch to the two-story window in the great room, this design is sure to please. The two-story foyer is flanked by a cozy den on the right and a formal dining room with a bay window on the left. A sunny nook is adjacent to the efficient kitchen, which offers a snack bar and a corner sink. The first-floor master suite features a double-door entry, a tray ceiling, a walk-in closet, and a bath with a corner tub and separate shower. Upstairs, two family bedrooms—each with a walk-in closet—share a full hall bath. A bonus room completes this level and is available for future development. A three-car garage easily shelters the family fleet.

first floor

second floor

PLAN: HPK1300131

STYLE: COUNTRY COTTAGE

FIRST FLOOR: 1,281 SQ. FT.

SECOND FLOOR: 611 SQ. FT.

TOTAL: 1,892 SQ. FT.

BEDROOMS: 4

BATHROOMS: 3

WIDTH: 30' - 0"

DEPTH: 58' - 6"

FOUNDATION: SLAB

■ Traditional stylings meld with the Southern feel of the nested gables and pediment-look entry of this four-bedroom home. A corner fireplace warms the living room, which is open to the dining and kitchen area. Secluded on the right, the master suite delights with a luxurious bath that boasts a double-sink vanity and twin walk-in closets that flank the garden tub. Two family bedrooms share a full bath on the second floor while a second full bath resides next to the fourth bedroom, making a perfect guest room.

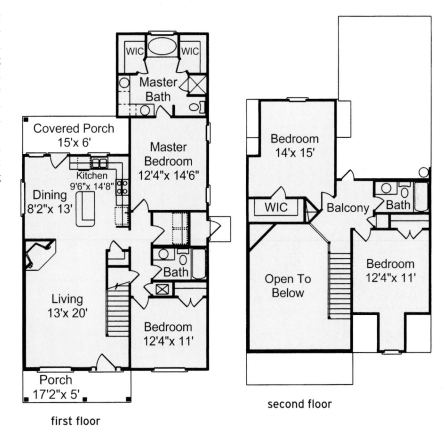

first floor

second floor

PLAN: HPK1300132

STYLE: EUROPEAN COTTAGE

FIRST FLOOR: 939 SQ. FT.

SECOND FLOOR: 788 SQ. FT.

TOTAL: 1,727 SQ. FT.

BONUS SPACE: 210 SQ. FT.

BEDROOMS: 3

BATHROOMS: 2½

WIDTH: 34' - 0"

DEPTH: 52' - 0"

FOUNDATION: UNFINISHED
WALKOUT BASEMENT

■ Designed for a narrow lot, this two-story home creates a package that offers maximum living space in a small footprint. The large great room features a fireplace and multiple windows. A delightful place to start the day, the bayed breakfast area enjoys plenty of sunshine. The formal dining room opens to the great room and is adorned with columns. On the second level, a master bedroom with a large walk-in closet and private bath is joined by two family bedrooms, a laundry, and a hall bath. Note the bonus room available for future expansion.

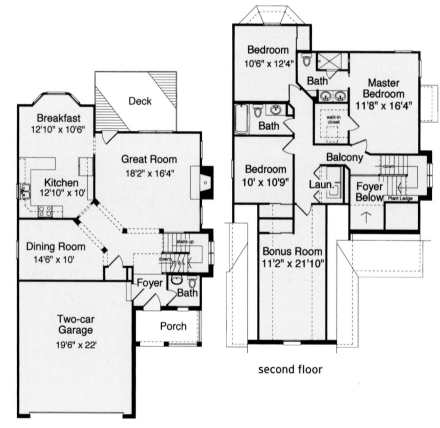

PLAN: HPK1300133

STYLE: CAPE COD

FIRST FLOOR: 1,251 SQ. FT.

SECOND FLOOR: 505 SQ. FT.

TOTAL: 1,756 SQ. FT.

BONUS SPACE: 447 SQ. FT.

BEDROOMS: 3

BATHROOMS: 2½

WIDTH: 50' - 0"

DEPTH: 39' - 0"

FOUNDATION: UNFINISHED WALKOUT BASEMENT, CRAWLSPACE, SLAB

■ Come home to a country gem with a unique portico entry and dazzling windows. Inside, the foyer directs family and guests to the two-story great room where a fireplace warms any gathering. Just ahead, the angled island kitchen serves casual snacks in the breakfast nook, and elegant meals in the dining room. The master suite is tucked to the rear for privacy, and enjoys a lavish spa bath. Upstairs, two bedrooms share a full bath and access to an expansive bonus room. Walk-in storage (not included in the square footage) is a wonderful amenity.

first floor

second floor

PLAN: HPK1300134

STYLE: EUROPEAN COTTAGE

FIRST FLOOR: 1,257 SQ. FT.

SECOND FLOOR: 558 SQ. FT.

TOTAL: 1,815 SQ. FT.

BONUS SPACE: 426 SQ. FT.

BEDROOMS: 3

BATHROOMS: 2½

WIDTH: 47' - 0"

DEPTH: 52' - 0"

FOUNDATION: CRAWLSPACE, SLAB

■ This suburban cottage design features a mix of stylish European and country accents, as well as a family-oriented floor plan. A charming front covered porch welcomes you inside, where the vaulted great room is flooded with light from two country-style dormers. A fireplace warms this room, which extends into the kitchen/dining area, accessing a rear screened porch. An island stovetop counter/snack bar will delight any chef, along with a walk-in storage pantry nearby. A ceiling fan cools the master suite, which provides His and Hers walk-in closets and a private whirlpool tub. Two other bedrooms, a sitting area, and a bonus room are found upstairs.

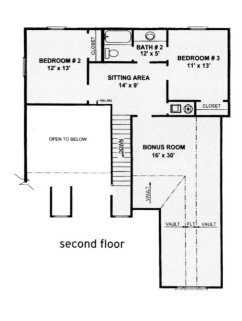

second floor

first floor

PLAN: HPK1300135

STYLE: FARMHOUSE

FIRST FLOOR: 1,529 SQ. FT.

SECOND FLOOR: 448 SQ. FT.

TOTAL: 1,977 SQ. FT.

BONUS SPACE: 292 SQ. FT.

BEDROOMS: 3

BATHROOMS: 2½

WIDTH: 49' - 0"

DEPTH: 59' - 0"

■ A cute veranda and dual-entry garage with a brick-and-siding exterior characterize this traditional home. Archways proliferate throughout the interior, creating an expansive effect. A dining room—convertible to a study, if one prefers—is directly to the left of the foyer, with the living room straight ahead. Through the living room to the left lies the kitchen, with breakfast nook, including an eating bar. An added feature here is a center wall that can be omitted for an open floor plan. The living room and master suite—with sloped ceilings, dual vanities and walk-in closet—let out onto the rear porch. A sloping attic, and bedrooms 2 and 3 are upstairs with a shared bath. This plan contains an option for a basement staircase behind the fireplace, and for a game room upstairs.

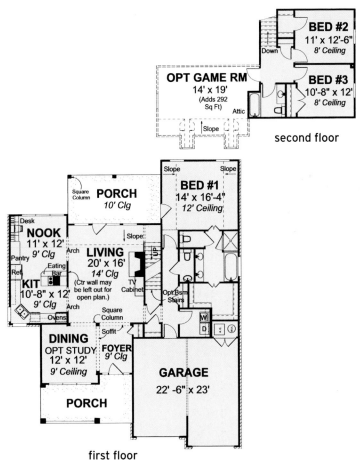

second floor

first floor

PLAN: HPK1300136

STYLE: TRADITIONAL	
FIRST FLOOR: 1,639 SQ. FT.	
SECOND FLOOR: 532 SQ. FT.	
TOTAL: 2,171 SQ. FT.	
BEDROOMS: 3	
BATHROOMS: 2½	
WIDTH: 49' - 0"	
DEPTH: 60' - 0"	

■ This traditional-style home's exterior is highlighted by a multigabled roof and 18th-Century style window panes. Elaborate grid-work on the garage entries complement this design. 2' x 4' horizontal wood paneling is well enhanced by a brick facade. The foyer is graced with an abundance of light from the dormer, and has a square column leading to the dining room, and an archway to the living room. On the main floor, the kitchen—with two pantries—is conveniently situated between the breakfast nook and server area, with the dining room located beyond. The nook also provides entry onto the home's rear porch. This house allows for the addition of a game room and basement. The upstairs bedrooms face the front and rear of the house, respectively, and are conjoined by a full bath.

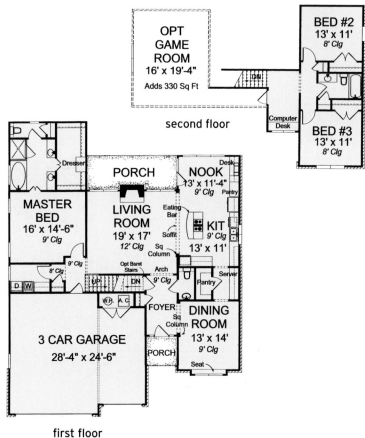

second floor

first floor

PLAN: HPK1300137

STYLE: TRADITIONAL

FIRST FLOOR: 1,178 SQ. FT.

SECOND FLOOR: 1,321 SQ. FT.

TOTAL: 2,499 SQ. FT.

BEDROOMS: 4

BATHROOMS: 2

WIDTH: 50' - 0"

DEPTH: 44' - 0"

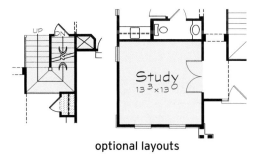

Study
13³×13⁰

optional layouts

■ A stone masonry facade and arched windows grace the exterior of this house, with Palladian glass dappling the sunlight on the inside. A flexible room on the main floor provides a possibility of five bedrooms in all. Laundry and bath are located behind the flex room, with kitchen, formal dining room, and family room forming one large area. A pantry and drop zone are secreted in the center of this level. Upstairs reside the remaining bedrooms (look at all of the walk-in closet space!), two more baths, linen closet, and perspective to the entryway below. The inhabitant of the master suite will live like royalty amidst its spaciousness.

first floor

second floor

PLAN: HPK1300138

STYLE:	FRENCH COUNTRY
FIRST FLOOR:	941 SQ. FT.
SECOND FLOOR:	819 SQ. FT.
TOTAL:	1,760 SQ. FT.
BEDROOMS:	3
BATHROOMS:	3
WIDTH:	50' - 0"
DEPTH:	44' - 6"
FOUNDATION:	CRAWLSPACE

■ A stone-accented entry and tall country shutters give this home a feeling of comfort and tradition. The foyer welcomes and leads to a truly open floor plan. An island defines the kitchen and adds a work area without distracting from the ample counter and cabinet space. The vaulted great room is lit up by large multipane windows and overlooks the rear porch, accessed by the sunny dining room. A den or guest room is tucked to the rear, adjacent to a corner-shower bath. Up a U-shaped staircase with an arched multilevel window, the master suite revels in a vaulted bedroom, lavish spa bath, and an immense walk-in closet. Two generous bedrooms, or make one a bonus area, share a large bath. A convenient laundry on this level is a thoughtful touch.

first floor

second floor

PLAN: HPK1300139

STYLE: COUNTRY COTTAGE
FIRST FLOOR: 1,658 SQ. FT.
SECOND FLOOR: 538 SQ. FT.
TOTAL: 2,196 SQ. FT.
BONUS SPACE: 496 SQ. FT.
BEDROOMS: 4
BATHROOMS: 2½
WIDTH: 50' - 0"
DEPTH: 56' - 0"
FOUNDATION: CRAWLSPACE

■ The brick accents of this home give it a European flavor. The vaulted foyer introduces the formal dining room plus a built-in shelf to the right and the den or Bedroom 4 to the left. The massive great room enjoys a vaulted ceiling and includes a cozy fireplace. The vaulted master bedroom features a walk-in closet and private access to the utility room. The private bath is entered through French doors and boasts dual vanities and an oversized soaking tub. Upstairs, two additional bedrooms share a hall with a large bonus room and a full bath with dual vanities—Bedroom 2 features a walk-in closet.

first floor

second floor

PLAN: HPK1300140

STYLE: CRAFTSMAN

FIRST FLOOR: 1,252 SQ. FT.

SECOND FLOOR: 985 SQ. FT.

TOTAL: 2,237 SQ. FT.

BONUS SPACE: 183 SQ. FT.

BEDROOMS: 4

BATHROOMS: 3

WIDTH: 40' - 0"

DEPTH: 51' - 0"

FOUNDATION: CRAWLSPACE, UNFINISHED BASEMENT

■ This cozy Craftsman plan conveniently separates living and sleeping quarters, with family living areas on the first floor and bedrooms on the second. The plan begins with a vaulted living/dining room, and moves on to a great room that provides a fireplace flanked by built-ins. The adjacent kitchen includes a built-in desk and adjoins a breakfast nook that opens to the rear property. To the rear of the plan, the den can be converted to a fourth bedroom. Upstairs, a master suite—with a spa tub and walk-in closet with built-in shelves—joins two bedrooms and a vaulted bonus room.

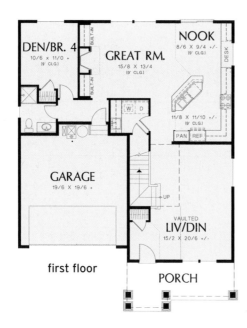

first floor

second floor

PLAN: HPK1300141

STYLE: CRAFTSMAN

FIRST FLOOR: 1,302 SQ. FT.

SECOND FLOOR: 516 SQ. FT.

TOTAL: 1,818 SQ. FT.

BEDROOMS: 3

BATHROOMS: 2½

WIDTH: 50' - 0"

DEPTH: 48' - 0"

■ This home offers Craftsman-style perfection. In the great room, a hearth creates a comforting atmosphere and windows on three sides lend wonderful views. The kitchen offers plenty of counter space and a snack bar. The adjoining breakfast area opens to the backyard. The master suite on the first level includes a walk-in closet and a dual-sink vanity in the bathroom. Two family bedrooms and a computer loft are found on the second level.

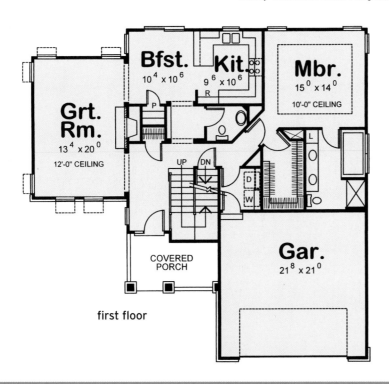

first floor

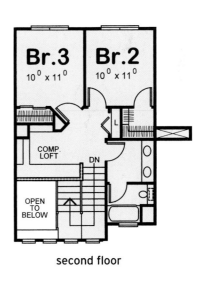

second floor

PLAN: HPK1300142

STYLE: CRAFTSMAN
FIRST FLOOR: 1,255 SQ. FT.
SECOND FLOOR: 1,128 SQ. FT.
TOTAL: 2,383 SQ. FT.
BEDROOMS: 4
BATHROOMS: 2½
WIDTH: 47' - 0"
DEPTH: 48' - 0"
FOUNDATION: CRAWLSPACE

■ Ideal for a narrow lot, this bungalow offers an open design with a practical flow. The first floor is highlighted by an island-cooktop, U-shaped kitchen that conveniently serves the adjacent family room, breakfast nook, and nearby dining room. Upstairs houses the master suite, two additional family bedrooms, a full bath, and an optional fourth bedroom/loft. A built-in bench on the front porch is perfect for outdoor gatherings.

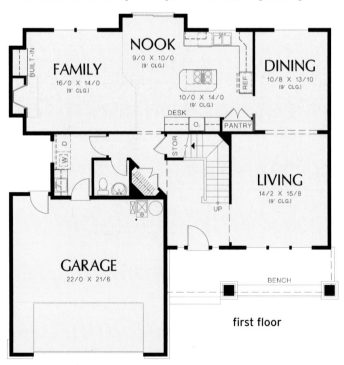

first floor

second floor

PLAN: HPK1300143

STYLE: CRAFTSMAN

FIRST FLOOR: 1,204 SQ. FT.

SECOND FLOOR: 1,264 SQ. FT.

TOTAL: 2,468 SQ. FT.

BONUS SPACE: 213 SQ. FT.

BEDROOMS: 3

BATHROOMS: 2½

WIDTH: 35' - 0"

DEPTH: 63' - 0"

FOUNDATION: CRAWLSPACE

■ A traditional design with untraditional amenities, this mid-size home is sure to please. The front-facing den, enhanced by French doors, is bathed in natural light. The great room sits at the heart of the home with an optional media center in the corner and a central fireplace along the right wall. The open design leads nicely into the adjoining dining room and kitchen. An island cooktop/serving bar conveniently serves the area. A future deck is accessible from the breakfast nook. Upstairs, the spacious master suite boasts a dual-sink vanity, a spa tub, a separate shower, a compartmented toilet, and an enormous walk-in closet. Two additional family bedrooms share a full bath. A bonus room and a practical second-floor laundry room complete this level.

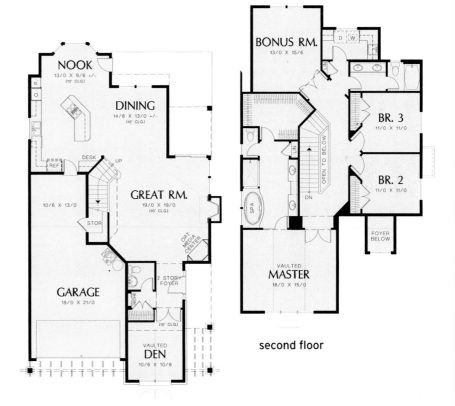

first floor

second floor

PLAN: HPK1300144

STYLE: CRAFTSMAN

FIRST FLOOR: 1,603 SQ. FT.

SECOND FLOOR: 471 SQ. FT.

TOTAL: 2,074 SQ. FT.

BEDROOMS: 3

BATHROOMS: $2\frac{1}{2}$

WIDTH: 50' - 0"

DEPTH: 56' - 0"

FOUNDATION: CRAWLSPACE

■ A covered porch opens the way to interior spaces—a main level with living spaces and master suite, and an upper level with two family bedrooms. Designed for the way you live, the great room is vaulted and open to a dining area and handy kitchen. A fireplace warms the gathering area. Corner built-ins in the dining room frame a window and door to the vaulted back porch. The front office also has space for optional built-ins. A side hallway leads back to the master suite. Upper level bedrooms enjoy the use of a full bath that separates them. A shop area in the garage is an added bonus.

first floor

second floor

PLAN: HPK1300327

STYLE: CRAFTSMAN

FIRST FLOOR: 1,294 SQ. FT.

SECOND FLOOR: 1,220 SQ. FT.

TOTAL: 2,514 SQ. FT.

BONUS SPACE: 366 SQ. FT.

BEDROOMS: 4

BATHROOMS: 3½

WIDTH: 38' - 0"

DEPTH: 76' - 0"

FOUNDATION: UNFINISHED BASEMENT

■ The unassuming facade of this traditional home offers few clues about how ideal this deisgn is for entertaining. The lack of unnecessary walls achieves a clean, smart layout that flows seamlessly. A side deck accessed from the living room and breakfast area extends the gathering outside. Upstairs houses all of the family bedrooms, including the master suite, enhanced by a spacious private deck. Two additional family bedrooms share a full bath. A fourth bedroom boasts a full bath and could be used as a recreation/exercise/guest room. The central study/loft area is perfect for a family computer.

optional layout

first floor

second floor

PLAN: HPK1300328

STYLE: CRAFTSMAN

FIRST FLOOR: 1,160 SQ. FT.

SECOND FLOOR: 1,531 SQ. FT.

TOTAL: 2,691 SQ. FT.

BEDROOMS: 3

BATHROOMS: 3½

WIDTH: 37' - 8"

DEPTH: 53' - 0"

FOUNDATION: FINISHED
WALKOUT BASEMENT

■ Stone and siding add color and texture to the exterior of this lovely period home. A covered porch introduces a front entry that leads directly into the living room, and through to the rear of the home. The open floor plan includes a great room with fireplace, dining area, and large kitchen with island and seating. A wall of windows across the rear of the home offers a view to the outdoors, and conveys natural light to the interior. Sliding doors from the great room lead to a deck that spans the width of the home. Split stairs lead to a second floor, where the master bedroom enjoys angled walls, a large walk-in closet, a garden bath with whirlpool tub, a double bowl vanity, a shower enclosure, and a view of the rear property. The simple lines remain true to the arts and crafts style.

second floor

basement

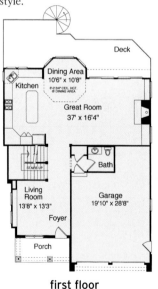

first floor

PLAN: HPK1300145

STYLE: CRAFTSMAN

FIRST FLOOR: 1,457 SQ. FT.

SECOND FLOOR: 1,185 SQ. FT.

TOTAL: 2,642 SQ. FT.

BEDROOMS: 3

BATHROOMS: 2½

WIDTH: 38' - 0"

DEPTH: 52' - 0"

FOUNDATION: SLAB

■ Traditional neighborhood design is captured in this home. Craftsman details with a modern layout anchor past and present, to offer a comfortable family design. The foyer introduces the parlor—the perfect spot to welcome guests—which sits off the open kitchen with snack bar. A morning room transitions the kitchen space to a large social room with built-ins and a fireplace. A formal dining room is just to the right of the kitchen. Upstairs, the master suite is framed by double doors, and offers a lovely sitting area that opens onto a covered porch. Two secondary bedrooms and a full bath complete this floor.

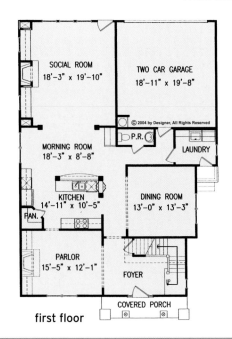

first floor

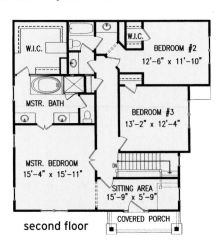

second floor

Flexible Designs for Families

©ALAN MASCORD DESIGN ASSOCIATES, INC. PHOTOGRAPH BY BOB GREENSPAN. THIS HOME, AS SHOWN IN THE PHOTOGRAPH, MAY DIFFER FROM THE ACTUAL BLUEPRINTS. FOR MORE DETAILED INFORMATION, PLEASE CHECK THE FLOOR PLANS CAREFULLY.

PLAN: HPK1300146

STYLE: TRADITIONAL

FIRST FLOOR: 1,082 SQ. FT.

SECOND FLOOR: 864 SQ. FT.

TOTAL: 1,946 SQ. FT.

BONUS SPACE: 358 SQ. FT.

BEDROOMS: 3

BATHROOMS: 2½

WIDTH: 40' - 0"

DEPTH: 52' - 0"

FOUNDATION: CRAWLSPACE

■ This home would look great in any neighborhood! From the covered front porch with a bench to rest on to the trio of gables, this design has a lot of appeal. Inside, the Craftsman styling continues with built-in shelves in the study, a warming fireplace in the great room, and plenty of windows to bring in the outdoors. The L-shaped kitchen is open to the nook and great room, and offers easy access to the formal dining area. Upstairs, two family bedrooms share a full bath and access to both a laundry room and a large bonus room. A vaulted master suite rounds out this floor with class. Complete with a walk-in closet and a pampering bath, this suite will be a haven for any homeowner.

first floor

second floor

PLAN: HPK1300147

STYLE: FLORIDIAN

SQUARE FOOTAGE: 1,576

BEDROOMS: 3

BATHROOMS: 2

WIDTH: 40' - 0"

DEPTH: 67' - 8"

FOUNDATION: SLAB

■ Though modest in size, this home boasts an interior courtyard with a solarium. The luxurious master suite surrounds the solarium and opens with double doors to the large open family room. The elegant dining room shares a volume ceiling with this space and connects via a serving bar to the gourmet kitchen. Besides the fireplace in the family room, there is also a sliding glass door to a covered patio. Two family bedrooms are to the rear of the plan and share a full bath. The utility area just off the foyer and breakfast nook with bright multi-pane windows lends convenience to the plan. Plans include three exterior choices.

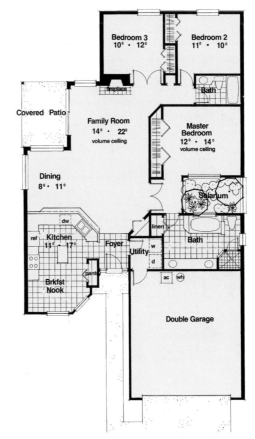

PLAN: HPK1300148

STYLE: TRADITIONAL

FIRST FLOOR: 1,619 SQ. FT.

SECOND FLOOR: 372 SQ. FT.

TOTAL: 1,991 SQ. FT.

BONUS SPACE: 82 SQ. FT.

BEDROOMS: 3

BATHROOMS: 3

WIDTH: 46' - 8"

DEPTH: 70' - 8"

■ Euro-French, country traditional sums up this exquisite hideaway. A complex roof line sits astride rustic exteriors and a chimney sure to charm! Cathedral-style ceilings adorn the main level. Enter your home and be greeted by a fireplace in the foyer on your immediate right, and a den on the left. Continue straight ahead to the great room, where you can view your enclosed deck and access your kitchen with accompanying eating area. A master suite with walk-in closet is to the right of the kitchen. A second bathroom and garage are accessed through the kitchen as well. Upstairs you will find plenty to do, including an office with built-in desk, and an extra kitchen!

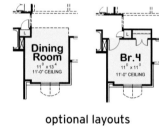

optional layouts

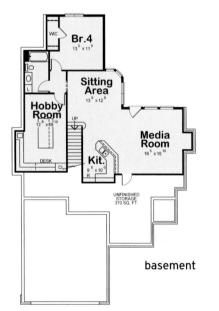

basement

first floor

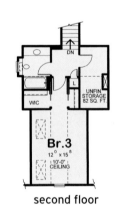

second floor

PLAN: HPK1300149

STYLE: TRADITIONAL

FIRST FLOOR: 1,062 SQ. FT.

SECOND FLOOR: 901 SQ. FT.

TOTAL: 1,963 SQ. FT.

BEDROOMS: 3

BATHROOMS: 2½

WIDTH: 42' - 0"

DEPTH: 48' - 4"

FOUNDATION: UNFINISHED BASEMENT

■ Classic inside and out, this is the plan for the family who values tradition. The facade is adorned with brick accents and a charming box-bay window; jack-arches top the rest of the windows. The entry opens on the left to the sunny dining room. Just ahead, past the stairs and powder room, is the family room, inviting with a fireplace and rear window wall. A second fireplace in the hearth room can be viewed from the breakfast nook and snack-bar-island kitchen. Upstairs, the master suite hosts His and Hers walk-in closets and a beautiful vaulted spa bath. Two secondary bedrooms share a full bath, and all bedrooms are in convenient proximity to the upper-level laundry. A fourth bedroom may be added over the dining room and would make a great home office or den.

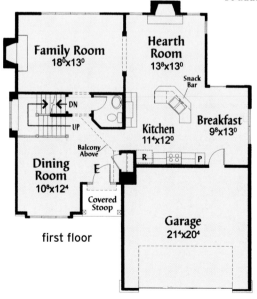

first floor

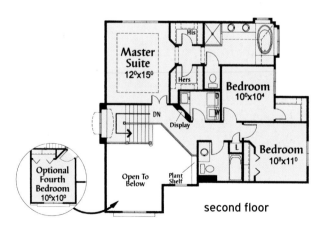

second floor

PLAN: HPK1300150

STYLE:	COUNTRY COTTAGE
FIRST FLOOR:	1,559 SQ. FT.
SECOND FLOOR:	475 SQ. FT.
TOTAL:	2,034 SQ. FT.
BONUS SPACE:	321 SQ. FT.
BEDROOMS:	4
BATHROOMS:	3
WIDTH:	50' - 0"
DEPTH:	56' - 4"
FOUNDATION:	CRAWLSPACE, SLAB, UNFINISHED WALKOUT BASEMENT

■ A careful blend of siding and stone lends eye-catching appeal to this traditional plan. Vaulted ceilings grace the great room, master bath, and dining room. The efficient kitchen offers pantry storage and a serving bar to the breakfast room. The master suite features a tray ceiling and a deluxe private bath. A bedroom/study is located on the first floor. Two second-floor bedrooms easily access a full bath. An optional bonus room offers plenty of room to grow—making it perfect for a guest suite, home office, or exercise room.

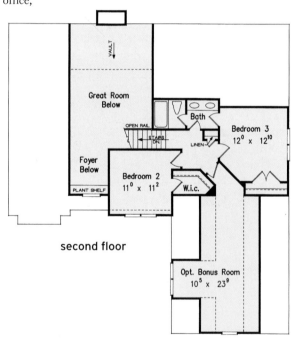

first floor

second floor

PLAN: HPK1300151

STYLE: COUNTRY COTTAGE

FIRST FLOOR: 1,293 SQ. FT.

SECOND FLOOR: 922 SQ. FT.

TOTAL: 2,215 SQ. FT.

BONUS SPACE: 235 SQ. FT.

BEDROOMS: 3

BATHROOMS: 3

WIDTH: 40' - 0"

DEPTH: 57' - 0"

FOUNDATION: CRAWLSPACE, UNFINISHED WALKOUT BASEMENT

■ Shingles and stone decorate the exterior of this charming design. Inside, decorative columns separate the living and dining rooms. The kitchen includes a pantry and a work island; the breakfast nook is conveniently nearby. Built-in cabinets flank the fireplace in the two-story family room. One family bedroom resides on the first floor, while the master suite and a second family bedroom are upstairs. An optional bonus room completes the second floor.

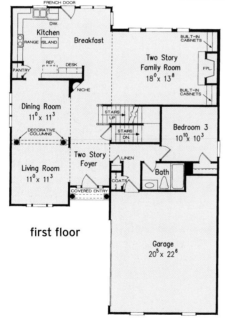

first floor

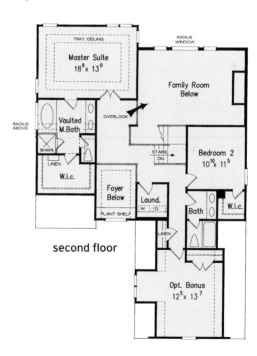

second floor

PLAN: HPK1300152

STYLE: COUNTRY COTTAGE
FIRST FLOOR: 1,355 SQ. FT.
SECOND FLOOR: 1,347 SQ. FT.
TOTAL: 2,702 SQ. FT.
BONUS SPACE: 285 SQ. FT.
BEDROOMS: 4
BATHROOMS: 4
WIDTH: 41' - 0"
DEPTH: 66' - 0"
FOUNDATION: CRAWLSPACE,
UNFINISHED WALKOUT
BASEMENT

■ Stone accents add a European feel to this narrow cottage, perfect in an established neighborhood or out in the country. Enter beneath a keystone arch to a two-story foyer; follow an angled hall to the family room where a coffered ceiling and fireplace create a welcoming atmosphere. The kitchen works hard so you don't have to, with a serving bar, stacked ovens, and easy access to the breakfast nook and dining room, lit by a box-bay window. The keeping room is to the rear, perfect for lazy mornings, curled up with a good book. Upstairs, the master suite delights in a detailed tray ceiling, bayed sitting area, and lavish bath. Two additional bedrooms join an optional bonus area (with a charming window seat) to complete the plan.

first floor

second floor

PLAN: HPK1300153

STYLE: COUNTRY COTTAGE

FIRST FLOOR: 1,196 SQ. FT.

SECOND FLOOR: 1,055 SQ. FT.

TOTAL: 2,251 SQ. FT.

BONUS SPACE: 206 SQ. FT.

BEDROOMS: 4

BATHROOMS: 3

WIDTH: 43' - 0"

DEPTH: 46' - 10"

FOUNDATION: CRAWLSPACE,
UNFINISHED WALKOUT
BASEMENT

■ This traditional country cottage has a classic facade and a floor plan that's ready to change with your family. The two-story foyer opens to the left to reveal a dining room with an oversize six-pane window. From here, the kitchen leads through to the breakfast area, charming with a French door and lots of natural light. The two-story grand room is highlighted by a fireplace framed by windows. A bedroom could easily serve as a home office, conveniently located near a full bath. Upstairs, two family bedrooms share a full bath; the master suite is resplendent with a private vaulted bath and an enormous walk-in closet with built-in shelving. A bonus room is limited only by your imagination.

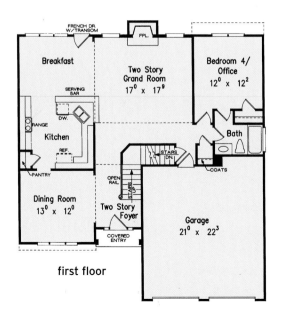

first floor

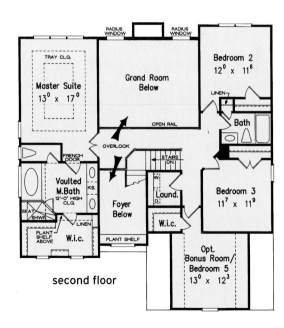

second floor

PLAN: HPK1300154

STYLE: GEORGIAN

FIRST FLOOR: 1,217 SQ. FT.

SECOND FLOOR: 1,390 SQ. FT.

TOTAL: 2,607 SQ. FT.

BEDROOMS: 5

BATHROOMS: 3

WIDTH: 50' - 0"

DEPTH: 40' - 4"

FOUNDATION: UNFINISHED

WALKOUT BASEMENT,

CRAWLSPACE, SLAB

■ Enter this beautiful five-bedroom Georgian home and you may never want to leave! An elegant, open floor plan reveals a family room, with a fireplace, leading to the breakfast area and U-shaped island kitchen. Upstairs, the master suite will amaze, with a sitting room, luxurious vaulted bath, and a walk-in closet so huge you have to see it to believe it! Three ample family bedrooms share a full bath. Don't miss the upper-level laundry room, positioned for ultimate convenience.

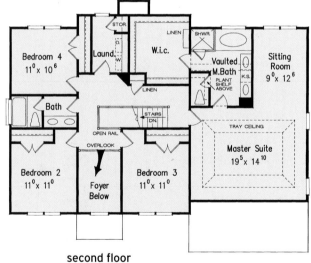

second floor

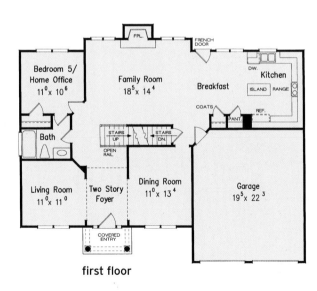

first floor

PLAN: HPK1300155

STYLE: COUNTRY COTTAGE
FIRST FLOOR: 1,458 SQ. FT.
SECOND FLOOR: 516 SQ. FT.
TOTAL: 1,974 SQ. FT.
BONUS SPACE: 168 SQ. FT.
BEDROOMS: 3
BATHROOMS: 2½
WIDTH: 50' - 0"
DEPTH: 46' - 0"
FOUNDATION: CRAWLSPACE,
UNFINISHED WALKOUT
BASEMENT

■ A covered porch welcomes family and friends to this appealing plan. Inside, arches create a formal air in the dining room and a vaulted ceiling adds space to the family room. A bay window brightens the breakfast room, which opens to the rear property. The first-floor master suite features a tray ceiling and a large private bath with a walk-in closet. Two second-floor family bedrooms, both with walk-in closets, share a full bath.

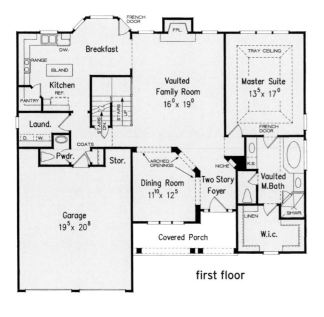

first floor

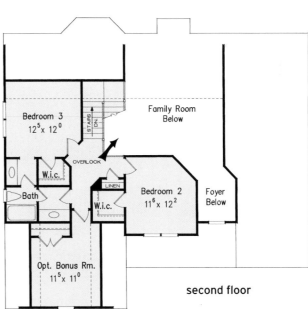

second floor

Flexible Designs for Families

PLAN: HPK1300156

STYLE: COUNTRY COTTAGE

FIRST FLOOR: 1,279 SQ. FT.

SECOND FLOOR: 1,071 SQ. FT.

TOTAL: 2,350 SQ. FT.

BEDROOMS: 4

BATHROOMS: 3

WIDTH: 50' - 0"

DEPTH: 42' - 6"

FOUNDATION: CRAWLSPACE,
UNFINISHED WALKOUT
BASEMENT

■ Rustic details complement brick and siding on the exterior of this home. The interior features vaulted living and family rooms and a convenient kitchen separating the dining and breakfast rooms. The living room provides a fireplace flanked by radius windows, and a French door in the breakfast room opens to the rear property. A bedroom to the back could be used as a study. Second-floor bedrooms include a master suite with a sitting area.

first floor

second floor

PLAN: HPK1300157

STYLE: CHATEAU STYLE

FIRST FLOOR: 1,441 SQ. FT.

SECOND FLOOR: 485 SQ. FT.

TOTAL: 1,926 SQ. FT.

BONUS SPACE: 226 SQ. FT.

BEDROOMS: 3

BATHROOMS: 2½

WIDTH: 49' - 0"

DEPTH: 50' - 10"

FOUNDATION: UNFINISHED
WALKOUT BASEMENT

■ Timeless style graces the facade of this stately two-story home. By facing the home with brick and surrounding the rest with siding, this design makes the most of your money. A two-story foyer opens on the left to reveal a formal living room. Ahead, the vaulted family room soars two-stories high, made cozy by a centered fireplace. Enjoy casual meals in the breakfast nook that opens to the angled kitchen. Tucked to the right, a pampering master suite provides a lovely private bath. Two upstairs bedrooms share a full bath and family-room overlook. Bonus space is perfect as an additional bedroom, or a play area.

first floor

second floor

PLAN: HPK1300158

STYLE: TRADITIONAL

FIRST FLOOR: 1,720 SQ. FT.

SECOND FLOOR: 545 SQ. FT.

TOTAL: 2,265 SQ. FT.

BONUS SPACE: 365 SQ. FT.

BEDROOMS: 3

BATHROOMS: 2½

WIDTH: 50' - 0"

DEPTH: 53' - 6"

FOUNDATION: WALKOUT
BASEMENT

■ The foyer opens to the living and dining areas, providing a spectacular entrance to this English Country cottage. Just beyond the dining room is a gourmet kitchen with a work island and a food bar opening to the breakfast room. Accented by a fireplace and built-in bookcases, the family room with a ribbon of windows is an excellent setting for family gatherings. Remotely located off the central hallway, the master suite includes rectangular ceiling detail and access to the rear deck, while the master bath features His and Hers vanities, a garden tub, and a spacious walk-in closet. The central staircase leads to the balcony overlook and two bedrooms with spacious closets and baths.

first floor

second floor

PLAN: HPK1300159

STYLE: FRENCH COUNTRY

FIRST FLOOR: 2,000 SQ. FT.

SECOND FLOOR: 934 SQ. FT.

TOTAL: 2,934 SQ. FT.

BEDROOMS: 3

BATHROOMS: 2½

WIDTH: 42' - 0"

DEPTH: 94' - 8"

FOUNDATION: CRAWLSPACE

■ This enchanting stone cottage is a beautiful example of French Country living. Inside, a dining room and study/guest suite flank the foyer. A hall niche is ready to display your treasures. Past the powder room, the gathering room is comfortable and inviting with a fireplace and French-door access to the terrace. An angled kitchen has an island cooktop for the ultimate in convenience. Separated for privacy, the master suite pampers with a soothing spa bath. Upstairs, two bedroom suites have private toilets and vanities and a shared shower/tub. A studio suite can be added as your family grows.

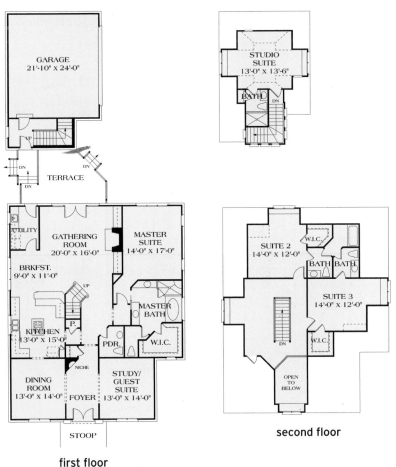

first floor

second floor

PLAN: HPK1300160

STYLE: FRENCH

FIRST FLOOR: 1,558 SQ. FT.

SECOND FLOOR: 546 SQ. FT.

TOTAL: 2,104 SQ. FT.

BONUS SPACE: 233 SQ. FT.

BEDROOMS: 3

BATHROOMS: 2½

WIDTH: 48' - 0"

DEPTH: 52' - 0"

FOUNDATION: UNFINISHED BASEMENT

■ This sturdy home with a brick exterior and intriguing gable lines is well suited to make life comfortable and enjoyable for most any family. The huge island kitchen, with French-door access to the backyard, opens to a cozy dining area that will surely be a center for family socializing. A fireplace joins the dining area with the living room. A front study or home office is an especially attractive feature. The master suite with a lavish bath and a walk-in closet is also located on the first level. Above, on the second floor, two more bedrooms share a bath. Off the kitchen, a laundry and a half-bath are near the entry to the garage.

first floor

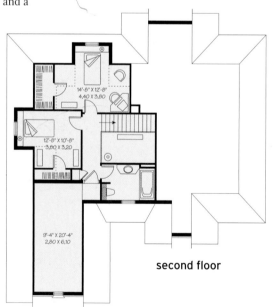

second floor

PLAN: HPK1300161

STYLE: COUNTRY COTTAGE

FIRST FLOOR: 1,164 SQ. FT.

SECOND FLOOR: 1,319 SQ. FT.

TOTAL: 2,483 SQ. FT.

BEDROOMS: 4

BATHROOMS: 3

WIDTH: 50' - 0"

DEPTH: 39' - 0"

FOUNDATION: UNFINISHED
WALKOUT BASEMENT

■ This charming cottage offers more space than you might think. A two-story living area is seen from the foyer where the U-shaped staircase leads you upstairs. The spacious kitchen/breakfast room even allows for a command center—the perfect place for the family computer. The first-floor bedroom provides space for an unexpected guest or can double as a home office. The master suite offers the option of a dramatic ceiling treatment with windows overlooking the rear of the house. A closet beyond the master bath makes room for all your clothes while also providing low storage. The other bedrooms also boast dramatic ceiling treatments, creating a sense of spaciousness.

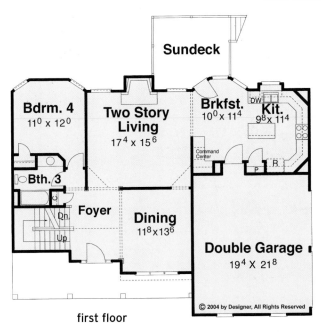

first floor

second floor

PLAN: HPK1300162

STYLE: TRADITIONAL
FIRST FLOOR: 1,075 SQ. FT.
SECOND FLOOR: 1,140 SQ. FT.
TOTAL: 2,215 SQ. FT.
BEDROOMS: 4
BATHROOMS: 3
WIDTH: 48' - 0"
DEPTH: 37' - 0"
FOUNDATION: UNFINISHED
WALKOUT BASEMENT

■ This traditional home takes a tried-and-true exterior style and pairs it with a brilliant floor plan for a peerless family design. The foyer is marked by decorative columns that also serve to define the adjacent dining room. Soaring two stories high, the family room enjoys a fireplace and a natural flow into the bayed breakfast nook and U-shaped island kitchen. A bedroom on this level is the ideal guest room or home office. Equipped to pamper and indulge, the second-floor master suite begins with French doors and continues with a stepped ceiling, window seat, built-in shelving, incredible spa bath, and a walk-in closet with enough storage for even the most dedicated shopper. Two additional bedrooms share this level along with a full bath, laundry room, and computer station.

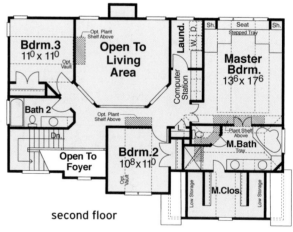

first floor

second floor

PLAN: HPK1300163

STYLE: TRADITIONAL

FIRST FLOOR: 1,492 SQ. FT.

SECOND FLOOR: 854 SQ. FT.

TOTAL: 2,346 SQ. FT.

BONUS SPACE: 810 SQ. FT.

BEDROOMS: 3

BATHROOMS: 3½

WIDTH: 44' - 0"

DEPTH: 48' - 0"

FOUNDATION: UNFINISHED
WALKOUT BASEMENT

■ Victorian detailing in the gables, transom windows, and heavy columns at the front porch add a touch of country elegance to this beautiful home. Inside, a two-story great room at the center of the plan adds air and space. Tray ceilings adorn all the bedrooms, which also have their own baths, walk-in closets, and porch access. The owners suite, with a private location on the first floor, has access to the rear porch, a luxurious garden tub, and extra-large shower. A loft on the second floor provides a great location for quiet contemplation. The basement has a two-car garage conveniently tucked under the house, as well as plenty of additional space for storage and a bonus room.

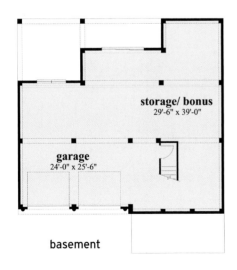

basement

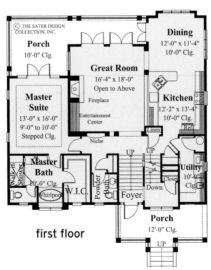

first floor

second floor

PLAN: HPK1300164

STYLE: TIDEWATER

FIRST FLOOR: 1,492 SQ. FT.

SECOND FLOOR: 854 SQ. FT.

TOTAL: 2,346 SQ. FT.

BEDROOMS: 3

BATHROOMS: 3½

WIDTH: 44' - 0"

DEPTH: 48' - 0"

FOUNDATION: ISLAND

BASEMENT

■ The staircase leading to a columned front porch lends a touch of grandeur to this residence. The great room is made inviting with a fireplace and twin sets of double doors opening to a wraparound porch that's also accessed by the master suite. This spacious suite features luxurious extras like His and Hers sinks, a separate garden tub and shower, and a huge walk-in closet. The kitchen provides plenty of counter space and overlooks the formal dining room. Upstairs, two additional bedrooms open up to a second-floor porch and have their own private baths and walk-in closets.

basement

first floor

second floor

PLAN: HPK1300165

STYLE: TIDEWATER

SQUARE FOOTAGE: 2,136

BONUS SPACE: 1,428 SQ. FT.

BEDROOMS: 3

BATHROOMS: 2

WIDTH: 44' - 0"

DEPTH: 63' - 0"

FOUNDATION: ISLAND

BASEMENT

■ This raised Tidewater design is well suited for many building situations, with comfortable outdoor areas that encourage year-round living. Horizontal siding and a steeply pitched roof call up a sense of the past, while a smart-space interior redefines the luxury of comfort with up-to-the-minute amenities. A vaulted ceiling highlights the great room, made comfy by a centered fireplace, extensive built-ins, and French doors that let in fresh air and sunlight. The formal dining room opens from the entry hall and features a triple-window view of the side property. A secluded sitting area in the master suite features a wide window and a door to a private area of the rear porch. Two secondary bedrooms share a full bath.

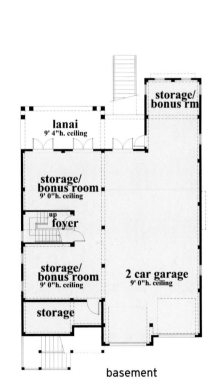

basement

first floor

PLAN: HPK1300166

STYLE: ITALIANATE

SQUARE FOOTAGE: 2,137

BEDROOMS: 3

BATHROOMS: 2

WIDTH: 44' - 0"

DEPTH: 61' - 0"

FOUNDATION: ISLAND
BASEMENT

■ The grand balustrade and recessed entry are just the beginning of this truly spectacular home. A hip vaulted ceiling highlights the great room—a perfect place to entertain, made cozy by a massive fireplace and built-in cabinetry. An angled snack counter provides an uninterrupted interior vista of the living area from the gourmet kitchen. To the rear of the plan, French doors open to a spacious lanai—a beautiful spot for enjoying the harmonious sounds of the sea. On the lower level, separate bonus spaces easily convert to hobby rooms or can be used for additional storage. An additional storage area promises room for unused toys and furnishings.

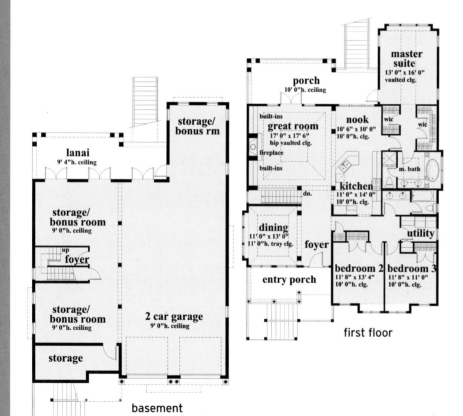

PLAN: HPK1300167

STYLE: VACATION

FIRST FLOOR: 1,212 SQ. FT.

SECOND FLOOR: 620 SQ. FT.

TOTAL: 1,832 SQ. FT.

BEDROOMS: 3

BATHROOMS: 2

WIDTH: 38' - 0"

DEPTH: 40' - 0"

FOUNDATION: UNFINISHED BASEMENT

■ A cross-gabled design with an oceanfront view means a bright, airy space at the center of the plan. A dual-facing fireplace also brings warmth to the gathering room as well as to the master bedroom. A walk-in closet and full bath, featuring a corner tub and dual vanities, serve the homeowners. Upstairs, two large bedrooms enjoy spacious closets and comfortably share a full bath. The broad wrap-around porch and sunroom present plenty of opportunities for vacation enjoyment.

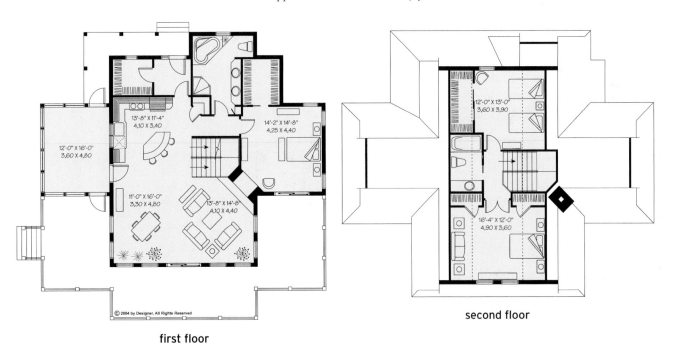

first floor

second floor

PLAN: HPK1300168

STYLE: COUNTRY COTTAGE

FIRST FLOOR: 1,440 SQ. FT.

SECOND FLOOR: 1,086 SQ. FT.

TOTAL: 2,526 SQ. FT.

BEDROOMS: 3

BATHROOMS: 3½

WIDTH: 48' - 0"

DEPTH: 60' - 0"

FOUNDATION: UNFINISHED
BASEMENT

■ Two beautiful decks on the front and at the back make this a wonderful plan to call home. A Palladian window provides plenty of natural light for the two-story living room. The country kitchen includes a large island snack bar and access to the front patio. A spacious first-floor master suite boasts a sitting area and a walk-through closet leading to a private bath. The second floor contains two bedrooms, two baths, and a reading room.

first floor

second floor

PLAN: HPK1300169

STYLE: VICTORIAN

FIRST FLOOR: 778 SQ. FT.

SECOND FLOOR: 810 SQ. FT.

TOTAL: 1,588 SQ. FT.

BEDROOMS: 3

BATHROOMS: 1½

WIDTH: 38' - 0"

DEPTH: 35' - 0"

FOUNDATION: UNFINISHED BASEMENT

■ This lovely two-story home draws heavily on the Queen Anne period with the covered porch that encompasses the lower half of the nested tower. Flanking the foyer on the right is the entertaining family room—great for gatherings. The gourmet kitchen enjoys plenty of counter space and is open to the breakfast area which accesses the rear porch. Completing this floor is a powder room with a utility room nearby. The second floor holds two family bedrooms and a luxurious master suite, all sharing a full bath that includes an oversized pampering tub—note the master bedroom accesses the bath through its own private pocket door.

first floor

second floor

Flexible Designs for Families

PLAN: HPK1300170

STYLE: FARMHOUSE

FIRST FLOOR: 957 SQ. FT.

SECOND FLOOR: 880 SQ. FT.

TOTAL: 1,837 SQ. FT.

BEDROOMS: 3

BATHROOMS: 2½

WIDTH: 48' - 0"

DEPTH: 41' - 2"

FOUNDATION: UNFINISHED BASEMENT

■ A wraparound porch and a wide variety of windows ornament the facade of this country home. Special amenities on the first floor include a fireplace—focused on the living room, but still visible from the cozy dining area—a bay-windowed sitting area to the front of the plan, and a large walk-in closet near the breakfast nook. Upstairs, three bedrooms—one a master suite with a private bath—all access another petite sitting area.

first floor

second floor

PLAN: HPK1300171

STYLE: COUNTRY

FIRST FLOOR: 880 SQ. FT.

SECOND FLOOR: 880 SQ. FT.

TOTAL: 1,760 SQ. FT.

BONUS SPACE: 256 SQ. FT.

BEDROOMS: 3

BATHROOMS: 2½

WIDTH: 42' - 0"

DEPTH: 40' - 0"

FOUNDATION: UNFINISHED BASEMENT

■ The family room located in the turret of the first floor benefits from the see-through fireplace and generous fenestration. A large dining area and island kitchen with breakfast nook round out the home's common areas. Three bedrooms reside upstairs, including a spacious master suite. Dual vanities located just outside the bath provide a quaint, mid-century feel. The other two bedrooms enjoy much closet space and comfortably share a full bath. A large bonus area above the garage awaits specification.

first floor

second floor

PLAN: HPK1300172

STYLE: VICTORIAN

FIRST FLOOR: 880 SQ. FT.

SECOND FLOOR: 880 SQ. FT.

TOTAL: 1,760 SQ. FT.

BONUS SPACE: 256 SQ. FT.

BEDROOMS: 3

BATHROOMS: 2½

WIDTH: 42' - 0"

DEPTH: 40' - 0"

FOUNDATION: UNFINISHED BASEMENT

■ This country Victorian design comes loaded with charm and amenities. The entry leads to open living space, defined by a two-sided fireplace and a large bay window. An island counter with a snack bar highlights the L-shaped kitchen. A quiet sitting area opens to the outdoors. Upstairs, the master suite allows plenty of sunlight from the turret's bay window and boasts a step-up tub, dual-sink vanity, and separate shower. Bonus space above the garage offers room for future expansion.

first floor

second floor

PLAN: HPK1300173

STYLE: VICTORIAN

FIRST FLOOR: 1,070 SQ. FT.

SECOND FLOOR: 970 SQ. FT.

TOTAL: 2,040 SQ. FT.

BEDROOMS: 3

BATHROOMS: 1½

WIDTH: 36' - 0"

DEPTH: 40' - 8"

FOUNDATION: UNFINISHED BASEMENT

■ Victorian styling can come in an affordable size, as this home shows. A sitting area inside the front hall connects with the family room for handling large parties. An enclosed room off the sitting area can be used as a study or extra bedroom. A combination half-bath and laundry is just inside the rear entrance for quick cleanup; the covered rear porch is accessed from a door just beyond the laundry area. For easy upkeep, the three bedrooms on the second floor share a full bath that includes a corner tub. One of the bedrooms offers access to a private balcony.

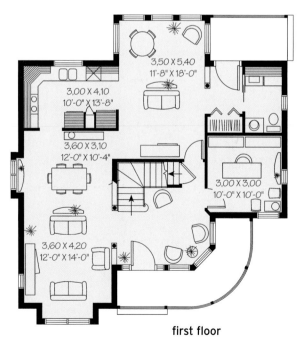

first floor

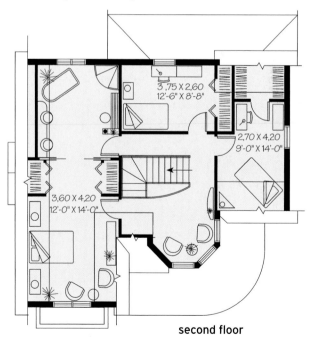

second floor

PLAN: HPK1300174

STYLE: COUNTRY COTTAGE
FIRST FLOOR: 1,155 SQ. FT.
SECOND FLOOR: 1,209 SQ. FT.
TOTAL: 2,364 SQ. FT.
BEDROOMS: 4
BATHROOMS: 2½
WIDTH: 46' - 0"
DEPTH: 36' - 8"
FOUNDATION: UNFINISHED
BASEMENT

■ With both farmhouse flavor and Victorian details, this plan features a wraparound veranda and a bayed area on the first and second floors as well as a turret on the second floor. Inside, the living room's many windows pour light in. The dining area begins with a bay window and is conveniently near the kitchen and breakfast area—also with a bay window. The U-shaped kitchen features an island workstation, ensuring plenty of space for cooking projects. A nearby lavatory is available for guests. The family room has an eye-catching corner-set fireplace. Upstairs, three family bedrooms share a full hall bath, while the master suite has a private bath and balcony, a large walk-in closet, and a sitting alcove, placed within the turret.

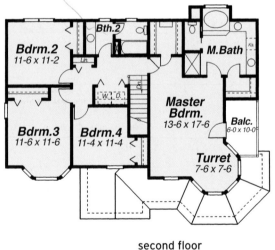

first floor

second floor

PLAN: HPK1300175

STYLE: EUROPEAN COTTAGE

FIRST FLOOR: 934 SQ. FT.

SECOND FLOOR: 1,108 SQ. FT.

TOTAL: 2,042 SQ. FT.

BEDROOMS: 4

BATHROOMS: 2½

WIDTH: 44' - 8"

DEPTH: 36' - 0"

FOUNDATION: UNFINISHED BASEMENT

■ This magnificent European adaptation is highlighted by hipped roofs, plenty of windows, cornice detailing, and an elegant entrance door adjacent to an impressive two-story turret. Inside are a magnificent living/dining area, U-shaped kitchen, breakfast bar, and comfortable family room. A gracious staircase leads upstairs to a deluxe master suite lavish in its efforts to pamper you. A well-lit home office and two secondary bedrooms share this level with a full bath.

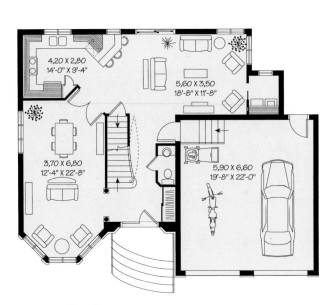

4,20 X 2,80
14'-0" X 9'-4"

5,60 X 3,50
18'-8" X 11'-8"

3,70 X 6,80
12'-4" X 22'-8"

5,90 X 6,60
19'-8" X 22'-0"

first floor

3,60 X 3,00
12'-0" X 10'-0"

3,30 X 3,60
11'-0" X 12'-0"

3,70 X 4,80
12'-4" X 16'-0"

BEDROOM OR OFFICE
3,00 X 3,00
10'-0" X 10'-0"

second floor

PLAN: HPK1300176

STYLE: FRENCH COUNTRY

FIRST FLOOR: 2,049 SQ. FT.

SECOND FLOOR: 458 SQ. FT.

TOTAL: 2,507 SQ. FT.

BEDROOMS: 4

BATHROOMS: 3

WIDTH: 42' - 0"

DEPTH: 76' - 7"

FOUNDATION: SLAB

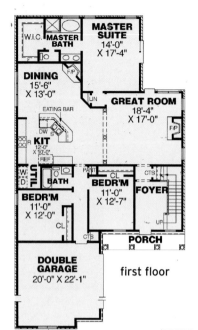

first floor

second floor

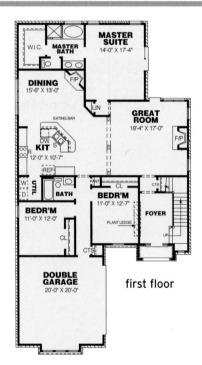

first floor

second floor

PLAN: HPK1300177

STYLE: FRENCH

FIRST FLOOR: 2,056 SQ. FT.

SECOND FLOOR: 458 SQ. FT.

TOTAL: 2,514 SQ. FT.

BEDROOMS: 4

BATHROOMS: 3

WIDTH: 42' - 0"

DEPTH: 76' - 5"

FOUNDATION: SLAB

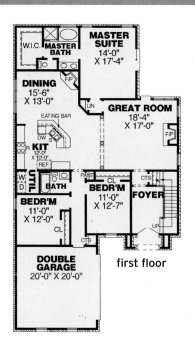

MASTER SUITE 14'-0" X 17'-4"

W.I.C. **MASTER BATH**

DINING 15'-6" X 13'-0"

GREAT ROOM 18'-4" X 17'-0"

EATING BAR

DW

KIT 12'-0" X 10'-0"

REF

UTIL

BATH

BEDR'M 11'-0" X 12'-7"

FOYER

UP

BEDR'M 11'-0" X 12'-0"

CL

DOUBLE GARAGE 20'-0" X 20'-0"

first floor

CL

BEDR'M GAMER'M 18'-9" X 17'-0"

BATH

ATTIC

DN

FOYER BELOW

PLANT LEDGE

second floor

PLAN: HPK1300178

STYLE: TRADITIONAL

FIRST FLOOR: 2,049 SQ. FT.

SECOND FLOOR: 458 SQ. FT.

TOTAL: 2,507 SQ. FT.

BEDROOMS: 4

BATHROOMS: 3

WIDTH: 42' - 0"

DEPTH: 74' - 11"

FOUNDATION: SLAB

PLAN: HPK1300179

STYLE: FRENCH

FIRST FLOOR: 1,568 SQ. FT.

SECOND FLOOR: 657 SQ. FT.

TOTAL: 2,225 SQ. FT.

BONUS SPACE: 329 SQ. FT.

BEDROOMS: 3

BATHROOMS: 2½

WIDTH: 45' - 0"

DEPTH: 58' - 0"

FOUNDATION: CRAWLSPACE

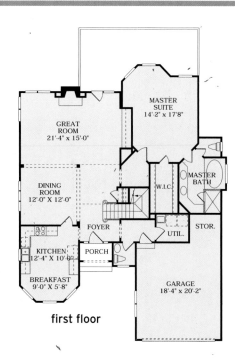

GREAT ROOM 21'-4" X 15'-0"

MASTER SUITE 14'-2" x 17'8"

DINING ROOM 12'-0" X 12'-0"

W.I.C.

MASTER BATH

FOYER

UTIL.

STOR.

KITCHEN 12'-4" X 10'-0"

PORCH

BREAKFAST 9'-0" X 5'-8"

GARAGE 18'-4" x 20'-2"

first floor

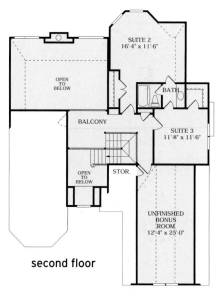

SUITE 2 16'-4" x 11'-6"

OPEN TO BELOW

BATH

BALCONY

SUITE 3 11'-8" x 11'-6"

OPEN TO BELOW

STOR.

UNFINISHED BONUS ROOM 12'-4" x 25'-0"

second floor

Flexible Designs For Families

PLAN: HPK1300180

STYLE: COUNTRY COTTAGE
FIRST FLOOR: 1,398 SQ. FT.
SECOND FLOOR: 515 SQ. FT.
TOTAL: 1,913 SQ. FT.
BONUS SPACE: 282 SQ. FT.
BEDROOMS: 3
BATHROOMS: 2½
WIDTH: 48' - 0"
DEPTH: 50' - 10"
FOUNDATION: CRAWLSPACE,
SLAB, UNFINISHED
WALKOUT BASEMENT

■ Varied rooflines, keystones, and arches set off a stucco exterior that's highlighted by a stone turret and a bay window. Inside, the formal dining room leads to a private covered porch for after-dinner conversation on pleasant evenings. The central kitchen boasts a built-in planning desk, an ample pantry, and an angled counter that overlooks the breakfast room. Sleeping quarters include a first-floor master suite with a vaulted bath and a plant shelf, and two second-floor family bedrooms that share a balcony overlook and a full bath.

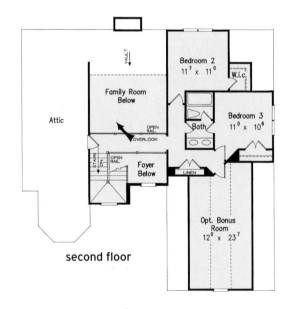

first floor

second floor

Great views and calming blue colors distinguish this master bedroom.

Distinctive Homes for Couples

A relaxing master suite is the perfect place to start and end your day

Among the features you'll find in the homes showcased in this chapter are sprawling, soothing master suites. The master bath, in particular, has earned a tremendous amount of attention from architects and designers as a haven for homeowners—and narrow-lot homes, as you'll see, are no exception.

The average square footage of master baths built today is at least double what it was a mere 20 years ago—a spacious trend that can be seen across every home style. Within that larger area, couples are carving out personal space for each of them. Dual vanities are featured in the master suite of every home in this chapter, along with a separate tub and shower. If one homeowner appreciates the therapeutic benefits of a whirlpool tub while their spouse enjoys the convenience of a quick shower these master suites will offer something for everyone.

With this added space and comfort in the master bath, homeowners are giving more and more consideration to the products they use within those spaces. Talk to your builder about the options available for bath fixtures, flooring, and more. Give careful thought to the styles you select, as well as their practicality: an antique-styled claw-foot tub looks terrific, but can be out of place in a contemporary home. Meanwhile, if you and your spouse prefer showers to long soaks in the tub, you may want to focus your resources on the latest full-body sprays and other shower amenities rather than the finest whirlpool tub.

STORE MORE

One reason that homeowners who are drawn to classic home styles still choose to build new, rather than buy an existing home, is storage space. We have outgrown the tiny, box-like closets of hundred-year-old homes, and demand much more, especially in our master suites.

The designers showcased in this chapter have created fabulous walk-in closet spaces, even within the confines of a narrow lot. Consider the configuration of your master suite and where you'd like your closet. Some are accessed through the master bath, while others open into the bedroom.

Whatever you choose, you'll be sure to delight in the amount of storage space your new home provides—it may even be time to expand that wardrobe.

Right: In floor plans like this one (page 222), walk-in closets aren't an afterthought—they are a prime feature of the master suite.

Bedtime Stories

With all the focus on the master bathroom, the bedroom has become almost an afterthought. But the designs highlighted here haven't forgotten where you'll rest your head.

Begin your search for the perfect bedroom by considering its size. You certainly want something that will comfortably accommodate your bed—and even that king-sized model you may be dreaming of.

While thinking about space, you may want to look for a master suite that includes a sitting area. A sitting area can be a great place to escape with a good book, or to slowly welcome the new day with a cup of coffee. In short, it can go a long way toward making your master suite a true private retreat.

Added amenities

You may want to look for other special features to add an even more personal touch to your master suite, depending upon how you plan to use the space. Some of the more luxurious master suites today incorporate a morning kitchen, where you can brew that first cup of coffee without leaving your bedroom.

Access to the outdoors can add a special touch to the master suite as well when the weather is right. A private balcony or patio can create a romantic getaway to enjoy sunsets, or a great spot to welcome the new day. ∎

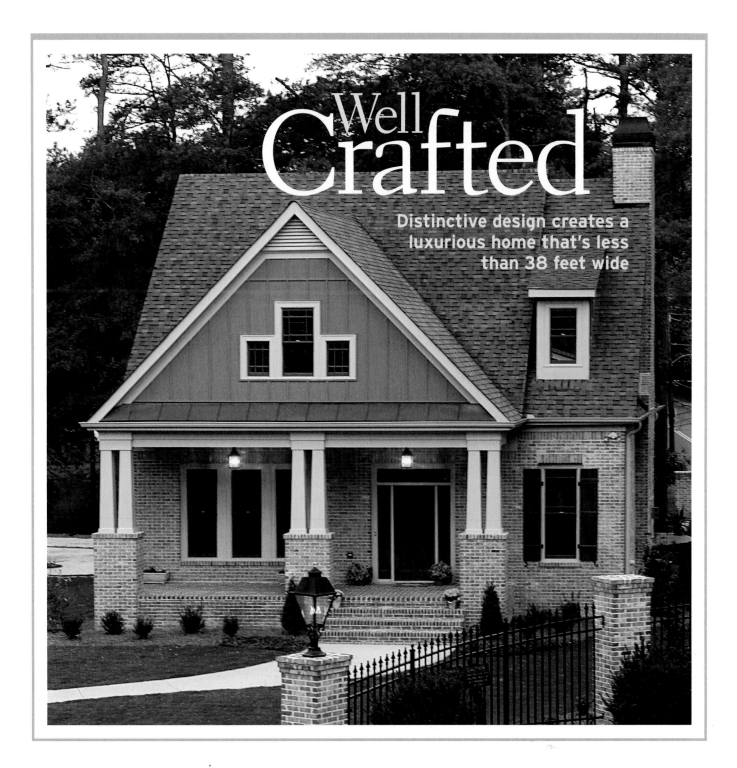

Well Crafted

Distinctive design creates a luxurious home that's less than 38 feet wide

Adding overhead windows like these, plus skylights, adds to the sense of space in a home. Below: As a result, this home is filled with natural light.

The wonderful attention to detail on this brick-and-siding exterior, with its distinctive Craftsman inspiration, hints at the home's message—a narrow facade can contain the height of luxury, both inside and out.

The beautiful but modest exterior gives way to a well-designed interior with a kitchen-centric layout. With four bedrooms, more than 3,200 square feet of living space, and easy access to the outdoors, this is a design that can offer it all in a concise package.

A spacious island anchors the kitchen, with a serving bar for quick meals. From there, the entire first floor is just steps away,

beginning with a casual keeping room that's connected to the breakfast area. This is a perfect spot where kids can play with their toys and a parent can keep an eye on them while preparing meals in the kitchen—and with the even larger living room nearby, kids don't necessarily have to pick up every time company comes over.

The living room features a large brick hearth with an optional niche above for a flat-screen television. Beamed ceilings, built-ins, and transom windows above add even more charm to this gorgeous room.

Both the living room and keeping room have access to the screened porch, a

Above: The living room has a fireplace and access to a screened porch to the left. Right: The kitchen enjoys a convenient location at the center of the home.

convenient room that's close enough to the kitchen to serve meals when the weather cooperates. Beyond that is an outdoor patio, providing a perfect spot for a grill or complete outdoor kitchen.

Even more spectacular features reside upstairs in this plan, including a flexible space above the garage that has its own full bath. Use it as a media room, game room, exercise room, or guest suite—in any case, it enjoys a terrific location at the back of the house, with privacy from the other bedrooms but easy access to the stairs and the main level.

The best of the second floor can be found in the master suite, which boasts an enormous bedroom and sitting area. A

Shed dormers on the back and side of the home increase space upstairs. The porch and patio add outdoor living areas.

A rear-loading garage saves space on a narrow-lot home.

first floor

second floor

PLAN: HPK1300329

STYLE: COUNTRY COTTAGE

FIRST FLOOR: 1,388 SQ. FT.

SECOND FLOOR: 1,835 SQ. FT.

TOTAL: 3,223 SQ. FT.

BEDROOMS: 4

BATHROOMS: 3½

WIDTH: 37' - 6"

DEPTH: 78' - 5"

FOUNDATION: UNFINISHED BASEMENT

decorative stepped ceiling adds interest and dormers usher in natural light. A walk-in closet offers plenty of space, while the master bath delivers on its promise of luxurious relaxation. ∎

PLAN: HPK1300181

STYLE: EUROPEAN COTTAGE

SQUARE FOOTAGE: 1,612

BEDROOMS: 2

BATHROOMS: 2

WIDTH: 42' - 0"

DEPTH: 67' - 4"

FOUNDATION: SLAB,
UNFINISHED BASEMENT

■ A brick-and-stone exterior with shake siding decorates the front of this delightful home. The large great room enjoys an 11-foot ceiling, gas fireplace, and access to the rear porch. The master bedroom suite offers a luxury bath with a dual-bowl vanity, whirlpool tub, and large walk-in closet. Access to the rear porch from the master suite is an unexpected feature. This home, designed for a narrow lot, offers spaciousness and luxurious living.

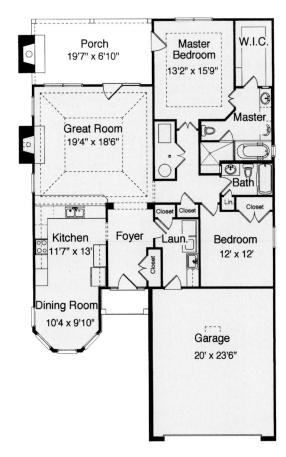

PLAN: HPK1300182

STYLE: EUROPEAN COTTAGE

FIRST FLOOR: 2,221 SQ. FT.

SECOND FLOOR: 602 SQ. FT.

TOTAL: 2,823 SQ. FT.

BEDROOMS: 2

BATHROOMS: 3

WIDTH: 50' - 0"

DEPTH: 70' - 4"

FOUNDATION: UNFINISHED
BASEMENT, SLAB

■ Just under 3,000 square feet, this two-story home is ideal for an empty-nester couple. The first-floor master suite is a blend of practicality and lavishness. The library adjacent to the master suite is an ideal location for a home office. The family bedroom on this level can serve as a guest suite or accomodations for an in-law. The open layout allows the design to flow without the use of unnecessary walls. An eating bar in the spacious kitchen cleverly serves the adjoining dining and great rooms. Access to the rear patio—equipped with an outdoor fireplace—from the dining room, welcomes alfresco meals and entertaining. With the majority of the living space on the first floor, a bonus room and full bath on the second floor is great for additional guests or visiting children.

second floor

first floor

PLAN: HPK1300183

STYLE: EUROPEAN COTTAGE

FIRST FLOOR: 2,230 SQ. FT.

SECOND FLOOR: 601 SQ. FT.

TOTAL: 2,831 SQ. FT.

BEDROOMS: 2

BATHROOMS: 3

WIDTH: 50' - 0"

DEPTH: 70' - 4"

FOUNDATION: UNFINISHED BASEMENT, SLAB

■ Although it might appear petite from the outside, once inside, this plan proves to be the perfect size for a couple. The first-floor master suite is a blend of practicality and lavishness. The library adjacent to the master suite is an ideal location for a home office. The family bedroom on this level can serve as a guest suite or accomodations for an in-law. The open layout allows the design to flow without the use of unnecessary walls. An eating bar in the spacious kitchen cleverly serves the adjoining dining and great rooms. Access to the rear patio—equipped with an outdoor fireplace—from the dining room, welcomes alfresco meals and entertaining. With the majority of the living space on the first floor, a bonus room and full bath on the second floor is great for additional guests or visiting children.

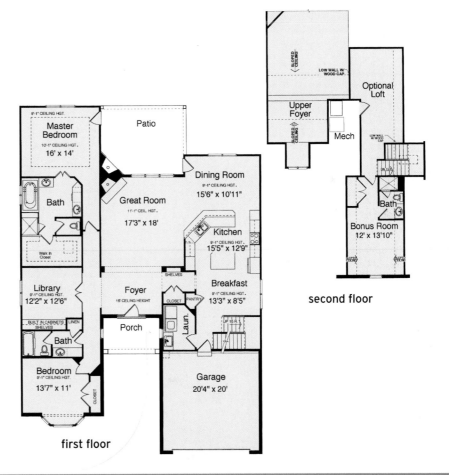

first floor

second floor

PLAN: HPK1300184

STYLE: COUNTRY COTTAGE

FIRST FLOOR: 2,037 SQ. FT.

SECOND FLOOR: 596 SQ. FT.

TOTAL: 2,633 SQ. FT.

BEDROOMS: 2

BATHROOMS: 3

WIDTH: 42' - 0"

DEPTH: 75' - 0"

FOUNDATION: UNFINISHED BASEMENT, SLAB

■ This beautiful home offers angles and varied ceiling heights throughout. The great room showcases these elements, and enjoys access to the covered porch and a view to the rear yard. Interior and exterior fireplaces provide a cozy atmosphere. Enjoyment of the great room expands into the formal dining area. The master bedroom suite offers a luxurious bath and access to the covered porch. Split stairs overlook the gallery, and lead to the second floor loft, full bath, and bonus room.

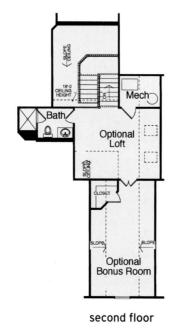

second floor

first floor

PLAN: HPK1300185

STYLE: COUNTRY COTTAGE

SQUARE FOOTAGE: 1,915

BEDROOMS: 3

BATHROOMS: 2

WIDTH: 46' - 0"

DEPTH: 60' - 2"

FOUNDATION: CRAWLSPACE

■ A sunny bay window and a shady recessed entry create an elegant impression in this lovely design. The sleeping quarters are arranged for privacy along the perimeter of the spacious living areas. The kitchen provides a generous work space, and the dining room is open to the gathering room with its fireplace. To the rear, a covered veranda is accessible from the dining room and the master suite. Note the lavish bath and huge walk-in closet in this suite.

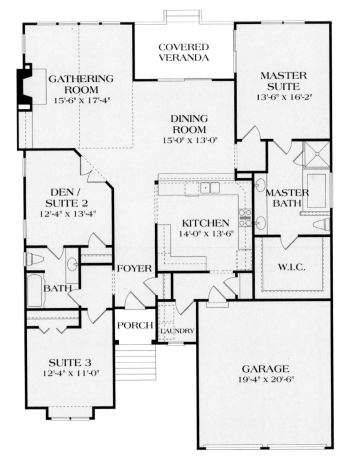

GATHERING ROOM
15'-6" x 17'-4"

COVERED VERANDA

MASTER SUITE
13'-6" x 16'-2"

DINING ROOM
15'-0" x 13'-0"

DEN / SUITE 2
12'-4" x 13'-4"

KITCHEN
14'-0" x 13'-6"

MASTER BATH

FOYER

BATH

W.I.C.

PORCH

LAUNDRY

SUITE 3
12'-4" x 11'-0"

GARAGE
19'-4" x 20'-6"

PLAN: HPK1300186

STYLE: TRADITIONAL

FIRST FLOOR: 1,897 SQ. FT.

SECOND FLOOR: 301 SQ. FT.

TOTAL: 2,198 SQ. FT.

BEDROOMS: 2

BATHROOMS: 3

WIDTH: 48' - 0"

DEPTH: 63' - 10"

FOUNDATION: UNFINISHED BASEMENT

■ Designed for a narrow lot, this delightful home offers an open great room and dining area with views to the rear yard, a deluxe master bedroom suite, private library or optional second bedroom and cozy screened porch. Multiple closets help keep an orderly home and an open kitchen, defined by an island with seating, makes time spent preparing meals a pleasurable experience. This home makes a perfect vacation retreat or empty-nester residence. A second-floor bedroom with a private bath offers privacy for overnight guests or for additional family members.

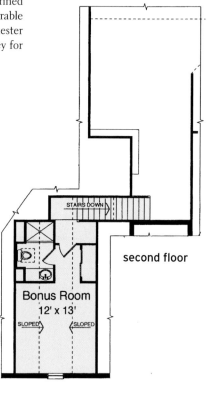

first floor

second floor

PLAN: HPK1300187

PLAN: HPK1300187

STYLE: TRANSITIONAL

SQUARE FOOTAGE: 1,462

BEDROOMS: 3

BATHROOMS: 2½

WIDTH: 46' - 0"

DEPTH: 59' - 4"

FOUNDATION: FINISHED WALKOUT BASEMENT

■ This transitional-style home is a great narrow-lot design. Inside, the foyer opens to the great room/dining area combination—here, a corner fireplace warms crisp evenings. The kitchen easily serves the dining area and optional screened porch, which is great for seasonal outdoor meals. The first-floor master suite includes a whirlpool bath and a walk-in closet. The laundry room leads to the two-car garage. Optional basement-level fixtures include a spacious recreation room, a hall bath, and two additional bedrooms—one easily converts to a library. Basement storage and unexcavated space is reserved for future developments.

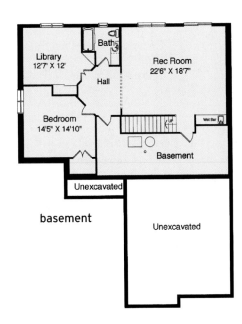

basement

first floor

PLAN: HPK1300188

STYLE: COUNTRY COTTAGE

SQUARE FOOTAGE: 1,422

BEDROOMS: 3

BATHROOMS: 2

WIDTH: 45' - 0"

DEPTH: 51' - 4"

FOUNDATION: UNFINISHED
WALKOUT BASEMENT

■ Homeowners can wait out rainy days on the front covered porch of this home and likewise enjoy sunny afternoons on the rear deck. They'll find spacious shelter inside in the large great room, easily accessible from the kitchen with a breakfast nook. With a corner fireplace and rear deck access, the great room will be buzzing with activity. Two secondary bedrooms—make one a library—share a full hall bath. The master suite is graciously appointed with a private bath and walk-in closet.

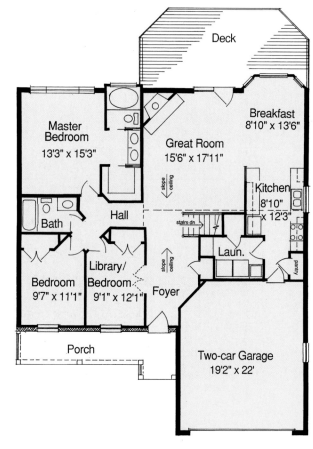

PLAN: HPK1300189

STYLE: TRADITIONAL

SQUARE FOOTAGE: 1,561

BEDROOMS: 2

BATHROOMS: 2

WIDTH: 50' - 0"

DEPTH: 50' - 0"

■ Clean lines characterize the elevation of this sophisticated ranch home. The volume entry with transom windows offers expansive views of the great room. Just off the entry, the formal living room serves as an optional third bedroom. Flexibility is also designed into the dining room and great room, which share a 10-foot ceiling. A thoughtfully designed kitchen with a pantry and corner sink serves the sunny breakfast area, which accesses a covered deck. The master suite includes a volume ceiling and a master bath with a whirlpool tub and skylight. One secondary bedroom is provided—or add one more by making the living room a bedroom.

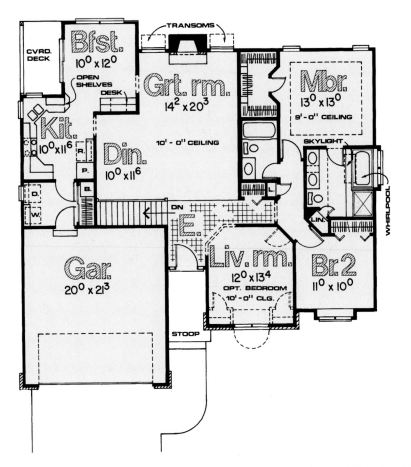

PLAN: HPK1300190

STYLE: TRADITIONAL

SQUARE FOOTAGE: 1,758

BEDROOMS: 2

BATHROOMS: 2

WIDTH: 48' - 0"

DEPTH: 63' - 0"

FOUNDATION: FINISHED
BASEMENT

■ Designed for a narrow lot, this one-story home offers an open great room with a cozy fireplace and dining area with excellent views to the backyard, rear deck and delightful screened porch—great for the summer. The conveniently located kitchen enjoys an island cooktop and plenty of cabinet and counter space. A library/bedroom is found at the entrance of the house while a secluded master bedroom is found to the rear left of the home for extra privacy. This master retreat boasts a dressing area, dual vanities, an angled soaking tub and a large walk-in closet. The future space in the basement holds a spacious recreation room for family entertainment, a large family bedroom, and another library/bedroom all sharing a full bath.

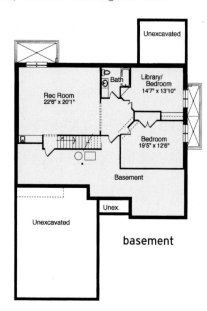

basement

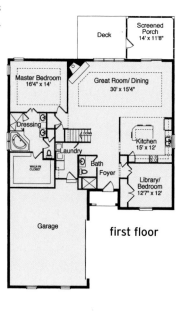

first floor

PLAN: HPK1300191

STYLE: TRADITIONAL

SQUARE FOOTAGE: 1,943

BEDROOMS: 2

BATHROOMS: 2

WIDTH: 35' - 0"

DEPTH: 75' - 0"

FOUNDATION: SLAB

■ This traditional-style home begins with a private side entrance and a covered entry porch. A large living room with a corner fireplace opens to the patio area. A laundry area is nestled between the garage, the U-shaped kitchen and the skylit dinette. Both the study and the master suite feature tray ceilings. The master suite also enjoys a double-sink vanity, a tub and separate shower, and two walk-in closets. A second bedroom features a walk-in closet and accesses a full hall bath.

for Couples

PLAN: HPK1300192

STYLE: EUROPEAN COTTAGE
SQUARE FOOTAGE: 1,673
BEDROOMS: 3
BATHROOMS: 2
WIDTH: 48' - 0"
DEPTH: 63' - 1"
FOUNDATION: SLAB

■ Quaint country charm pervades the facade of this one-story ranch plan. The living room at the heart of the floor plan features a fireplace and a 10-foot ceiling. The island kitchen and dining area are nearby. A rear covered patio leads to an even larger patio area, accessible from the living room and the master bedroom. Note the coffered ceiling and fine bath that are part of the master suite. Twin family rooms share a bath that includes double sinks in the left wing of the home.

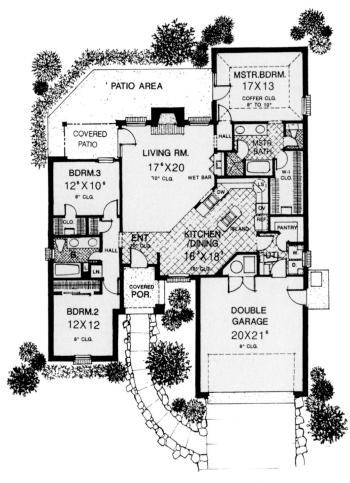

PLAN: HPK1300193

STYLE: TIDEWATER

FIRST FLOOR: 1,143 SQ. FT.

SECOND FLOOR: 651 SQ. FT.

TOTAL: 1,794 SQ. FT.

BEDROOMS: 2

BATHROOMS: 2½

WIDTH: 32' - 0"

DEPTH: 57' - 0"

FOUNDATION: ISLAND
BASEMENT

■ This intriguing home is full of elegant Victorian detail and many amenities. Beyond the grand staircase and central foyer are the living areas; on the left is the dining room and on the right is the kitchen, which provides plenty of counter space and a pantry. The great room includes a fireplace and built-in cabinets. Towards the front of the first floor is a family bedroom with a private bath, a utility room, and a powder room. The master suite (with a master bath) and a loft open to the great room below and dominate the second floor.

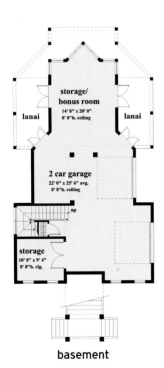

basement

first floor

second floor

PLAN: HPK1300194

STYLE:	ITALIANATE
FIRST FLOOR:	1,143 SQ. FT.
SECOND FLOOR:	651 SQ. FT.
TOTAL:	1,794 SQ. FT.
BONUS SPACE:	476 SQ. FT.
BEDROOMS:	2
BATHROOMS:	2½
WIDTH:	32' - 0"
DEPTH:	57' - 0"
FOUNDATION:	SLAB

■ Italian Country elegance graces the exterior of this casa bellisima, swept in Mediterranean enchantment. The covered entryway extends into the foyer, where straight ahead the two-story great room spaciously enhances the interior. This room features a warming fireplace and offers built-in cabinetry. The open dining room extends through double doors to the veranda on the left side of the plan. The adjacent kitchen features efficient pantry space. A family bedroom with a bath, a powder room, and a utility room also reside on this main floor. Upstairs, a vaulted master suite with a vaulted private bath and deck share the floor with a loft area, which overlooks the great room. Downstairs, the basement-level bonus room and storage area share space with the two-car garage. Two lanais open on either side of the bonus room for additional outdoor patio space.

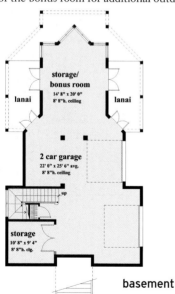

basement

first floor

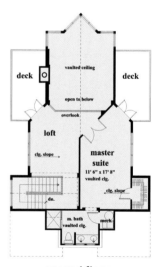

second floor

PLAN: HPK1300195

STYLE: FLORIDIAN

FIRST FLOOR: 906 SQ. FT.

SECOND FLOOR: 714 SQ. FT.

TOTAL: 1,620 SQ. FT.

BEDROOMS: 2

BATHROOMS: 2½

WIDTH: 40' - 0"

DEPTH: 37' - 0"

FOUNDATION: UNFINISHED BASEMENT

■ A unique tower with an observation deck will make this design a standout in any location. Inside, an impressive entry with a wrapping stair leads to three levels of livability. The main level includes a gallery leading to a formal dining room, a counter-filled kitchen on the left and a vaulted great room on the right. Five French doors on the main level access a covered porch spanning the width of the home. The upper level houses the master bedroom, with a sumptuous bath and a private deck, a guest bedroom and a large hall bath. On the lower level, the split two-car garage offers additional storage space.

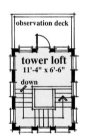

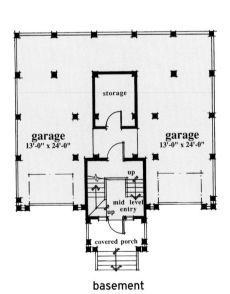

basement

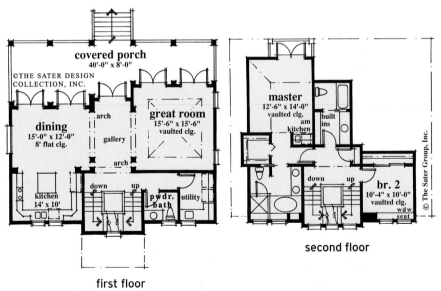

first floor

second floor

©THE SATER DESIGN COLLECTION, INC.

© The Sater Group, Inc.

PLAN: HPK1300196

STYLE: BUNGALOW

FIRST FLOOR: 1,143 SQ. FT.

SECOND FLOOR: 651 SQ. FT.

TOTAL: 1,794 SQ. FT.

BONUS SPACE: 651 SQ. FT.

BEDROOMS: 2

BATHROOMS: 2½

WIDTH: 32' - 0"

DEPTH: 57' - 0"

FOUNDATION: UNFINISHED
WALKOUT BASEMENT

■ This traditional country cabin is a vacationer's dream. Stone and vertical wood siding rustically camouflage the exterior; the inside pampers in lavish style. An elegant entryway extends into the foyer, where straight ahead, the two-story great room visually expands the lofty interior. This room provides a warming fireplace and offers built-in cabinetry. Double doors open to a fresh veranda, which wraps around to the rear deck—a perfect place to enjoy the outdoors. Upstairs, a vaulted ceiling enhances the master suite and its private bath. A private deck from the master suite can be accessed through a set of double doors. The loft area overlooking the great room accesses a second deck. The basement level hosts a bonus room, storage area, and two-car garage.

second floor

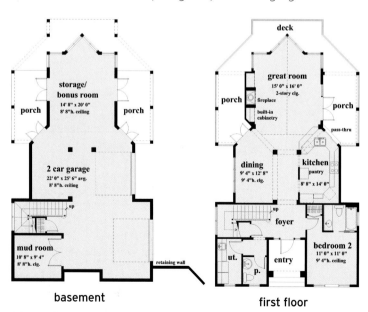

basement

first floor

PLAN: HPK1300197

STYLE: TIDEWATER

FIRST FLOOR: 1,671 SQ. FT.

SECOND FLOOR: 846 SQ. FT.

TOTAL: 2,517 SQ. FT.

BEDROOMS: 3

BATHROOMS: 2

WIDTH: 44' - 0"

DEPTH: 55' - 0"

FOUNDATION: ISLAND
BASEMENT

■ Exotic tropical breezes will find their way through the joyful rooms of this just-right cottage, bringing with them a sense of tranquility and contentment. The great room provides such luxurious amenities as a vaulted ceiling, built-ins, a grand fireplace and an overlook from the upper-level gallery hall. An efficient island kitchen is nestled between a sunny nook and the formal dining room, which is elegantly defined by regal columns. Pocket doors open to a private study to the left of the foyer. Secondary sleeping quarters on this level include two family bedrooms that share a full bath, with a laundry conveniently placed nearby. The upper level is dedicated to the expansive master suite, which boasts a private veranda, tray ceiling, sitting room and walk-in closet. The lower level provides a three-car garage, a lanai and a bonus room for future development.

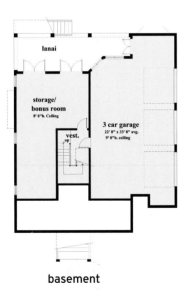

basement

first floor

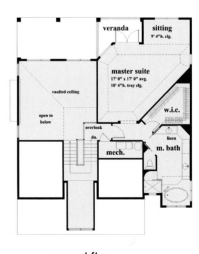

second floor

PLAN: HPK1300198

STYLE: BUNGALOW

FIRST FLOOR: 1,671 SQ. FT.

SECOND FLOOR: 846 SQ. FT.

TOTAL: 2,517 SQ. FT.

BONUS SPACE: 518 SQ. FT.

BEDROOMS: 3

BATHROOMS: 2

WIDTH: 44' - 0"

DEPTH: 55' - 0"

FOUNDATION: ISLAND

BASEMENT

■ An array of elegant details creates a welcoming entry to this new-century home, with massive stone pillars, a matchstick pediment, and a stunning turret. The main-level foyer leads up to the spacious living area and down to the lower-level bonus room, which boasts a covered porch, ski storage, mudroom, and three-car garage. On the main level, a vaulted ceiling highlights the great room, and a fireplace warms the open interior. French doors bring in a feeling of nature and provide access to the rear covered porch. Secondary sleeping quarters reside to the right of the plan, connected by a gallery hall that offers a full bath.

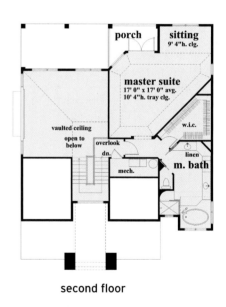

second floor

basement

first floor

PLAN: HPK1300199

STYLE: ITALIANATE

FIRST FLOOR: 1,266 SQ. FT.

SECOND FLOOR: 1,324 SQ. FT.

TOTAL: 2,590 SQ. FT.

BEDROOMS: 3

BATHROOMS: 2½

WIDTH: 34' - 0"

DEPTH: 63' - 2"

FOUNDATION: SLAB

■ This modern take on the Italian villa boasts plenty of indoor/outdoor flow. Four sets of double doors wrap around the great room and dining area and open to the stunning veranda. The great room is enhanced by a coffered ceiling and built-in cabinetry, and the entire first floor is bathed in sunlight from a wall of glass doors overlooking the veranda. The dining room connects to a gourmet island kitchen. Upstairs, a beautiful deck wraps gracefully around the family bedrooms. The master suite is a skylit haven enhanced by a sitting bay, which features a vaulted octagonal ceiling and a cozy two-sided fireplace. Private double doors access the sundeck from the master suite, the secondary bedrooms, and the study.

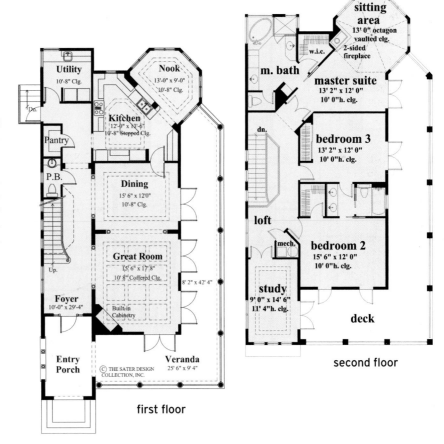

first floor

second floor

PLAN: HPK1300202

STYLE: TRANSITIONAL
FIRST FLOOR: 1,233 SQ. FT.
SECOND FLOOR: 824 SQ. FT.
TOTAL: 2,057 SQ. FT.
BEDROOMS: 3
BATHROOMS: 3
WIDTH: 31' - 10"
DEPTH: 77' - 10"
FOUNDATION: CRAWLSPACE

■ Traditional styling distinguishes this narrow-lot home. As one enters the foyer, the large living room and dining room—both with volume ceilings—are visible beyond. A flex room that can be used as a guest suite or home office/study opens off the foyer. A roomy covered porch is accessed from the breakfast room and provides space for outdoor entertaining. Upstairs, the master suite has all the amenities, including access to a private second-story covered porch. Another bedroom and bath complete this efficiently designed plan.

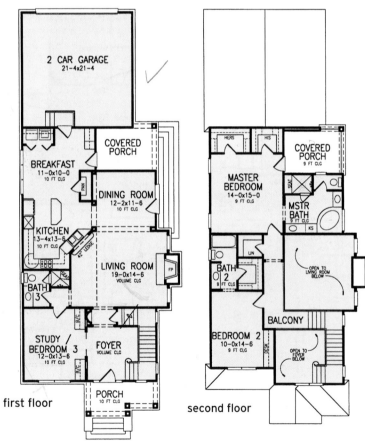

first floor

second floor

PLAN: HPK1300203

STYLE: COUNTRY COTTAGE
FIRST FLOOR: 832 SQ. FT.
SECOND FLOOR: 278 SQ. FT.
TOTAL: 1,110 SQ. FT.
BEDROOMS: 2
BATHROOMS: 2
WIDTH: 32' - 0"
DEPTH: 34' - 0"
FOUNDATION: PIER
(SAME AS PILING)

■ Designed for the relaxing coastal lifestyle, this casual beach house aims to please, with three well-planned levels. The lower level has French doors to the front for privacy and opens to reveal a carport, covered porch, tons of storage (great for sandy surfboards), and an enclosed entry/utility area. The main level features a two-story living room with a wonderful porch that stretches the length of the house. The kitchen is efficient and easily serves the dining area. The master bedroom has an ample walk-in closet and is conveniently adjacent to a full bath. Upstairs, an additional bedroom has a semiprivate bath and accesses the observation room for amazing ocean sunset views.

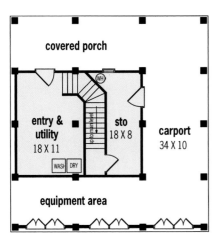

basement

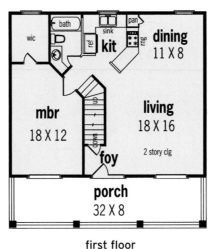

first floor

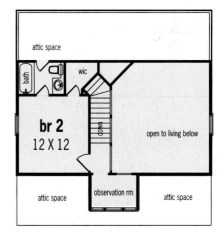

second floor

PLAN: HPK1300204

STYLE: EUROPEAN COTTAGE

FIRST FLOOR: 741 SQ. FT.

SECOND FLOOR: 584 SQ. FT.

TOTAL: 1,325 SQ. FT.

BEDROOMS: 1

BATHROOMS: 1½

WIDTH: 33' - 0"

DEPTH: 26' - 0"

FOUNDATION: UNFINISHED WALKOUT BASEMENT

■ This home is absolutely full of windows, and a large deck enhances the outdoor living possibilities. Picture the wall of windows facing the seashore, with the sound of waves lulling you into a calm, comfortable feeling. Inside, an open floor plan includes a family/dining room, an L-shaped kitchen with a snack bar, and a full bath with laundry facilities. A special treat is the bumped-out hot tub room, almost entirely surrounded by windows. Upstairs, choose either the one- or two-bedroom plan. Both include a full bath and access to the upper balcony.

first floor

second floor

PLAN: HPK1300205

STYLE: TRADITIONAL

FIRST FLOOR: 1,407 SQ. FT.

SECOND FLOOR: 625 SQ. FT.

TOTAL: 2,032 SQ. FT.

BEDROOMS: 3

BATHROOMS: 2½

WIDTH: 40' - 0"

DEPTH: 56' - 0"

FOUNDATION: CRAWLSPACE

■ Captivating and just the right size, this striking home is sided in a pleasing mix of materials: cedar shingles, lap siding, cedar battens and stone. A dormer window over the garage complements the charming exterior. A versatile home office with built-ins and a storage area sits to the left of the foyer. The stairway climbs to an upper level that houses two bedrooms with built-in counters. A shared hall bath boasts a huge walk-in linen closet. The living room, enhanced by a vaulted ceiling, features a fireplace and built-in media center. The dining room has a recessed niche for a hutch. The master suite sits on the main level, complete with a vaulted salon, a bath with spa tub and separate shower, and a massive walk-in closet. Look for a laundry room and half-bath nearby.

second floor

first floor

PLAN: HPK1300206

STYLE: TRADITIONAL

SQUARE FOOTAGE: 1,208

BEDROOMS: 3

BATHROOMS: 2

WIDTH: 48' - 0"

DEPTH: 29' - 0"

FOUNDATION: UNFINISHED

BASEMENT

■ Here is a rustic cottage that provides plenty of amenities. An open interior takes full advantage of outdoor views and allows flexible space. The family room boasts a fireplace and vistas that extend to the rear property. The dining room features a double window and French-door access to the sundeck. Wrapping counters in the kitchen provide plenty of space for food preparation. The master suite provides a compartmented bath, front-property views, and two wardrobes. The secondary bedrooms share a hall with linen storage.

PLAN: HPK1300207

STYLE: TRADITIONAL

SQUARE FOOTAGE: 1,574

BEDROOMS: 2

BATHROOMS: 2

WIDTH: 50' - 0"

DEPTH: 65' - 0"

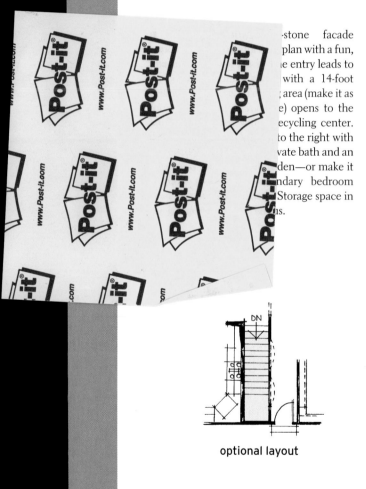

...-stone facade
...plan with a fun,
... entry leads to
... with a 14-foot
... area (make it as
...e) opens to the
...ecycling center.
... to the right with
...vate bath and an
...den—or make it
...ndary bedroom
...Storage space in
...s.

optional layout

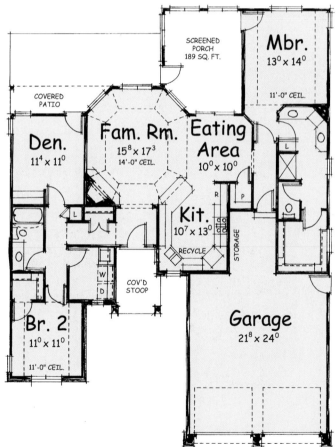

PLAN: HPK1300208

STYLE: CONTEMPORARY

SQUARE FOOTAGE: 1,797

BEDROOMS: 3

BATHROOMS: 2

WIDTH: 45' - 0"

DEPTH: 45' - 2"

FOUNDATION: UNFINISHED
WALKOUT BASEMENT

■ This attractive bungalow home offers a large living area in a moderate square footage. The entry hall contains a spacious closet and access to an optional bedroom/den. Visually open to the dining and great rooms, the kitchen provides an abundance of counter space and cabinets, a pantry and easy access to the laundry room. The master suite features the luxury of a whirlpool tub, double-bowl vanity, compartmented bath and walk-in closet. Two bedrooms or one and a den share a full hall bath. For outdoor enjoyment, a large deck featuring a hot tub is located off the dining room. A two-car garage is located under the home.

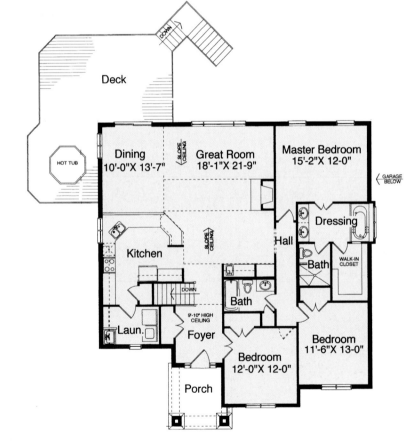

PLAN: HPK1300209

STYLE: FRENCH

SQUARE FOOTAGE: 1,994

BEDROOMS: 3

BATHROOMS: 2

WIDTH: 49' - 0"

DEPTH: 68' - 0"

FOUNDATION: CRAWLSPACE, SLAB

■ French accents inspire this European-influenced creation. A quaint courtyard introduces guests to this family compound. Inside, the central kitchen opens to the morning room. A sunken family room with sloped ceilings features a fireplace and access to the rear porch. The master bedroom, with a private bath and walk-in closet, is placed on the right side of the plan. Two additional family bedrooms reside on the left and share a full bath.

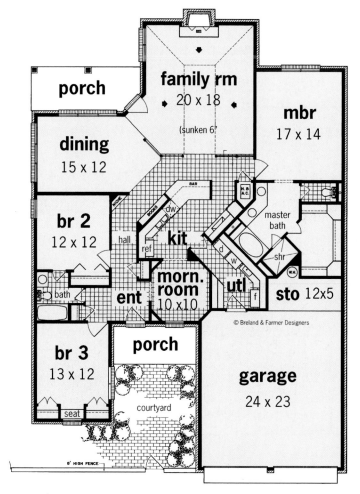

PLAN: HPK1300210

STYLE: FRENCH

SQUARE FOOTAGE: 1,891

BEDROOMS: 2

BATHROOMS: 2

WIDTH: 49' - 0"

DEPTH: 64' - 0"

FOUNDATION: CRAWLSPACE, SLAB

■ The gated courtyard adds privacy and personality to this charming two-bedroom home. The open interior includes a sunken family room with a sloped ceiling, a gracious fireplace, built-ins, and access to a rear porch. A brilliantly sunny dining room sits opposite an open and cleverly angled kitchen—allowing for ease of service between the dining room and the morning room. The living room could be used as a third bedroom or a study. The master suite includes a dual-bowl vanity, a separate bath and shower, and a large walk-in closet.

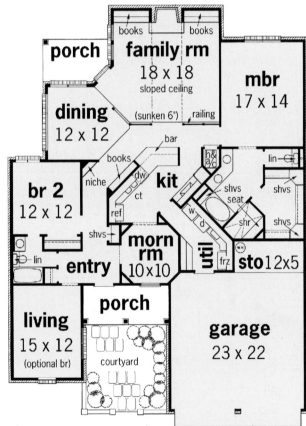

PLAN: HPK1300211

STYLE: MEDITERRANEAN

SQUARE FOOTAGE: 1,723

BEDROOMS: 2

BATHROOMS: 2

WIDTH: 45' - 0"

DEPTH: 62' - 6"

FOUNDATION: UNFINISHED
BASEMENT

■ A New-Age contemporary touch graces the exterior of this impressive yet affordable home. The entry leads to the formal areas in the open dining room and vaulted living room. The kitchen overlooks a quaint morning room, which leads to a rear deck that's a perfect spot for outdoor activities. With a walk-in closet and private bath, home-owners will be pampered in the master suite. The second bedroom, the two-car garage, and a utility room complete the plan.

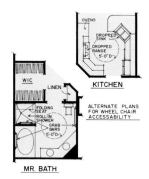

PLAN: HPK1300212

STYLE:	CONTEMPORARY
SQUARE FOOTAGE:	1,590
BEDROOMS:	3
BATHROOMS:	2
WIDTH:	43' - 0"
DEPTH:	59' - 0"
FOUNDATION:	SLAB

■ This stunner in stucco features enormous arched windows and a high pillared entrance in front, and a side-loading, double-capacity garage to the left. A tiled floor foyer opens to the living area (living and dining room), with volume ceiling and plenty of natural light streaming in. The kitchen feeds off of the dining area, where it shares an open plan with the family room. A handy washer and dryer open directly off of the kitchen, as does a garage entrance and pantry. The family room has optional space for a fireplace or entertainment center. Sliding glass doors lead to the patio, complete with an optional summer kitchen. The master suite lets off of the family area, and has a bath with a spa-style tub, huge walk-in closet, and double vanities.

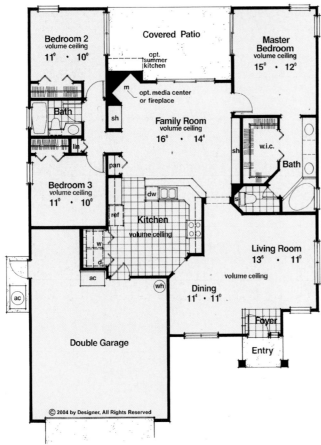

PLAN: HPK1300213

STYLE: COUNTRY COTTAGE

FIRST FLOOR: 814 SQ. FT.

SECOND FLOOR: 267 SQ. FT.

TOTAL: 1,081 SQ. FT.

BEDROOMS: 2

BATHROOMS: 2

WIDTH: 28' - 0"

DEPTH: 34' - 6"

FOUNDATION: UNFINISHED
BASEMENT, CRAWLSPACE, SLAB

■ This plan easily fits into established neighborhoods, with a canted bay window, traditional trim, and stucco finish. An upper-level bedroom—with private bath—overlooks the vaulted living room or can be finished off for more privacy. The appealing master suite features a sunny sitting area and walk-in closet. The efficient kitchen offers angles and looks out over the dining area and the cozy living room. Note the warming fireplace in the living room.

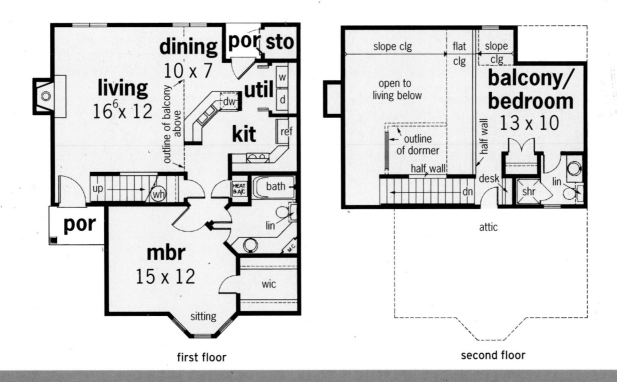

first floor

second floor

PLAN: HPK1300214

STYLE: COUNTRY COTTAGE

SQUARE FOOTAGE: 1,902

BEDROOMS: 3

BATHROOMS: 2

WIDTH: 50' - 0"

DEPTH: 53' - 0"

FOUNDATION: CRAWLSPACE, UNFINISHED WALKOUT BASEMENT

■ This home begins with several attractive exterior features—gables, a hipped roof, muntin windows and a sunburst. Inside, high ceilings in the foyer and grand room are sure to impress. The grand room shares a see-through fireplace with a vaulted sun room. The right side of the plan houses three bedrooms, one a master suite with a tray-ceilinged sitting room at the entrance, and two family bedrooms that share a full bath in the hall. The kitchen, with wrap-around counters and a serving bar, is conveniently located between the breakfast area and the formal dining room.

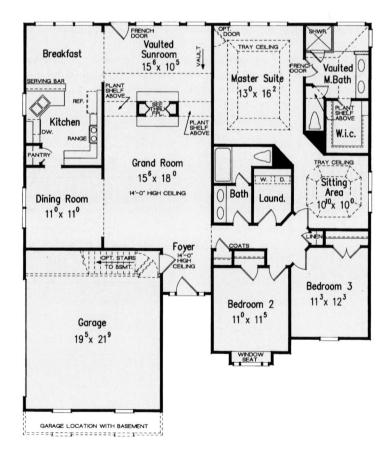

PLAN: HPK1300215

STYLE: CAPE COD

FIRST FLOOR: 1,506 SQ. FT.

SECOND FLOOR: 426 SQ. FT.

TOTAL: 1,932 SQ. FT.

BEDROOMS: 3

BATHROOMS: 2½

WIDTH: 50' - 0"

DEPTH: 52' - 6"

FOUNDATION: CRAWLSPACE, UNFINISHED WALKOUT BASEMENT

■ A Craftsman cottage with careful detailing, this sweet country home is sure to please. From the covered porch, the foyer reveals an open floor plan. The dining room, defined by columns, leads into the vaulted family room. Here, a fireplace framed by windows makes this comfortable space feel cozy. The vaulted breakfast and keeping rooms are bathed in light; easy access to the gourmet kitchen includes a serving-bar island. The master suite features a vaulted spa bath with a radius window and a garden tub. Upstairs, two bedrooms share a full bath.

first floor

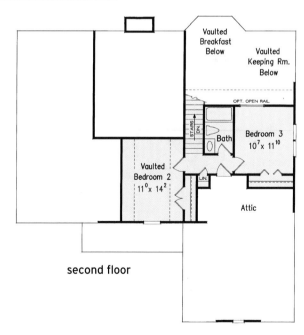

second floor

PLAN: HPK1300218

STYLE: CRAFTSMAN

FIRST FLOOR: 1,675 SQ. FT.

SECOND FLOOR: 614 SQ. FT.

TOTAL: 2,289 SQ. FT.

BEDROOMS: 3

BATHROOMS: 2½

WIDTH: 48' - 0"

DEPTH: 56' - 0"

FOUNDATION: CRAWLSPACE

■ With a nod to the details of the Arts and Crafts movement, this appealing bungalow has an eye-catching covered front porch, cedar-shingle accents, and light-catching windows. The main foyer separates a cozy den on the left from the formal dining room on the right. A butler's pantry connects the dining room and the convenient kitchen. An angled peninsula containing the cooktop joins the kitchen to a casual nook. There is patio access here for outdoor entertaining. A gas fireplace, skylights, and a built-in media center in the great room create a comfortable place in which to relax. Exquisite in design, the master suite includes a bath with a spa tub, dual lavatories, separate shower, walk-in closet and compartmented toilet. On the upper level is a hall bath with dual lavatories to serve the two family bedrooms on this floor.

second floor

first floor

PLAN: HPK1300219

STYLE: COUNTRY COTTAGE

FIRST FLOOR: 1,390 SQ. FT.

SECOND FLOOR: 764 SQ. FT.

TOTAL: 2,154 SQ. FT.

BONUS SPACE: 282 SQ. FT.

BEDROOMS: 3

BATHROOMS: 3½

WIDTH: 42' - 0"

DEPTH: 57' - 4"

FOUNDATION: CRAWLSPACE, UNFINISHED WALKOUT BASEMENT

■ Diverse rooflines and window styles blend to project a sense of splendor, which is continued throughout the interior of this Southern-style home. With a soaring two-story vault ceiling and an extended-hearth fireplace, the family room assumes center stage in this design. The island kitchen, located between the formal dining room and breakfast corner, is well suited to serve both. A fully furnished master suite, with French doors separating the bath from the sleeping area, occupies the entire left wing. Upstairs, a similar-size suite offers posh quarters for overnight guests. A third bedroom, and space for a fourth, also are on this floor. All the upstairs bedrooms share access to a balcony overlooking the family room.

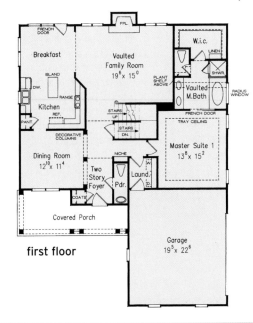

first floor

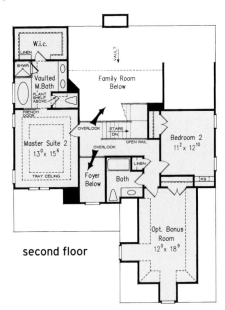

second floor

PLAN: HPK1300220

STYLE: COUNTRY COTTAGE

FIRST FLOOR: 935 SQ. FT.

SECOND FLOOR: 1,105 SQ. FT.

TOTAL: 2,040 SQ. FT.

BEDROOMS: 3

BATHROOMS: 2½

WIDTH: 44' - 0"

DEPTH: 39' - 0"

FOUNDATION: CRAWLSPACE, UNFINISHED WALKOUT BASEMENT, SLAB

■ Classic siding and an inviting front porch make this home welcome in any neighborhood. Enter to the two-story foyer; the dining room is on the left, elegantly serving up formal meals. Follow a short hall past the laundry room and decorative niche to the country-style island kitchen. Open planning creates excellent flow to the breakfast area and hearth-warmed great room. Upstairs, an enchanting master suite pampers with a soothing bath and optional sitting room. Secondary bedrooms share a full bath and balcony overlook.

first floor

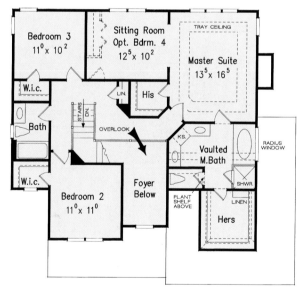

second floor

PLAN: HPK1300221

STYLE: COUNTRY COTTAGE

FIRST FLOOR: 737 SQ. FT.

SECOND FLOOR: 840 SQ. FT.

TOTAL: 1,577 SQ. FT.

BEDROOMS: 3

BATHROOMS: 2½

WIDTH: 36' - 0"

DEPTH: 42' - 0"

FOUNDATION: UNFINISHED BASEMENT, SLAB

■ Loaded with charm, this mountain cottage takes on the ambiance of a country Victorian with rustic appeal. The two-story foyer opens to a sweep-back staircase, lit by a double-hung window. A spacious hearth-warmed living area views the dining room (with rear patio access) and efficient kitchen. To the left, a built-in desk is perfect as a small office or family organization center. Upstairs, a cathedral ceiling in the master suite adds drama; the private bath soothes and relaxes.

first floor

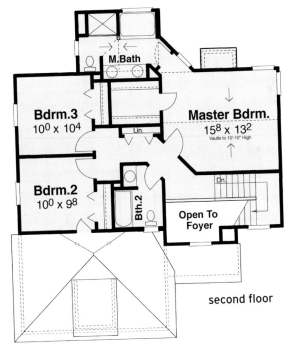

second floor

Distinctive Homes for Couples

PLAN: HPK1300224

STYLE: CRAFTSMAN	
SQUARE FOOTAGE: 1,850	
BEDROOMS: 3	
BATHROOMS: 2	
WIDTH: 44' - 0"	
DEPTH: 68' - 0"	
FOUNDATION: CRAWLSPACE	

■ With all of the tantalizing elements of a cottage, and the comfortable space of a family-sized home, this Arts and Crafts one-story is the best of both worlds. Exterior accents such as stone wainscot, cedar shingles under the gable ends, and mission-style windows enhance this effect. Three bedrooms are aligned along the right of the interior, situated behind the garage, shielding them from street noise. Bedroom 3 and the master bedroom have walk-in closets; a tray ceiling decorates the master salon. Living and dining areas include a large great room, a dining room with sliding glass doors to a rear patio, and a private den with window seat and vaulted ceiling. A warming hearth lights the great room—right next to a built-in media center. The open corner kitchen features a 42-inch snack bar counter, and giant walk-in pantry.

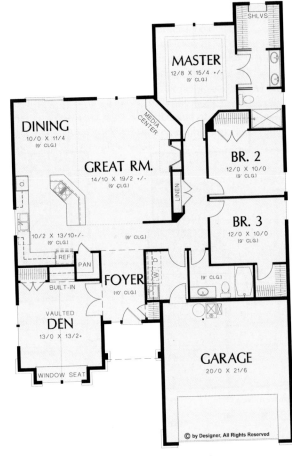

PLAN: HPK1300225

STYLE: FARMHOUSE

FIRST FLOOR: 1,950 SQ. FT.

SECOND FLOOR: 1,005 SQ. FT.

TOTAL: 2,955 SQ. FT.

BEDROOMS: 3

BATHROOMS: 2½

WIDTH: 45' - 0"

DEPTH: 54' - 0"

FOUNDATION: CRAWLSPACE

■ This traditional country farmhouse features enormous windows with glazed sash design, rounded columns on the porch, and a matching detached garage. The front entrance offers immediate access through French doors to a vaulted den with built-in shelves and lots of natural light on the right. The great room, with corner gas fireplace, is enjoined by an archway to the kitchen and dining area. The rear porch is accessible through sliding doors from the dining room. The kitchen features a center preparation island and walk-in pantry. The kingly master suite is accessed through double doors off the main hallway, and features a vaulted ceiling, unique angled walk-in closet, and a spa. The main floor also offers a utility room, linen closet, and half bath located by the den. A game room and two bedrooms are found upstairs. One bedroom has its own balcony, and the two share a full bath.

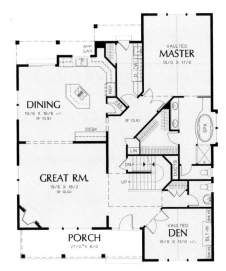

first floor

second floor

PLAN: HPK1300226

STYLE: FARMHOUSE

FIRST FLOOR: 694 SQ. FT.

SECOND FLOOR: 558 SQ. FT.

TOTAL: 1,252 SQ. FT.

BEDROOMS: 2

BATHROOMS: 1½

WIDTH: 28' - 0"

DEPTH: 40' - 0"

FOUNDATION: UNFINISHED BASEMENT

■ A glass-door entrance welcomes visitors into the picturesque charm of this countryside home. A large wraparound porch leads to a relaxing outdoor lounge area—perfect for summer afternoons. The island kitchen opens to an eating area across from the living room. A powder room, laundry area, and the one-car garage complete this floor. Upstairs, two family bedrooms are linked by a full bath.

first floor

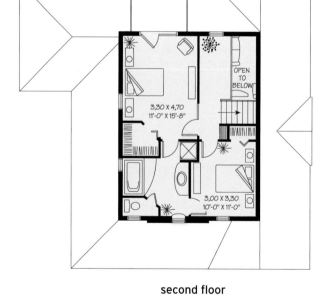

second floor

PLAN: HPK1300227

STYLE: COUNTRY COTTAGE

SQUARE FOOTAGE: 1,732

BEDROOMS: 3

BATHROOMS: 2

WIDTH: 46' - 0"

DEPTH: 66' - 0"

FOUNDATION: SLAB, CRAWLSPACE

■ Simple Victorian detailing marks the exterior of this interesting plan. The interior surrounds a private courtyard. The entry leads to the two-car garage, the courtyard, and two family bedrooms and their shared bath. Each bedroom is equipped with a walk-in closet. French doors accent the remainder of the home; they are found in the master bedroom, the dining area, and on each side of the living-room fireplace. A wet bar in the living room ensures successful entertaining. The master bathroom is a garden retreat with access to the courtyard and a planter inside next to the garden tub. A skylight brings natural light into this incredible room.

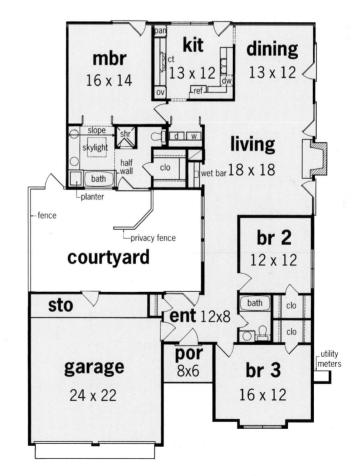

Distinctive Homes for Couples

THIS HOME, AS SHOWN IN THE PHOTOGRAPH, MAY DIFFER FROM THE ACTUAL BLUEPRINTS. BUILDER: ASHLEY DEVELOPMENT. FOR MORE DETAILED INFORMATION, PLEASE CHECK THE FLOOR PLANS CAREFULLY.

PLAN: HPK1300330

STYLE: TRANSITIONAL
FIRST FLOOR: 1,362 SQ. FT.
SECOND FLOOR: 1,737 SQ. FT.
TOTAL: 3,099 SQ. FT.
BEDROOMS: 3
BATHROOMS: 2½
WIDTH: 37' - 10"
DEPTH: 52' - 4"
FOUNDATION: FINISHED
WALKOUT BASEMENT

■ An exquisitely designed entry and Palladian window decorate the exterior of this narrow-lot home. A high ceiling in the foyer and adjacent staircase with wood trim creates an elegant entry. A spacious gallery introduces the formal dining room and great room. The wall of windows and doors across the rear wall showcase the exterior view. The gourmet kitchen enjoys a chef's island, walk-in pantry and snack bar with seating. The second floor loft and hall provide a dramatic view to the foyer, and lead to three bedrooms and a laundry room. The master bedroom suite enjoys a soothing bath and raised ceiling—windows offer a spectacular view from the whirlpool tub and shower. With an array of high-end amenities, this house makes a wonderful narrow-lot choice.

first floor

Deck

Great Room
21'3" x 15'7"

Breakfast
14'6" x 10'8"

Kitchen
14'6" x 14'7"

Dining Room
14'4" x 11'2"

Gallery

PANTRY

Bath

CLOSET

Garage
18'7" x 21'

Foyer

second floor

SEAT

Master Bath

Master Bedroom
18'7" x 14'
9'-10" HIGH @ CENTER

WALK-IN CLOSET

Office/Bedroom
12' x 11'8"
9'-10" HIGH @ CENTER

Hall

Laun.

Loft

WOOD RAIL

Bath

WALK-IN CLOSET

Foyer Below

Bedroom
16'10" x 11'8"

SLOPED

SLOPED

PLAN: HPK1300228

STYLE: TRANSITIONAL

SQUARE FOOTAGE: 1,911

BEDROOMS: 3

BATHROOMS: 2

WIDTH: 45' - 0"

DEPTH: 78' - 5"

FOUNDATION: CRAWLSPACE

■ Clean lines and an efficient floor plan make this striking home surprisingly economical to build. Stucco and decorative shutters create a welcoming facade as you enter from the covered stoop. Inside, the island kitchen is created for family get-togethers, with lots of space and an open design that encourages conversation from the naturally lit dining room. The gathering room has a dramatic vaulted ceiling and a warming fireplace. At the rear, the master suite accesses a covered lanai and enjoys a sumptuous bath. Two secondary bedrooms are on the far left, or make one a comfortable den.

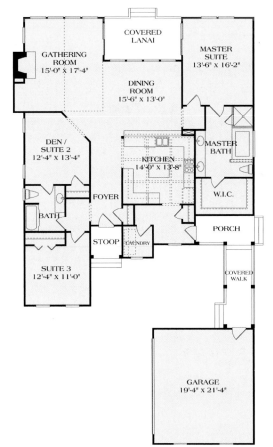

PLAN: HPK1300229

STYLE: COUNTRY COTTAGE
SQUARE FOOTAGE: 1,792
BONUS SPACE: 255 SQ. FT.
BEDROOMS: 3
BATHROOMS: 2
WIDTH: 50' - 0"
DEPTH: 62' - 6"
FOUNDATION: CRAWLSPACE, UNFINISHED WALKOUT BASEMENT

■ The country charm of this Cape Cod-style home belies the elegance inside. The beautiful foyer, accented by columns that define the formal dining room, leads to the family room. Here, the vaulted space is warm and cozy, courtesy of an extended-hearth fireplace. The kitchen is open and welcoming with angled counters that offer plenty of workspace. The laundry is conveniently located near the garage entrance. In the master suite, the star is the vaulted compartmented bath. Two additional bedrooms—both with ample closets and one with a raised ceiling—complete the plan. An optional upstairs addition includes a fourth bedroom and a full bath.

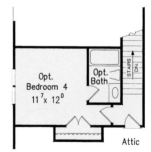

PLAN: HPK1300230

STYLE: TRADITIONAL

SQUARE FOOTAGE: 1,208

BEDROOMS: 3

BATHROOMS: 2

WIDTH: 48' - 0"

DEPTH: 29' - 0"

FOUNDATION: UNFINISHED BASEMENT

■ The details of the exterior of this small, attractive Colonial-style home include wood siding, shuttered windows, a gabled room and a stunning entry with sidelights. At the front of the house, the family room offers a fireplace to warm the cold night air. Beyond lies the dining room and U-shaped kitchen, which share a door to the sun deck. Two family bedrooms located at the middle of the home share a bathroom that contains a laundry. To the left of the house is the master bedroom with two closets, an optional plant shelf, and a bathroom with dual sinks and a linen closet.

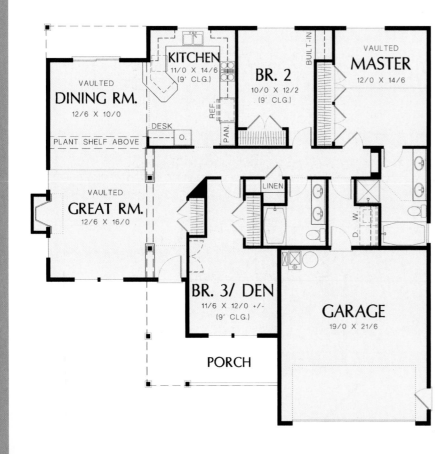

PLAN: HPK1300231

STYLE: TRADITIONAL

SQUARE FOOTAGE: 1,557

BEDROOMS: 3

BATHROOMS: 2

WIDTH: 50' - 0"

DEPTH: 50' - 0"

FOUNDATION: CRAWLSPACE

■ A wraparound porch sets off this sweet country facade. The gallery foyer opens to a vaulted great room with a fireplace and leads to the formal dining room. Advanced amenities such as a vaulted ceiling and a plant shelf complement views of nature through tall windows and sliding glass doors. A planning desk, pantry, and peninsula counter highlight the gourmet kitchen, which boasts a window over the sink. A flex room easily converts from a secondary bedroom to a den or home office. A second bedroom enjoys a view of the rear property; nearby, a full bath offers two sinks.

PLAN: HPK1300232

STYLE: COUNTRY COTTAGE

SQUARE FOOTAGE: 1,532

BEDROOMS: 3

BATHROOMS: 2

WIDTH: 38' - 0"

DEPTH: 66' - 0"

FOUNDATION: UNFINISHED
BASEMENT, SLAB

■ Designed for a narrow lot, this Tudor adaptation provides curb appeal and a great floor plan. The modest front entry is highlighted by a dormer that flows into a cathedral ceiling. Open planning positions the living room, dining area and bowed kitchen for optimum spaciousness. The curved bar separating the kitchen can accommodate a cafe-style table, defining the space. The master suite is secluded with a sitting area and splendid private bath. Two additional bedrooms share a full bath near the front of the home.

Opt. Study
10^8 x 12^8

optional layout

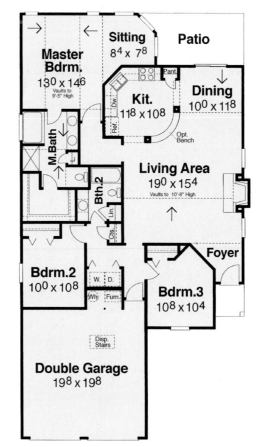

PLAN: HPK1300233

STYLE: COUNTRY COTTAGE

SQUARE FOOTAGE: 1,546

BEDROOMS: 2

BATHROOMS: 2

WIDTH: 37' - 0"

DEPTH: 64' - 0"

FOUNDATION: SLAB

■ A smart layout allows many extras to be incorporated into this compact design. For instance, the vaulted family room doubles as a full-sized foyer for a big welcome. In lieu of a separate formal dining room, the casual dining room functions as a breakfast nook, enjoying views toward the patio and accommodating seating at the serving bar. The second bathroom remains close enough to the center of the home to be used by guests. The master suite is surprisingly roomy and features a tray ceiling, sitting area, full-sized walk-in, and a gorgeous bath. Private access to the patio is a great customizable option.

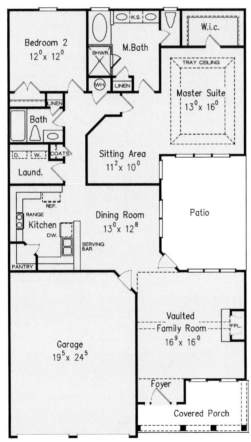

PLAN: HPK1300234

STYLE: COUNTRY COTTAGE

SQUARE FOOTAGE: 1,546

BEDROOMS: 3

BATHROOMS: 2

WIDTH: 37' - 0"

DEPTH: 65' - 5"

FOUNDATION: SLAB

■ Petite in proportions and scaled for narrow lots—great first-home builders, city in-fill, and empty nesters—this design considers modern comforts. A casual foyer connects with the vaulted family room adding warmth to the space with a fireplace. A series of windows face the large side patio, extending private living space to the outdoors. The dining room also enjoys the patio view and the convenience of the nearby C-shaped kitchen with walk-in pantry and serving bar. A short, wide hallway makes room for two family bedrooms and a full hall bath. The master suite, enhanced by a tray ceiling, is outfitted with a walk-in closet, roomy bath with dual-sink vanities, separate shower and tub, and a private toilet.

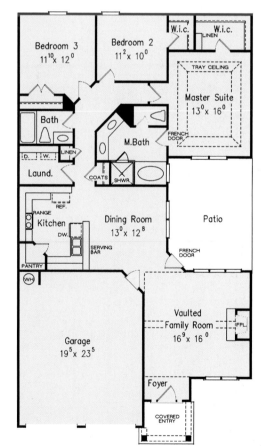

PLAN: HPK1300235

STYLE: COUNTRY COTTAGE
SQUARE FOOTAGE: 1,437
BEDROOMS: 2
BATHROOMS: 2
WIDTH: 37' - 0"
DEPTH: 64' - 5"
FOUNDATION: SLAB

■ A two-car garage topped by twin dormers, and a covered and pillared front porch capture a timeless essence on the facade of this country home. In one story you get two bedrooms and two full baths, perfect for a small family, empty nesters, or even as a vacation home. The long foyer leads directly into a great room filled with amenities such as a fireplace flanked by built-in shelves, decorative colums, French-door access to a vast side patio, and a vaulted ceiling. From there you can enter the dining room, wisely placed adjacent to the kitchen with convenient serving bar. The master suite leaves nothing to be desired; pass through the French doors into the master bath and discover the dual-sink vanity and access to a spacious walk-in closet.

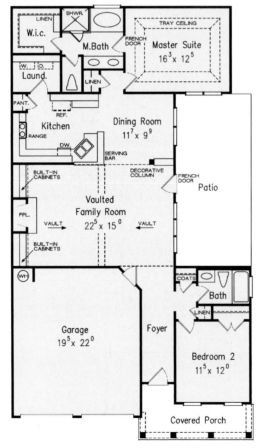

PLAN: HPK1300236

STYLE: CRAFTSMAN

SQUARE FOOTAGE: 1,393

BONUS SPACE: 160 SQ. FT.

BEDROOMS: 2

BATHROOMS: 2

WIDTH: 32' - 0"

DEPTH: 63' - 0"

FOUNDATION: UNFINISHED
WALKOUT BASEMENT, SLAB

■ Modest living at its best, this unassuming exterior reveals a practical, contemporary design. A fireplace in the vaulted family room warms the space. A side patio and covered porch offer outdoor living space. The kichen bar conveniently serves the adjoining dining room. A hallway leads to the master suite on the left and a second bedroom and hall bath on the right. The vaulted master suite boasts sliding door access to a private sitting room. An optional layout offers a sunroom.

optional layout

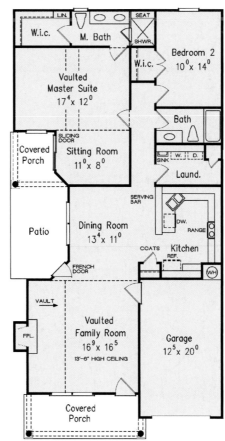

PLAN: HPK1300237

PLAN: HPK1300237

STYLE: CRAFTSMAN

SQUARE FOOTAGE: 1,407

BEDROOMS: 2

BATHROOMS: 2

WIDTH: 32' - 0"

DEPTH: 61' - 7"

FOUNDATION: SLAB, UNFINISHED WALKOUT BASEMENT

■ Country cottage comfort awaits the owner of this home. Enter into a spacious, vaulted family room with built-in cabinets, a window seat, and a fireplace with TV niche that is perfect for relaxing. Together with the adjoining dining room this space is also great for entertaining, and has easy access to a traditional country kitchen with its built-in pantry and separate laundry area. To the rear is a private vaulted master bedroom suite, a second bedroom, and second bath. Surrounded by family room, dining room, and master bedroom, a sheltered patio extends the offer of an outdoor living room.

optional layout

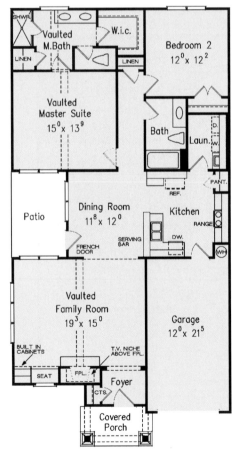

PLAN: HPK1300238

STYLE: TRADITIONAL

SQUARE FOOTAGE: 1,583

BEDROOMS: 3

BATHROOMS: 2

WIDTH: 34' - 0"

DEPTH: 77' - 2"

■ Perfect for narrow, long lots, this home evokes images of quaint seaside villages that dot the New England coastline. In row house fashion, this home lives larger than its modest square footage. The open floor plan provides distinct room definition by using columns and a convenient kitchen pass-through in the common areas. A study/bedroom offers flexibility for changing needs, and each bedroom is positioned for privacy. The fireplace can be seen from every common room, and a screened porch creates an outdoor haven. The master suite features a cathedral ceiling, a spacious walk-in closet, and a well-appointed master bath with a double vanity, garden tub, and separate shower.

© 2003 Donald A. Gardner, Inc.

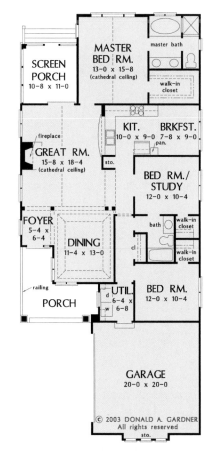

PLAN: HPK1300239

STYLE: TRADITIONAL	
SQUARE FOOTAGE: 1,858	
BEDROOMS: 3	
BATHROOMS: 2	
WIDTH: 50' - 0"	
DEPTH: 59' - 8"	

■ The wraparound covered porch adds charm as it provides a generous amount of outdoor living space. Inside, the foyer opens to the great room with its cathedral ceiling and cozy fireplace. To the rear, the formal dining room and breakfast nook are situated near the island kitchen for efficiency and convenience. The sleeping quarters are on the right where the master suite enjoys a luxurious private bath with a double-sink vanity. Two additional family bedrooms share a full bath, one doubles as a study.

PLAN: HPK1300240

STYLE: TRADITIONAL

FIRST FLOOR: 960 / 960 SQ. FT.

SECOND FLOOR: 533 / 533 SQ. FT.

TOTAL: 1,493 / 1,493 SQ. FT.

BEDROOMS: 3 / 3

BATHROOMS: 2½ / 2½

WIDTH: 64' - 0"

DEPTH: 50' - 8"

FOUNDATION: UNFINISHED
BASEMENT

■ A country front covered porch welcomes you inside to a charming and traditional duplex home. Just inside, a powder room and hall closet flank the foyer. The U-shaped kitchen overlooks the dining area and two-story great room, featuring a fireplace. The first-floor master suite enjoys His and Hers walk-in closets and a private bath. A laundry room connecting to the garage completes the first floor. Upstairs, Bedrooms 2 and 3 share a full hall bath and a balcony hall overlooking the great room and kitchen below.

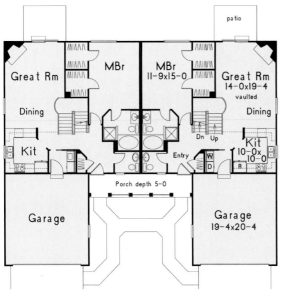

first floor

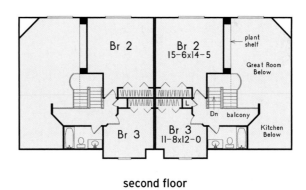

second floor

PLAN: HPK1300241

STYLE: MEDITERRANEAN

SQUARE FOOTAGE: 996 / 996

BEDROOMS: 2 / 2

BATHROOMS: 2 / 2

WIDTH: 60' - 0"

DEPTH: 55' - 0"

FOUNDATION: UNFINISHED BASEMENT

■ Perfectly suited to warmer climates, this beautiful stucco duplex features stunning European and Mediterranean accents. Enter one of the units through the front porch or the single-car garage. The kitchen provides a walk-in pantry, space for a washer and dryer, and a combined dining/great room with a vaulted ceiling warmed by a fireplace. Access the rear patio for outdoor grilling. The master suite features a linen closet, private bath and walk-in closet. The second family bedroom is located near the full hall bath. Designed for the young or growing family, this charming duplex home is both economical and stylish for any neighborhood setting.

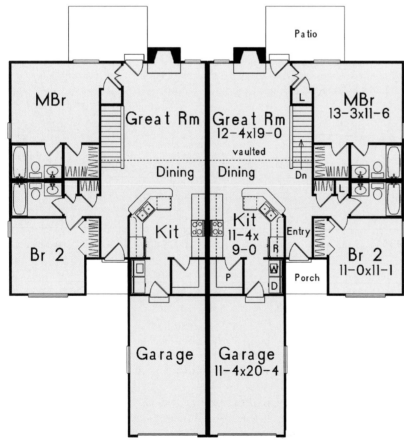

The clean lines and bright facade of this home, found on page 303, capture the best of contemporary styling.

Contemporary & Urban In-fill Plans

These designs are created to fit in—and stand out in—downtown settings

It may not gather the momentum of the post-World War II rush to suburbia, but there is a distinct movement afoot for people to return to urban areas. From large cities to smaller towns, "downtown" is seeing a revival—and its appeal spans generations, from 20-somethings to baby boomers.

The pace of the city seems to fit today's caffeinated lifestyles; the ease of having everything at your fingertips—or at least within a couple blocks' walk—carries a tremendous appeal. The cultural draw of a downtown area, even in smaller towns, is something that few suburbs can match.

The challenge in these areas is that lot sizes are generally small, and in many cases the existing housing has outgrown its usefulness. Whether building new or replacing an old structure, construction in urban areas is booming.

That boom requires careful planning from the start, as designers create narrow-lot plans that meet the needs of both the site and the homeowners. This chapter collects 54 home plans that were designed with these challenges in mind. You'll find a wide variety of styles—from contemporary to classic—that could fit in a number of urban settings. Some locations call for the crisp, clean lines of modern style; in other spots, particularly if you are replacing an existing structure, you may want a design that more closely matches the historic styling nearby.

Exquisite Interiors

Whatever style you choose for the exterior of your home, you'll find contemporary, luxurious options for inside. A growing trend in home design is to wrap a contemporary-styled layout in a classic exterior, thereby getting a design built for the way today's family lives, but with a timeless exterior.

As a result, you will find homes that include open, flowing floor plans and luxurious master suites, much like those featured in other chapters of this book. There are relatively few formal living rooms—instead, you'll see an emphasis on great rooms or larger family rooms located near the kitchen. These spaces tend to be more casual, and big enough to accommodate either the entire family or a group of guests.

Garage Works

A number of plans in this chapter include front-facing—or even drive-under garages, a feature that adds space and convenience to an urban home. Most original urban architecture doesn't include a garage, since much of it was developed before the rise of the automobile. Now, with limited parking space and security concerns, guaranteeing your car a sheltered parking spot is a valuable commodity.

The added storage space a garage can provide is another welcome commodity in a narrow-lot plan. Attic and other storage space might be limited by the home's width, so a little extra room in the garage can make a big difference. Most drive-under garages boast even more storage space, since that level of the home is generally reserved for the basement. ∎

PORCH SWING

While quaint front porches can make attractive conversation pieces on today's homes, they were literally conversation places in years gone by. When designs like the one pictured here first appeared on the American landscape, neighbors could greet each other and even carry on conversations from their own front porches.

Porches are often associated with the charm of the country, but they were a staple of early urban architecture as well. Incorporate one in your new downtown home and you'll not only enjoy the benefits of charm and added living space, but it will also help your new home fit naturally with its surroundings.

Right: Two porches extend the living space and lend a welcoming feel to the front of this classic town house design. See page 283 for details.

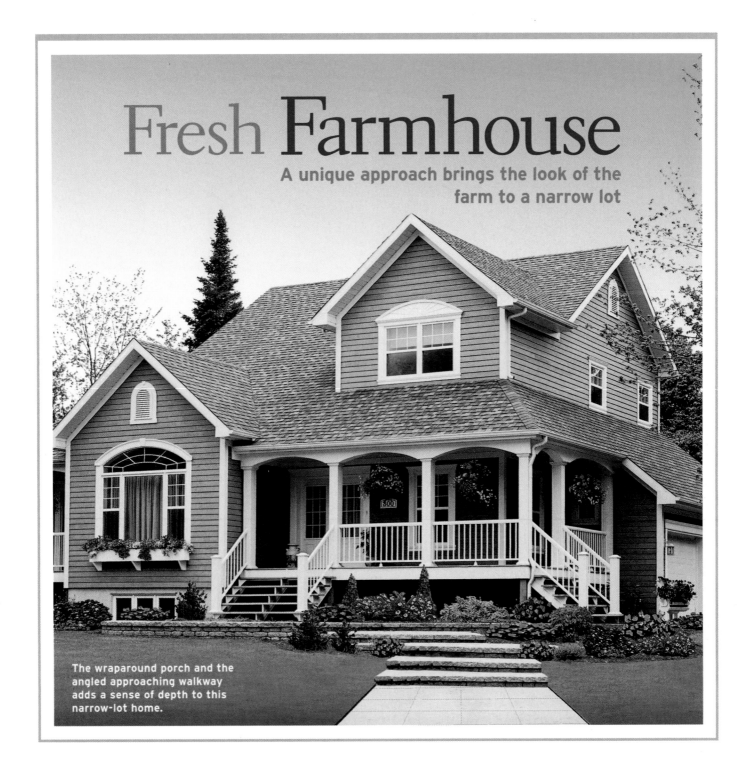

Fresh Farmhouse

A unique approach brings the look of the farm to a narrow lot

The wraparound porch and the angled approaching walkway adds a sense of depth to this narrow-lot home.

Bright windows in the
family room overlook
the front yard.

You don't need sprawling acres of land to capture the refreshing feel of a farmhouse. This design brings country style to a 50-foot-wide footprint that would fit just as well in town as it would on a dirt road.

The home delivers a floor plan that offers both a living room and a family room, but in an open design that ensures the living room won't be forgotten like the small front rooms in so many classic Colonials. Instead, this living room opens easily into both the dining room and kitchen, creating a comfortable, welcoming atmosphere. A small porch off the dining room adds to its charm.

The galley-style kitchen features a built-in breakfast table, with another small porch attached. Linked to the dining room and living room on one side and the family room on the other, the kitchen easily serves as the center of the home. The living room is large and comfortable, with a fireplace at the center and windows on three sides.

Elsewhere on the first floor you'll find a quiet home office with windows overlooking

the front yard. It's situated right next to the front door—perfect for a home-based business that welcomes the occasional client. You'll also find a coat closet next to both of the entrances and a laundry/utility room near the two-car garage.

Upstairs the master bedroom is, fittingly, the largest room in the house, with plenty of space to relax. A corner walk-in closet and a spacious master bath with separate shower add to the suite.

Two additional bedrooms, each with a spacious closet, share a full bath. The upstairs hallway includes an overlook that's

Above: The dining room has access to a front porch. Top Right: A built-in breakfast nook saves space in the kitchen. Right: The luxurious master bath includes a plant niche tucked into a dormer.

PLAN: HPK1300331

STYLE: ADAM STYLE

FIRST FLOOR: 1,792 SQ. FT.

SECOND FLOOR: 899 SQ. FT.

TOTAL: 2,691 SQ. FT.

BEDROOMS: 4

BATHROOMS: 2½

WIDTH: 32' - 9"

DEPTH: 99' - 5"

FOUNDATION: SLAB

■ Tall, elegant windows and a stately chimney deck out the facade of this stunning Town home. The robust mix of Colonial balance and natural symmetry lends an inviting look to the exterior. Inside, a row of columns sets off the dining area, which provides views to the side courtyard. Informal spaces share a door to the side property—a great place to linger or start a walk into town. The secluded master suite provides a dressing area and two walk-in closets. Upstairs, a cluster of secondary bedrooms share a spacious hall bath.

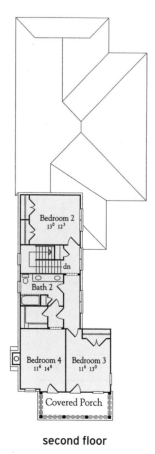

first floor

second floor

PLAN: HPK1300244

STYLE: TRADITIONAL

FIRST FLOOR: 911 SQ. FT.

SECOND FLOOR: 1,029 SQ. FT.

TOTAL: 1,940 SQ. FT.

BEDROOMS: 3

BATHROOMS: 2½

WIDTH: 20' - 10"

DEPTH: 75' - 10"

FOUNDATION: CRAWLSPACE

■ With irresistible charm and quiet curb appeal, this enchanting cottage conceals a sophisticated interior that's prepared for busy lifestyles. Built-in cabinetry in the great room frames a massive fireplace, which warms the area and complements the natural views. An open kitchen provides an island with a double sink and snack counter. Planned events are easily served in the formal dining room with French doors that lead to the veranda. On the upper level, a central hall with linen storage connects the sleeping quarters. The master suite boasts a walk-in closet and a roomy bath with a dual-sink vanity. Each of two secondary bedrooms has plenty of wardrobe space and porch access.

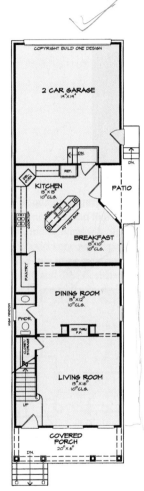

first floor

second floor

PLAN: HPK1300247

STYLE: TRADITIONAL

FIRST FLOOR: 1,260 SQ. FT.

SECOND FLOOR: 1,057 SQ. FT.

TOTAL: 2,317 SQ. FT.

BEDROOMS: 5

BATHROOMS: 2½

WIDTH: 35' - 0"

DEPTH: 56' - 0"

FOUNDATION: SLAB

■ At home in the city, this narrow-lot design takes advantage of street views. A rear-loading, two-car garage is accessed via a rear porch and breakfast room. The adjoining C-shaped kitchen is only steps from the formal dining room. A warming fireplace can be enjoyed in the great room (and even from the dining room). A first-floor master suite provides convenience and comfort. Two walk-in closets, dual-sink vanity, soaking tub, and enclosed shower pamper and dissolve stress. The second floor is home to four bedrooms—or three bedrooms and a loft. A roomy laundry area is located on the second floor.

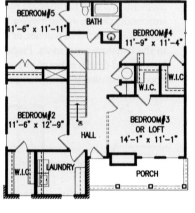

second floor

first floor

PLAN: HPK1300332

STYLE: FRENCH

FIRST FLOOR: 1,135 SQ. FT.

SECOND FLOOR: 1,092 SQ. FT.

TOTAL: 2,227 SQ. FT.

BEDROOMS: 3

BATHROOMS: 2½

WIDTH: 28' - 8"

DEPTH: 74' - 2"

FOUNDATION: CRAWLSPACE

■ Stylish square columns line the porch and portico of this townhome, which has received the Builder's Choice National Design and Planning Award and the Award of Merit in Architecture. Inside, an open arrangement of the formal rooms is partially defined by a through-fireplace. Brightened by a triple window, the breakfast nook is an inviting place for family and friends to gather. A single door opens to the outside, where steps lead down to the rear property—a good place to start a walk into town. The kitchen features a food-prep island and a siz-able pantry. Upstairs, the master suite offers a fireplace and access to the portico.

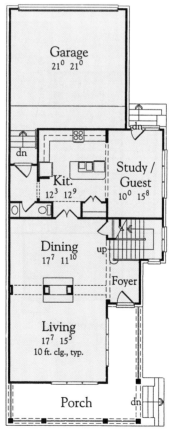

Garage
21⁰ 21⁰

dn

Kit.
12³ 12⁹

dn

Study /
Guest
10⁰ 15⁸

Dining
17⁷ 11¹⁰

up

Foyer

Living
17⁷ 15⁵
10 ft. clg., typ.

Porch

dn

first floor

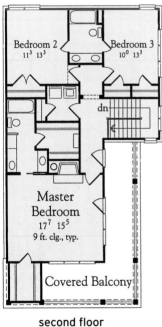

Bedroom 2
11³ 13³

Bedroom 3
10⁰ 13³

dn

Master
Bedroom
17⁷ 15⁵
9 ft. clg., typ.

Covered Balcony

second floor

PLAN: HPK1300335

STYLE: COLONIAL
FIRST FLOOR: 1,260 SQ. FT.
SECOND FLOOR: 1,160 SQ. FT.
TOTAL: 2,420 SQ. FT.
BEDROOMS: 4
BATHROOMS: 3
WIDTH: 43' - 5"
DEPTH: 68' - 3"
FOUNDATION: CRAWLSPACE

■ A wealth of outdoor living space extends the confines of this narrow-lot home, creating a sense of spaciousness. A fireplace in the living room adds ambiance and warmth. A second fireplace in the family room is a nice touch. The U-shaped kitchen is both practical and efficient. A first-floor bedroom, with full bath, can be used as a study or guest suite. On the second floor, the master bedroom shares access to a screened porch with bedroom 4. An additional bedroom and a full bath complete this level.

second floor

first floor

PLAN: HPK1300336

STYLE: ADAM STYLE
FIRST FLOOR: 1,587 SQ. FT.
SECOND FLOOR: 1,191 SQ. FT.
TOTAL: 2,778 SQ. FT.
BEDROOMS: 3
BATHROOMS: 2½
WIDTH: 21' - 8"
DEPTH: 93' - 8"
FOUNDATION: SLAB

■ Box-paneled shutters add a touch of class to this Town design—a home that is simply the ultimate in comfort and style. A winding staircase highlights a refined foyer that sets the pace for the entire home. Fireplaces warm the formal and casual rooms, which can accommodate all occasions. The well-organized kitchen provides a snack bar for easy meals and serves the formal dining room with ease. Upstairs, two secondary bedrooms share a full bath and a study that could be used as a computer room. The master suite boasts two walk-in closets, an indulgent bath and a private porch.

first floor

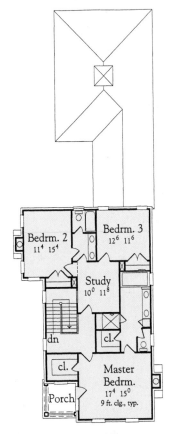

second floor

PLAN: HPK1300337

STYLE: COLONIAL

FIRST FLOOR: 1,442 SQ. FT.

SECOND FLOOR: 1,456 SQ. FT.

TOTAL: 2,898 SQ. FT.

BEDROOMS: 3

BATHROOMS: 3

WIDTH: 41' - 8"

DEPTH: 53' - 0"

FOUNDATION: FINISHED BASEMENT

■ Designed for a narrow lot, this stately two story home offers views out the rear from two decks, a screened porch, as well as the dining room, and great room. The formal great room combines with the dining area and kitchen to create one large living space. The gourmet kitchen enjoys a clear view to the rear and includes a snack bar with seating and a walk-in pantry. Split stairs lead to a second floor balcony, home office, and two bedrooms. The master bedroom suite enjoys a whirlpool tub, shower enclosure, double bowl vanity, gas fireplace, and windows to the rear and side. Every part of this home is designed wtih an eye for function and aesthetics.

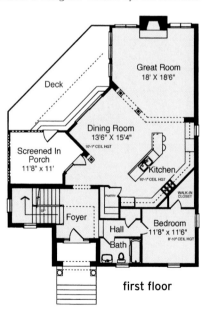

first floor

second floor

PLAN: HPK1300338

STYLE: ADAM STYLE

FIRST FLOOR: 1,369 SQ. FT.

SECOND FLOOR: 856 SQ. FT.

TOTAL: 2,225 SQ. FT.

BEDROOMS: 4

BATHROOMS: 2½

WIDTH: 36' - 2"

DEPTH: 71' - 6"

FOUNDATION: SLAB

■ The lovely facade of this Town or Village home is beautifully decorated with a double portico. A front bay window provides a stunning accent to the traditional exterior, while allowing natural light within. The formal living room features a fireplace and opens to the dining room, which leads outdoors. The gourmet kitchen has a walk-in pantry. The master suite is a relaxing space that includes a sitting bay, access to the side grounds, walk-in closet and soothing bath. A winding staircase offers an overlook to the living room.

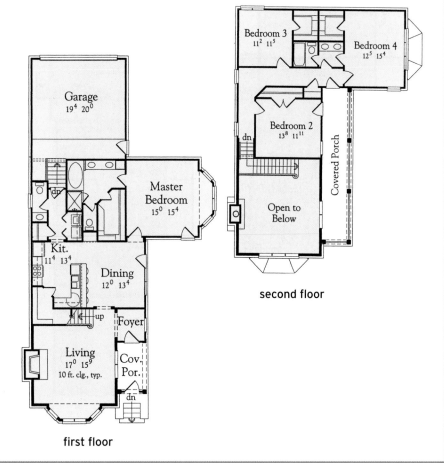

first floor

second floor

© The Sater Design Collection, Inc.

PLAN: HPK1300251

STYLE: COUNTRY COTTAGE

FIRST FLOOR: 1,372 SQ. FT.

SECOND FLOOR: 1,617 SQ. FT.

TOTAL: 2,989 SQ. FT.

BEDROOMS: 5

BATHROOMS: $5\frac{1}{2}$

WIDTH: 50' - 0"

DEPTH: 83' - 10"

FOUNDATION: PIER

(SAME AS PILING)

■ Sun-kissed porticos and wide-open decks capture views and permit breezes to whisper through rooms all around this coastal cottage. Inspired by Caribbean manors and refined in the architecture of Charleston Row houses, the style is brought into the 21st Century with a highly functional floor plan that is fully engaged with the outdoors. The foyer links the entry with public living spaces as well as a private room that flexes to accommodate guests or harbor a quiet library or conservatory. Built-in cabinetry and a stepped ceiling subdue the scale of the media room. The central stairs create a fluid connection with the spacious living room, formal dining room, and kitchen. An upper veranda features an alfresco kitchen that extends the function of the dining room.

first floor

second floor

PLAN: HPK1300252

STYLE: ITALIANATE

FIRST FLOOR: 874 SQ. FT.

SECOND FLOOR: 880 SQ. FT.

TOTAL: 1,754 SQ. FT.

BEDROOMS: 3

BATHROOMS: 2½

WIDTH: 34' - 0"

DEPTH: 43' - 0"

FOUNDATION: ISLAND
BASEMENT

■ A stately tower adds a sense of grandeur to contemporary high-pitched rooflines on this dreamy Mediterranean-style villa. Surrounded by outdoor views, the living space extends to a veranda through three sets of French doors. Decorative columns announce the dining area, which boasts a 10-foot ceiling and views of its own. Tall arch-top windows bathe a winding staircase with sunlight or moonlight. The upper-level sleeping quarters include a master retreat that offers a bedroom with views and access to the observation deck. Secondary bedrooms share a full bath and linen storage. Bedroom 3 features a walk-in closet and French doors to the deck.

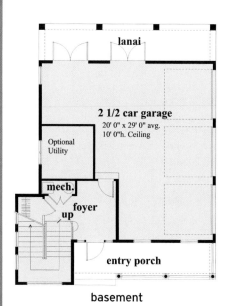

basement

first floor

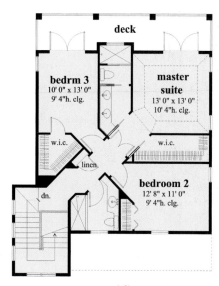

second floor

PLAN: HPK1300253

STYLE: CRAFTSMAN

FIRST FLOOR: 1,005 SQ. FT.

SECOND FLOOR: 620 SQ. FT.

TOTAL: 1,625 SQ. FT.

BEDROOMS: 2

BATHROOMS: 2½

WIDTH: 30' - 0"

DEPTH: 44' - 6"

FOUNDATION: FINISHED

WALKOUT BASEMENT

■ A mixture of materials and modern styling creates a lovely home plan for the small family. The main level provides formal living and dining rooms as well as a kitchen area. The quiet study may be converted to an additional bedroom as space is needed. A laundry and powder room are located nearby. The vaulted master bedroom boasts a private bath with a double-bowl vanity and a walk-in closet. Bedroom 2 provides its own bath.

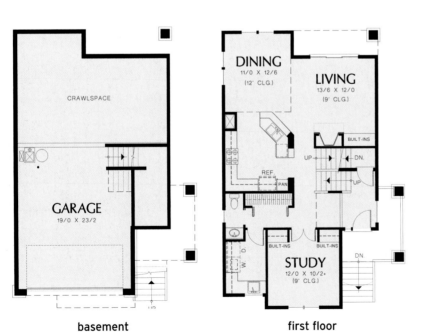

basement

first floor

second floor

PLAN: HPK1300254

STYLE: CRAFTSMAN

FIRST FLOOR: 993 SQ. FT.

SECOND FLOOR: 642 SQ. FT.

TOTAL: 1,635 SQ. FT.

BEDROOMS: 2

BATHROOMS: 2½

WIDTH: 28' - 0"

DEPTH: 44' - 0"

FOUNDATION: FINISHED
WALKOUT BASEMENT

■ This modern three-level home is just right for a young family. The main level features a study, kitchen, dining room, laundry, and two-story living room with a corner fireplace. A rear patio makes summertime grilling fun. The master bedroom is vaulted and features a double-bowl vanity bath and walk-in closet. Bedroom 2 offers its own full bath as well. The basement level boasts a spacious garage and storage area.

basement

first floor

second floor

PLAN: HPK1300255

STYLE: CRAFTSMAN

FIRST FLOOR: 897 SQ. FT.

SECOND FLOOR: 740 SQ. FT.

TOTAL: 1,637 SQ. FT.

BEDROOMS: 3

BATHROOMS: 2½

WIDTH: 30' - 0"

DEPTH: 42' - 6"

FOUNDATION: UNFINISHED WALKOUT BASEMENT

■ With a garage on the ground level, this home takes a much smaller footprint and is perfect for narrow-lot applications. Take a short flight of stairs up to the entry, which opens to a receiving hall and then to the living and dining combination. The living room features a fireplace flanked by bookshelves. The island kitchen and nook are to the rear, near a half-bath. Upstairs are two family bedrooms sharing a full bath and the vaulted master suite, with a private bath and dual walk-in closets.

CRAWLSPACE

UP

GARAGE
19/0 X 23/2

UP

basement

NOOK
15/0 X 10/0
(9' CLG.)

REF. DESK

DN. UP

PAN.

UP

DINING
15/0 X 10/10
(9' CLG.)

BUILT-INS

LIVING
17/0 X 12/6
(9' CLG.)

BUILT-INS

first floor

BR. 2
10/0 X 12/0

LINEN

BR. 3
10/0 X 12/0

DN.

LINEN

OPEN TO BELOW

W/D

SH.

SH.

SH.

(VAULTED)
MASTER
14/10 X 12/2

second floor

PLAN: HPK1300256

STYLE: TRADITIONAL

FIRST FLOOR: 1,554 SQ. FT.

SECOND FLOOR: 1,130 SQ. FT.

TOTAL: 2,684 SQ. FT.

BEDROOMS: 4

BATHROOMS: 2½

WIDTH: 40' - 0"

DEPTH: 67' - 0"

FOUNDATION: SLAB

© The Sater Design Collection, Inc.

■ Clapboard siding and a standing-seam room set off this cottage elevation—a comfortable seaside retreat with an easy going style. A central turret anchors a series of varied gables and rooflines, evoking the charm of Caribbean style. Square columns and a spare balustrade define the perimeter of a spacious entry porch, which leads to a gallery-style foyer. Pocket doors seclude a forward study featuring a step ceiling and views of the front property. An open arrangement of the formal rooms progresses into the plan without restrictions, bounded only by wide views of the outdoors. Retreating glass doors permit the living and dining spaces to extend to the veranda. Upstairs, the master suite adjoins a spare room that could serve as a study, and leads out to a rear deck.

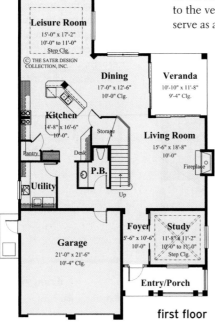

first floor

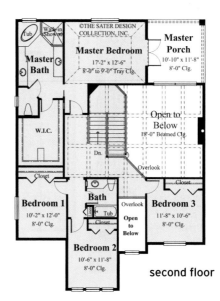

second floor

PLAN: HPK1300259

STYLE: BUNGALOW

FIRST FLOOR: 874 SQ. FT.

SECOND FLOOR: 880 SQ. FT.

TOTAL: 1,754 SQ. FT.

BEDROOMS: 3

BATHROOMS: 2½

WIDTH: 34' - 0"

DEPTH: 43' - 0"

FOUNDATION: UNFINISHED WALKOUT BASEMENT

■ A magnificent turret provides a great accent to the well-crafted look of this historic exterior. French doors open the main-level living areas to the outside. Built-in cabinetry frames the massive fireplace, which warms the decor and atmosphere. Arches and columns help define the interior space, lending a sense of privacy to the dining area—a stunning space with views and access to the covered porch. On the upper level, two secondary bedrooms share a full bath. Double doors lead to the master retreat.

second floor

first floor

basement

PLAN: HPK1300260

STYLE: TIDEWATER
FIRST FLOOR: 1,266 SQ. FT.
SECOND FLOOR: 1,324 SQ. FT.
TOTAL: 2,590 SQ. FT.
BEDROOMS: 3
BATHROOMS: 2½
WIDTH: 34' - 0"
DEPTH: 63' - 2"
FOUNDATION: CRAWLSPACE

■ This Floridian-style home boasts an impressive balcony that is sure to catch the eye. A large veranda borders two sides of the home. The entry leads into a long foyer, which runs from the entrance to the rear of the design. The coffered great room enjoys a fireplace, built-in cabinetry, and French doors to the veranda; the dining room also accesses the veranda. The island kitchen leads into a bayed nook, perfect for Sunday morning breakfasting. The second floor is home to two family bedrooms—both with access to the deck—a study, and a luxurious master suite. A vaulted sitting area, full bath, and deck access are just some of the highlights of the master suite.

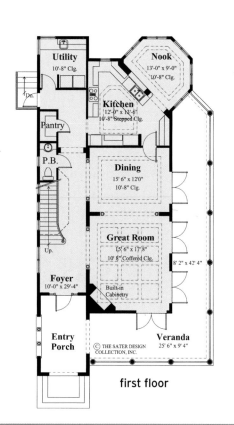

first floor

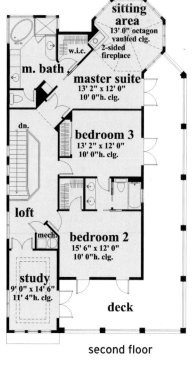

second floor

PLAN: HPK1300261

STYLE: BUNGALOW

FIRST FLOOR: 1,542 SQ. FT.

SECOND FLOOR: 971 SQ. FT.

TOTAL: 2,513 SQ. FT.

BEDROOMS: 3

BATHROOMS: 3

WIDTH: 46' - 0"

DEPTH: 51' - 0"

FOUNDATION: ISLAND
BASEMENT

■ Stonework and elements of Craftsman style make a strong statement but are partnered here with a sweet disposition. Sidelights and transoms enrich the elevation and offer a warm welcome to a well-accoutered interior with up-to-the-minute amenities. A wealth of windows allows gentle breezes to flow through the living space, and French doors extend an invitation to enjoy the rear covered porch. Nearby, a well-organized kitchen offers a pass-through to the great room, and service to the formal dining room through a convenient butler's pantry. Upstairs, the master suite sports a private sitting area that opens to an upper deck through French doors. The upper-level gallery provides an overlook to the great room and connects the master retreat with a secondary bedroom that opens to the deck.

second floor

basement

first floor

PLAN: HPK1300262

STYLE: BUNGALOW

FIRST FLOOR: 1,342 SQ. FT.

SECOND FLOOR: 511 SQ. FT.

TOTAL: 1,853 SQ. FT.

BEDROOMS: 3

BATHROOMS: 2

WIDTH: 44' - 0"

DEPTH: 40' - 0"

FOUNDATION: UNFINISHED
BASEMENT

■ Matchstick details and a careful blend of stone and siding lend a special style and spirit to this stately retreat. Multipane windows take in the scenery and deck out the refined exterior of this cabin-style home designed for a life of luxury. An open foyer shares its natural light with the great room—a bright reprieve filled with its own outdoor light. Dinner guests may wander from the coziness of the hearth space into the crisp night air through lovely French doors. The master retreat is an entire wing of the main level.

second floor

first floor

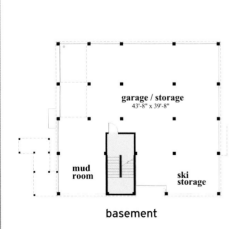

basement

PLAN: HPK1300263

STYLE: CRAFTSMAN
FIRST FLOOR: 436 SQ. FT.
SECOND FLOOR: 792 SQ. FT.
THIRD FLOOR: 202 SQ. FT.
TOTAL: 1,430 SQ. FT.
BEDROOMS: 2
BATHROOMS: 2
WIDTH: 16' - 0"
DEPTH: 54' - 0"
FOUNDATION: CRAWLSPACE

■ For an in-fill lot, a lake site, or seaside retreat, this plan offers three floors of living and a very narrow footprint to make it conform to your needs. A high-pitched roofline accommodates an enchanting dormer window, and a covered porch screens the setback entry. The lower floor at garage level holds a bedroom with full bath and laundry alcove. Built-ins include a desk and drawers along one wall. Outdoor access leads to convenient storage for lawn equipment and other essentials. The main level upstairs holds a vaulted living room with built-in media center, an L-shaped booth seating for dining, an island kitchen with double-door pantry and display shelves, and the master suite. An outdoor deck lies just beyond the living area. A cozy vaulted study loft is graced by a huge built-in bookshelf.

first floor

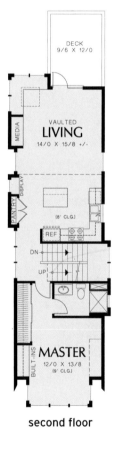

second floor

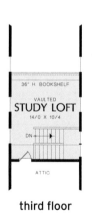

third floor

PLAN: HPK1300340

STYLE: TRADITIONAL

FIRST FLOOR: 1,440 SQ. FT.

SECOND FLOOR: 1,440 SQ. FT.

TOTAL: 2,880 SQ. FT.

BONUS SPACE: 140 SQ. FT.

BEDROOMS: 4

BATHROOMS: 2½

WIDTH: 30' - 0"

DEPTH: 56' - 0"

FOUNDATION: UNFINISHED BASEMENT

■ The impressive exterior gives way to an interior without boundaries. The lack of unnecessary walls creates a feeling of spaciousness. Access to the sun-deck from the family room extends the living space, encouraging entertaining. The second floor houses the master suite and three additional family bedrooms. Bedrooms 2 and 3 enjoy private access to a front-facing covered porch. A second-floor laundry room is an added convenience. The finished basement, boasting a sizable recreation room, completes this plan.

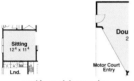

optional layouts

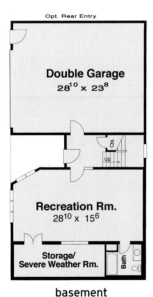

basement

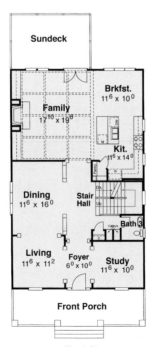

first floor

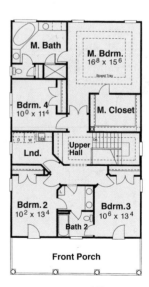

second floor

PLAN: HPK1300341

STYLE: PRAIRIE

FIRST FLOOR: 1,198 SQ. FT.

SECOND FLOOR: 1,570 SQ. FT.

TOTAL: 2,768 SQ. FT.

BEDROOMS: 4

BATHROOMS: $3\frac{1}{2}$

WIDTH: 38' - 0"

DEPTH: 75' - 0"

FOUNDATION: CRAWLSPACE

■ Ideal for a narrow city-lot, this urban in-fill home is a city dweller's dream. The open, first-floor layout offers easy interaction between rooms. Access to a rear deck from the living room and breakfast area makes outdoor dining a possibility. The sleeping quarters are housed upstairs, including the master suite and three additional family bedrooms. Bedroom 4 boasts a private, full bath, a linen storage closet, and the command center control panel for the home automation system. The second-floor laundry room is an added convenience.

first floor

second floor

PLAN: HPK1300342

STYLE: TRADITIONAL

FIRST FLOOR: 1,379 SQ. FT.

SECOND FLOOR: 1,794 SQ. FT.

TOTAL: 3,173 SQ. FT.

BEDROOMS: 4

BATHROOMS: 3½

WIDTH: 38' - 0"

DEPTH: 80' - 0"

FOUNDATION: UNFINISHED
BASEMENT

■ Bold columns distinguish the covered porch on this traditional home. Inside, the minimal use of walls is refreshing and opens the floor plan by adjoining living spaces. Access to the rear patio from the breakfast area makes alfresco meals a possibility. The second floor houses the spacious master suite, enhanced by a tray ceiling and private balcony. Two adjacent family bedrooms are separated by a Jack-and-Jill bath. A short hallway leads to the second-floor laundry room. The family computer station sits outside of bedroom 4—equipped with a full, private bath—useful as an ideal guest suite.

first floor

second floor

PLAN: HPK1300266

STYLE: EUROPEAN COTTAGE

FIRST FLOOR: 1,664 SQ. FT.

SECOND FLOOR: 1,404 SQ. FT.

TOTAL: 3,068 SQ. FT.

BEDROOMS: 4

BATHROOMS: 2½

WIDTH: 42' - 4"

DEPTH: 50' - 4"

FOUNDATION: UNFINISHED BASEMENT

■ This spacious four-bedroom design offers plenty of extras. Open living and dining areas boast distinctive styling, including the lovely archways from the foyer. Among the extras in the dining area are a serving bar and built-in space for a buffet. The large kitchen offers ample counter space and opens to the breakfast area with a telephone desk, pantry, and double French doors to the patio. The family room features a TV alcove over the gas fireplace. The study, accessed from the front foyer, overlooks the front yard. The luxurious master bedroom boasts its own separate sitting room with a vaulted ceiling.

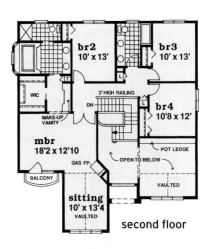

second floor

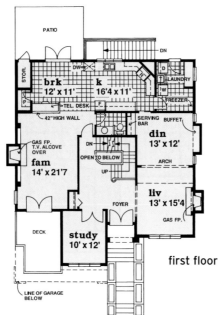

first floor

PLAN: HPK1300267

STYLE: CONTEMPORARY

FIRST FLOOR: 988 SQ. FT.

SECOND FLOOR: 1,137 SQ. FT.

TOTAL: 2,125 SQ. FT.

BEDROOMS: 3

BATHROOMS: 2½

WIDTH: 48' - 0"

DEPTH: 40' - 0"

FOUNDATION: UNFINISHED BASEMENT

■ This home features fancy roof detailing and keystone arches, which give it a European aura. Multiple windows in the turret provide natural light in the living room and the master bedroom. The U-shaped kitchen shares a snack bar with the family room. The master suite's walk-in closet leads to the private bath, which enjoys two vanities with an angled shower and a garden tub. This home features a two-car garage, which can be substituted by an office with a sitting area.

4,80 X 2,80
16'-0" X 9'-4"

5,70 X 3,60
19'-0" X 12'-0"

3,70 X 6,90
12'-4" X 23'-0"

3,30 X 5,50
11'-0" X 18'-4"

3,40 X 7,30
11'-4" X 24'-4"

first floor

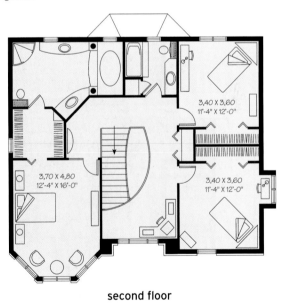

3,40 X 3,60
11'-4" X 12'-0"

3,70 X 4,80
12'-4" X 16'-0"

3,40 X 3,60
11'-4" X 12'-0"

second floor

PLAN: HPK1300272

STYLE:	NW CONTEMPORARY
FIRST FLOOR:	1,317 SQ. FT.
SECOND FLOOR:	1,146 SQ. FT.
TOTAL:	2,463 SQ. FT.
BEDROOMS:	4
BATHROOMS:	2½
WIDTH:	40' - 0"
DEPTH:	54' - 0"
FOUNDATION:	CRAWLSPACE

■ This striking stucco home incorporates fine design elements throughout the plan, including a columned formal living and dining area with a boxed ceiling and a fireplace. A gourmet kitchen accommodates the most elaborate—as well as the simplest—meals. The large family room is just off the kitchen for easy casual living. A lovely curved staircase leads to a balcony overlooking the foyer. The master bedroom contains many fine design features, including a luxury bath with a vaulted ceiling and a spa-style bath. Three comfortable family bedrooms share a full hall bath.

first floor

second floor

PLAN: HPK1300273

STYLE: SW CONTEMPORARY

FIRST FLOOR: 1,383 SQ. FT.

SECOND FLOOR: 1,156 SQ. FT.

TOTAL: 2,539 SQ. FT.

BEDROOMS: 4

BATHROOMS: 2½

WIDTH: 40' - 0"

DEPTH: 59' - 0"

FOUNDATION: UNFINISHED
BASEMENT, CRAWLSPACE

■ This well-planned stucco home is suited for a narrow lot. Its interior begins with a two-story foyer that displays a sweeping, curved staircase, an art niche, and a plant ledge. The vaulted ceiling in the living room is enhanced by a full-height window and a fireplace. Columns separate the living and dining rooms; the dining room has a tray ceiling. The step-saving kitchen is adjacent to a carousel breakfast room with a French door to the rear yard. A gas fireplace warms the family room, which features a room-divider display counter and sliding glass doors. A den with a tray ceiling rounds out the first floor. The master suite boasts a tray ceiling, window seat, raised whirlpool tub, and separate shower. Three family bedrooms share a full bath.

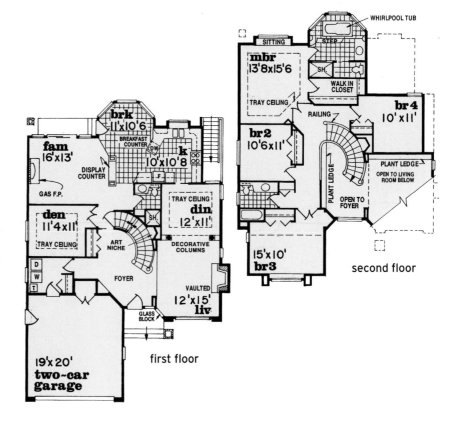

PLAN: HPK1300274

STYLE: SW CONTEMPORARY

FIRST FLOOR: 1,463 SQ. FT.

SECOND FLOOR: 872 SQ. FT.

TOTAL: 2,335 SQ. FT.

BEDROOMS: 3

BATHROOMS: 3

WIDTH: 44' - 0"

DEPTH: 58' - 10"

FOUNDATION: CRAWLSPACE,
UNFINISHED BASEMENT

■ Two different facades are available for this home: a California stucco or a traditional brick-and-siding version. The interior plan begins with a vaulted foyer hosting a sweeping curved staircase spilling into a sunken living room with a masonry fireplace and vaulted ceiling. The kitchen features a pantry, center cooking island, built-in desk, and sunny breakfast bay. A den with a walk-in closet and nearby bath can easily double as a guest room. The master suite on the second floor boasts a drop ceiling, bayed sitting area, and lavish bath. The family bedrooms share a full bath.

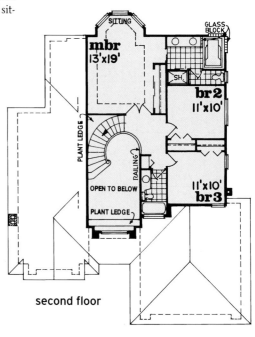

first floor

second floor

PLAN: HPK1300275

STYLE: CONTEMPORARY

FIRST FLOOR: 908 SQ. FT.

SECOND FLOOR: 576 SQ. FT.

TOTAL: 1,484 SQ. FT.

BEDROOMS: 3

BATHROOMS: 2

WIDTH: 26' - 0"

DEPTH: 48' - 0"

FOUNDATION: UNFINISHED BASEMENT

■ Picture yourself driving up to the lake after a long week at work and pulling into the driveway of this gorgeous vacation home. In the foyer, you can hang your coat in the closet and store the toys for the kids. Days are naturally lit by sunlight streaming in through the abundant fenestration throughout the home, but be sure to enjoy the view off the screened porch as well. With a full kitchen at your disposal, you can create a meal to be enjoyed either leisurely at the island or more formally in the dining room. Curl up with a good book and a glass of wine and enjoy the glow of the wood-burning fireplace in the family room, or invite friends over for a movie. They can stay over in the first-floor bedroom with nearby full bath. Then retreat upstairs where you can tuck the kids into their room and fall fast asleep in yours.

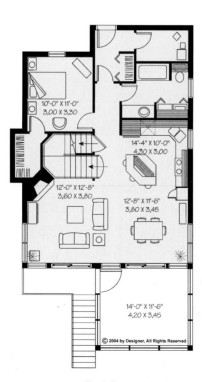

10'-0" X 11'-0"
3,00 X 3,30

14'-4" X 10'-0"
4,30 X 3,00

12'-0" X 12'-8"
3,60 X 3,80

12'-8" X 11'-6"
3,80 X 3,45

14'-0" X 11'-6"
4,20 X 3,45

© 2004 by Designer, All Rights Reserved

first floor

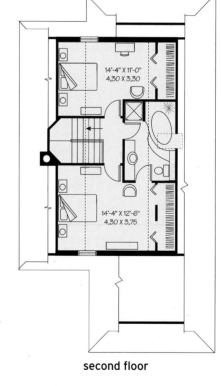

14'-4" X 11'-0"
4,30 X 3,30

14'-4" X 12'-6"
4,30 X 3,75

second floor

PLAN: HPK1300276

STYLE: NW CONTEMPORARY

FIRST FLOOR: 1,022 SQ. FT.

SECOND FLOOR: 813 SQ. FT.

TOTAL: 1,835 SQ. FT.

BEDROOMS: 3

BATHROOMS: 2½

WIDTH: 36' - 0"

DEPTH: 33' - 0"

FOUNDATION: SLAB

■ This home is quite a "looker" with its steeply sloping rooflines and large sunburst and multipane windows. This plan not only accommodates a narrow lot, but it also fits a sloping site. The angled corner entry gives way to a two-story living room with a tiled hearth. The dining room shares an interesting angled space with this area and enjoys easy service from the efficient kitchen. The family room offers double doors to a refreshing balcony. A powder room and laundry room complete the main level. Upstairs, a vaulted master bedroom enjoys a private bath; two other bedrooms share a bath.

first floor

second floor

PLAN: HPK1300277

STYLE: CRAFTSMAN

MAIN LEVEL: 1,106 SQ. FT.

UPPER LEVEL: 872 SQ. FT.

TOTAL: 1,978 SQ. FT.

BEDROOMS: 3

BATHROOMS: 2½

WIDTH: 38' - 0"

DEPTH: 35' - 0"

FOUNDATION: SLAB,
UNFINISHED BASEMENT

■ Though this home gives the impression of the Northwest, it will be the winner of any neighborhood. From the foyer, the two-story living room is just a couple of steps up and features a through-fireplace. The U-shaped kitchen has a cooktop work island, an adjacent nook, and easy access to the formal dining room. A spacious family room shares the fireplace with the living room, is enhanced by built-ins, and also offers a quiet deck for stargazing. The upstairs consists of two family bedrooms sharing a full bath and a vaulted master suite complete with a walk-in closet and sumptuous bath. A two-car, drive-under garage has plenty of room for storage.

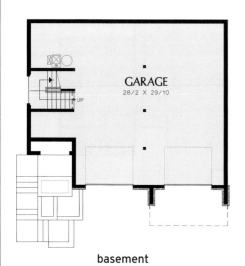

basement

main level

upper level

© 2000 Donald A. Gardner, Inc.

PLAN: HPK1300280

STYLE: RESORT LIFESTYLES

FIRST FLOOR: 1,500 SQ. FT.

SECOND FLOOR: 1,112 SQ. FT.

TOTAL: 2,612 SQ. FT.

BEDROOMS: 4

BATHROOMS: 3

WIDTH: 42' - 0"

DEPTH: 49' - 6"

■ Porches front and back, a multitude of windows, and a narrow facade make this elevated pier foundation perfect for beach property or any waterfront lot. The main living areas are positioned at the rear of the home for the best views of the water. The great room features a vaulted ceiling, fireplace, and back porch access. The kitchen is open, sharing space with a bayed breakfast area and lovely sun room. The first floor includes a bedroom/study and full bath, while the master suite and two more family bedrooms can be found upstairs. The master suite boasts a private porch and sitting room with bay window.

first floor

second floor

PLAN: HPK1300281

STYLE: CAPE COD

FIRST FLOOR: 803 SQ. FT.

SECOND FLOOR: 1,182 SQ. FT.

TOTAL: 1,985 SQ. FT.

BEDROOMS: 4

BATHROOMS: 2½

WIDTH: 36' - 0"

DEPTH: 43' - 4"

FOUNDATION: UNFINISHED
WALKOUT BASEMENT,
CRAWLSPACE

■ This narrow-lot home would be perfect nestled into an in-fill lot or standing prominently in a new development. Either way, its classic style will make it a standout. Enter to a foyer that is lit by a second-story arched window. Subtle angles direct traffic into the family room, where a warming fireplace awaits. An efficient kitchen opens to both the sunny breakfast nook and formal dining room, catering to any occasion. Upstairs, four bedrooms include a vaulted master suite with a lavish bath. A laundry room on this level is a thoughtful touch.

first floor

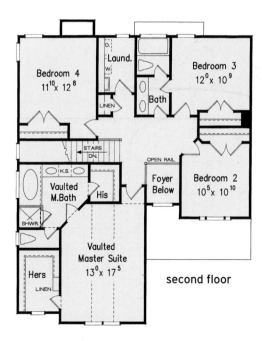

second floor

PLAN: HPK1300282

STYLE: TRADITIONAL

FIRST FLOOR: 1,347 SQ. FT.

SECOND FLOOR: 537 SQ. FT.

TOTAL: 1,884 SQ. FT.

BEDROOMS: 3

BATHROOMS: 2½

WIDTH: 32' - 10"

DEPTH: 70' - 10"

FOUNDATION: CRAWLSPACE

■ This old-fashioned townhouse design features an attractive two-story floor plan. Two front covered porches enhance the traditional facade. Inside, the foyer introduces an island kitchen that overlooks the dining room. A formal two-story living room, located at the rear of the plan, is warmed by a fireplace. The first-floor master suite enjoys a private bath and huge walk-in closet. A powder room, laundry room, and two-car garage complete the first floor. Upstairs, two secondary bedrooms—one with a walk-in closet—share a full hall bath. Bedroom 3 features a private balcony overlooking the front property. Optional storage is available on the second floor.

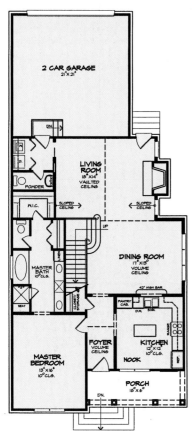

first floor

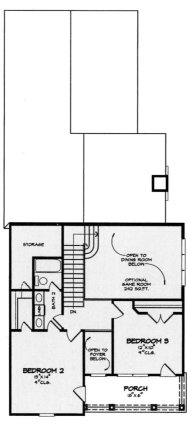

second floor

PLAN: HPK1300343

STYLE: ADAM STYLE

FIRST FLOOR: 774 SQ. FT.

SECOND FLOOR: 754 SQ. FT.

THIRD FLOOR: 260 SQ. FT.

TOTAL: 1,788 SQ. FT.

BEDROOMS: 2

BATHROOMS: 2½

WIDTH: 20' - 0"

DEPTH: 40' - 0"

FOUNDATION: UNFINISHED BASEMENT

■ The luxury of detached housing, combined with the convenience and sophistication of city living, serves as the primary focus of this home. Provocative touches, such as a corner fireplace in the great room, a generous open floor plan, third-floor loft, and an expansive master suite, highlight the Neo-Traditional design. The warmth of the fireplace, windows across the rear (overlooking a courtyard), and angled rear entry are alluring touches. With an expansive rear patio and porch, emphasis is placed on a balance of indoor-outdoor living.

first floor

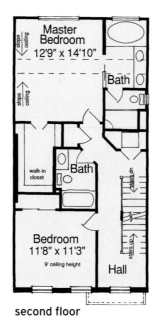

second floor

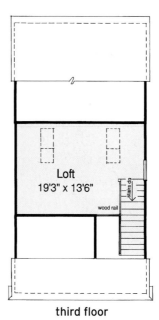

third floor

A large deck and a second-floor balcony are just two reasons this beautiful Tudor cottage, found on page 371, would make a perfect vacation home.

Affordable Dream Homes

A smaller square footage doesn't have to reduce the luxury found within

Moving away from the dreaded McMansions and other excesses of our nation's recent home-building history, the hottest trend in new homes today calls for smaller, well-crafted houses. Homeowners aren't asking for more space than they need, but they want the space that they build to be as nice as possible.

This trend, as you'll see, fits perfectly with narrow-lot homes. Plans like the 47 showcased in this chapter may have a small footprint, but they pack plenty of luxury within their walls.

We've titled this chapter "Affordable Dream Homes" because their smaller square footage allows you to save over a large, sprawling home. But there's no need for these designs to fall short of your dreams. With the money you save by not going overboard on the square footage, you can invest in quality where you'll notice it most—in rooms or exteriors that you enjoy every day.

PHOTOS BY BOB GREENSPAN

Outer Space

If you're a believer in first impressions, your home's exterior might be one place you wish to splurge. This could mean a variety of alternative treatments—like fiber cement siding instead of vinyl, for example. Other considerations could include upgraded windows or increased attention to the home's architectural trim.

There are other exterior options where you could splurge and enjoy not just a better look but a better lifestyle as well. Consider incorporating a deck or patio if your home plan doesn't already call for one, and if you're prepared to spend a little more, use the very best low-maintenance materials. That will give you more time to enjoy your outdoor spaces.

Inside Extravagance

Adding a level of luxury to your interiors can be as simple as paying special attention to detail. Little things—like built-in bookshelves and cabinets—can go a long way, especially in a narrow-lot home where space may be at a premium. Other details can include architectural trim, like chair rails or crown moldings, or decorative ceiling treatments. You'll see many of these elements noted in the floor plans in this chapter, and you can work with your builder to add them when necessary as well.

You may also consider splurging on one particular room in your home. Perhaps you want the perfect master suite or the kitchen of your dreams—these are the most common rooms to be remodeled down the road, so it makes sense to make them as good as can be during the building stage. Other options might be less common but more suitable for your tastes—perhaps a home theater to enjoy that DVD collection or a nicely outfitted rec room in the basement.

Make it Yours

If you are looking to add a personal touch that means a little more than an added detail or improved product in your home, keep in mind that you can customize any plan. Whether it's adding space to a bedroom, moving a garage, or another modification, turn to page 376 for details on how to use our Customization Service. ■

HOT KITCHENS

No room in the home provides a better stage to showcase your personal tastes than the kitchen—and not just with what you cook. It's where we inevitably spend the most time, whether with family or entertaining, and your kitchen's styling and products can be translated to fit your personality.

Are you a hard-core cook? Fill your kitchen with sparkling high-performance appliances and plenty of counter space, including a prep sink, to provide you the perfect setting to prepare your cuisine. If ordering in is more your thing, your money will be better spent on attractive elements like cabinets and countertops rather than top-of-the-line appliances.

Left: Rich wood tones give this kitchen, inside the home on page 354, a comfortable feel.

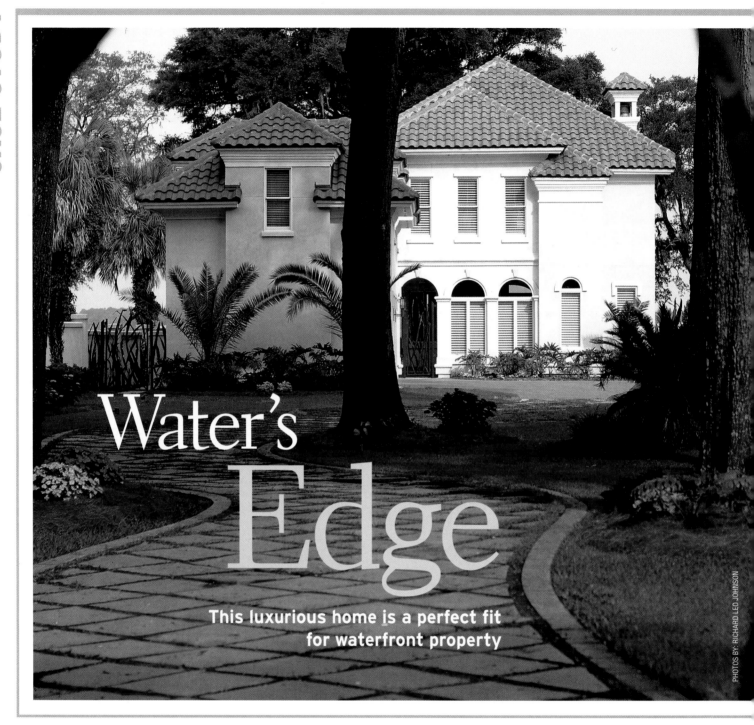

Water's
Edge

This luxurious home is a perfect fit for waterfront property

PHOTOS BY: RICHARD LEO JOHNSON

Covered porches wrap around two sides of this Floridian home, blurring the lines between indoors and out and expanding the living space of this beautiful narrow-lot home. From the unique courtyard entry to the enormous master suite, this home fits on a 50-foot-wide lot but has no limits on luxury.

Its clever design begins with those signature covered porches—one on each level—overlooking the spa and lap pool. The outdoor attractions, both man-made and natural, will draw your eye outside from almost any spot in this home. But don't let it distract you from the beauty within.

The kitchen and dining room, at the center of the first floor, are perfect examples. The dining area occupies a bay window looking out to the porch and pool, and it opens easily into the great room. The island kitchen also connects to the great room, where a serving bar invites guests to pull up chairs and spend time with the chef.

Left: Make your way up a windy drive and peek past the trees for a glimpse at the splendor of this home. Above: Smart storage spaces, as on each side of this hallway, keep the clutter to a minimum. Right: Open design and a serving bar connect the kitchen to the great room.

The long center hallway provides through-the-house views, accentuating the space in the home.

A wall of curved glass dominates the corner of the great room, expanding its shape in two directions. Three sets of French doors open to the porch. Turning back inside, a fireplace and TV niche highlight a wall filled with built-ins.

Three bedrooms reside upstairs, but one will grab your attention—the master suite. It fills at least half the floor, and like the great room below it features a curved wall of glass and three sets of French doors. An angled wall provides the bed with ideal views every morning. His and Hers walk-in closets provide plenty of storage space, and the master

Wraparound covered porches—on both the first and second floors—expand the living space.

Enjoy sunrises and relaxing evenings on the second-floor porch.

The master bath beckons with a soaking tub and separate shower designed to fit two people.

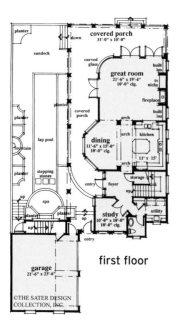

first floor

planter
covered porch
31'-0" x 10'-0"
down
sundeck
curved glass
built ins
great room
21'-6" x 19'-4"
10'-0" clg.
tv niche
fireplace
planter
covered porch
arch
built ins
planter
arch
kitchen
dining
11'-6" x 15'-0"
10'-0" clg.
lap pool
arch
11' x 15'
fountain
planter
arch
storage
entry
foyer
up
stepping stones
spa
up
study
10'-0" x 10'-0"
10'-0" clg.
utility
planter
planter
up
entry
garage
21'-6" x 23'-6"
©THE SATER DESIGN COLLECTION, INC.

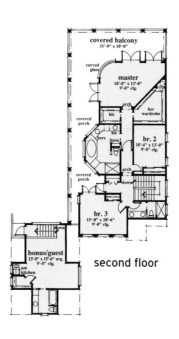

second floor

covered balcony
31'-0" x 10'-0"
curved glass
master
18'-0" x 13'-0"
9'-0" clg.
his
her wardrobe
covered porch
arch
his
hers
linen
br. 2
10'-4" x 13'-0"
9'-0" clg.
covered porch
arch
down
br. 3
15'-0" x 10'-6"
9'-0" clg.
down
bonus/guest
13'-0" x 15'-6" avg.
9'-0" clg.
am kitchen

PLAN: HPK1300283

STYLE: ITALIANATE

FIRST FLOOR: 1,293 SQ. FT.

SECOND FLOOR: 1,154 SQ. FT.

TOTAL: 2,447 SQ. FT.

BONUS SPACE: 426 SQ. FT.

BEDROOMS: 3

BATHROOMS: 2½

WIDTH: 50' - 0"

DEPTH: 90' - 0"

FOUNDATION: SLAB

bath is sure to pamper. Its whirlpool tub fits perfectly in a bay window, with a separate shower and His and Hers vanities nearby.

As if that weren't enough, bonus space above the garage offers yet another treat—a possible guest suite. A full bath and a morning kitchen will make any visitor feel at home—and with a house like this, you're sure to have plenty of visitors. ∎

PLAN: HPK1300284

STYLE: PLANTATION
FIRST FLOOR: 2,236 SQ. FT.
SECOND FLOOR: 1,208 SQ. FT.
TOTAL: 3,444 SQ. FT.
BONUS SPACE: 318 SQ. FT.
BEDROOMS: 4
BATHROOMS: 4
WIDTH: 42' - 6"
DEPTH: 71' - 4"
FOUNDATION: PIER
(SAME AS PILING)

■ This spacious home offers a front porch and a second-floor balcony as well as a wraparound porch in the rear. The elegant foyer, with its grand staircase, is flanked by the dining room on the left and the study on the right. The island kitchen adjoins the family room and the sunny breakfast nook. The master suite, with an elaborate private bath, is secluded in the back for privacy. Three additional bedrooms—one with a sitting room—share two full baths on the second floor.

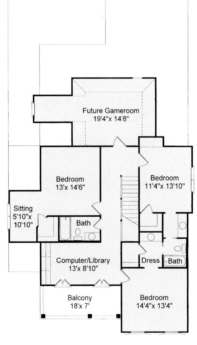

first floor

second floor

PLAN: HPK1300285

STYLE: PLANTATION

FIRST FLOOR: 1,742 SQ. FT.

SECOND FLOOR: 1,624 SQ. FT.

TOTAL: 3,366 SQ. FT.

BEDROOMS: 4

BATHROOMS: 3

WIDTH: 42' - 10"

DEPTH: 77' - 0"

FOUNDATION: PIER
(SAME AS PILING)

■ Elegant Southern living is the theme of this seaside townhouse. The narrow-lot design allows for comfortable urban living. Inside, the living room is warmed by a fireplace, while the island kitchen serves the breakfast room and casual den. A first-floor guest bedroom is located at the front of the design. The dining room is reserved for more formal occasions. Upstairs, the gracious master suite features a private second-floor porch, two walk-in closets, and a private bath. Two additional bedrooms share a hall bath on this floor.

first floor

Deck 25'8"x 9'

Porch 25'8"x 8'

Den 13'8"x 12'9"

Breakfast 16'6"x 10'

Living 25'4"x 18'

Kitchen 13'8"x 15'

Dining 13'8"x 12'

Porch

Bath

Bedroom 15'8"x 11'

second floor

Porch

Master Bedroom 20'x 18'

Master Bath

WIC

WIC

Utility

Balcony

Bedroom 13'8"x 12'

Bath

Bedroom 15'8"x 11'

PLAN: HPK1300288

STYLE: BUNGALOW
FIRST FLOOR: 1,266 SQ. FT.
SECOND FLOOR: 1,324 SQ. FT.
TOTAL: 2,590 SQ. FT.
BEDROOMS: 3
BATHROOMS: 2½
WIDTH: 34' - 0"
DEPTH: 63' - 2"
FOUNDATION: CRAWLSPACE

■ Tall windows and a lofty deck bestow spectacular views across the front of this rustic hideaway—perfect for any region. The wraparound porch extends the living and dining space to the soul-stirring beauty of the outdoors. A beam ceiling highlights the great room, creating a pleasing mix of style and warmth. A food-preparation island and walk-in pantry extend the facility of the kitchen, which easily serves occasions, planned or casual. A powder room is placed just off the foyer. Upper-level sleeping quarters include two secondary bedrooms that share a compartmented bath. The master suite features a handsome bedroom with a vaulted sitting bay and a two-sided fireplace shared with the bath.

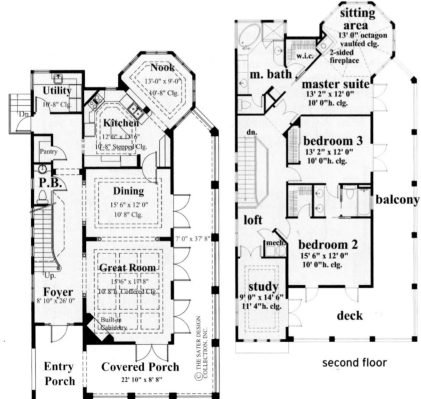

first floor

second floor

PLAN: HPK1300289

STYLE: BUNGALOW

FIRST FLOOR: 1,383 SQ. FT.

SECOND FLOOR: 595 SQ. FT.

TOTAL: 1,978 SQ. FT.

BEDROOMS: 3

BATHROOMS: 2

WIDTH: 48' - 0"

DEPTH: 48' - 8"

FOUNDATION: UNFINISHED WALKOUT BASEMENT

■ The stone facade and woodwork detail give this home a Craftsman appeal. The foyer opens to a staircase up to the vaulted great room, which features a fireplace flanked by built-ins and French-door access to the rear covered porch. The open dining room with a tray ceiling offers convenience to the spacious kitchen. Two family bedrooms share a bath and enjoy private porches. An overlook to the great room below is a perfect introduction to the master suite. The second level spreads out the luxury of the master suite with a spacious walk-in closet, a private porch, and a glorious master bath with a garden tub, dual vanities, and a compartmented toilet.

basement

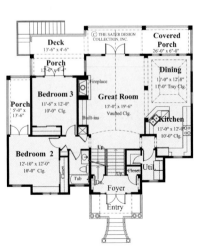

first floor

second floor

PLAN: HPK1300290

PLAN: HPK1300290

STYLE: FLORIDIAN

FIRST FLOOR: 1,684 SQ. FT.

SECOND FLOOR: 1,195 SQ. FT.

TOTAL: 2,879 SQ. FT.

BONUS SPACE: 674 SQ. FT.

BEDROOMS: 3

BATHROOMS: 3

WIDTH: 45' - 0"

DEPTH: 52' - 0"

FOUNDATION: PIER

(SAME AS PILING)

■ Asymmetrical rooflines set off a grand turret and a two-story bay that allow glorious views from the front of this home. Arch-top clerestory windows bring natural light into the great room, which shares a corner fireplace and a wet bar with the dining room. Two guest suites are located on this floor. A winding staircase leads to a luxurious master suite that shares a fireplace with the bath and includes a morning kitchen, French doors to the balcony, and a double walk-in closet. Down the hall, a study and a balcony overlooking the great room complete the plan.

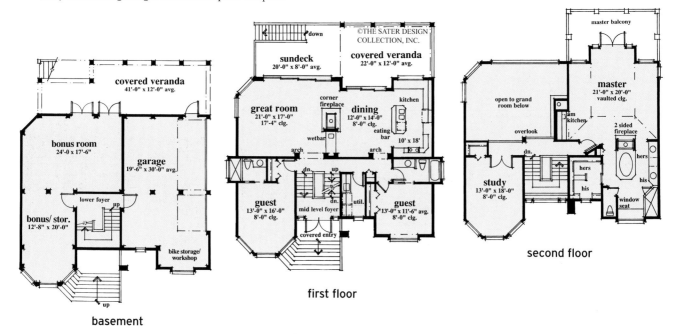

basement

first floor

second floor

PLAN: HPK1300291

PLAN: HPK1300291

STYLE: EUROPEAN COTTAGE

FIRST FLOOR: 1,637 SQ. FT.

SECOND FLOOR: 1,022 SQ. FT.

TOTAL: 2,659 SQ. FT.

BONUS SPACE: 532 SQ. FT.

BEDROOMS: 3

BATHROOMS: 3½

WIDTH: 50' - 0"

DEPTH: 53' - 0"

FOUNDATION: PIER
(SAME AS PILING)

■ Variable rooflines, a tower, and a covered front porch all combine to give this home a wonderful ambiance. Enter through the midlevel foyer and head either up to the main living level or down to the garage. On the main level, find a spacious light-filled great room sharing a fireplace with the dining room. A study offers access to the rear covered veranda. The efficient island kitchen is open to the dining room, offering ease in entertaining. A guest suite with a private full bath completes this level. Upstairs, a second guest suite with its own bath and a deluxe master suite with a covered balcony, sundeck, walk-in closet, and lavish bath are sure to please.

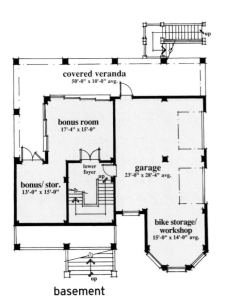

basement

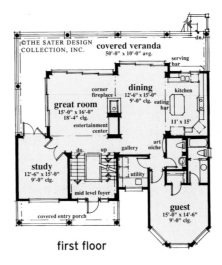

first floor

second floor

PLAN: HPK1300292

STYLE: TIDEWATER
FIRST FLOOR: 1,342 SQ. FT.
SECOND FLOOR: 511 SQ. FT.
TOTAL: 1,853 SQ. FT.
BEDROOMS: 3
BATHROOMS: 2½
WIDTH: 44' - 0"
DEPTH: 40' - 0"
FOUNDATION: ISLAND BASEMENT

■ Detailed fretwork complements a standing-seam roof on this tropical cottage. An arch-top transom provides an absolutely perfect highlight to the classic clapboard facade. An unrestrained floor plan offers cool digs for kicking back and a sensational retreat for guests—whether the occasion is formal or casual. French doors open to a rear porch from the great room letting in fresh air and the sights and sounds of the great outdoors. Inside, the master bedroom leads to a dressing space with linen storage and a walk-in closet. The lavish bath includes a garden tub, oversized shower, and a wraparound vanity with two sinks. Two secondary bedrooms on the upper level share a spacious loft that overlooks the great room. One of the bedrooms opens to a private deck.

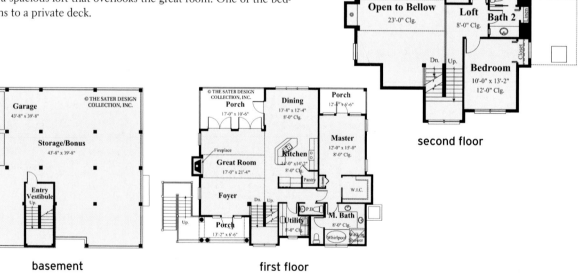

basement

first floor

second floor

PLAN: HPK1300293

STYLE: FLORIDIAN

FIRST FLOOR: 1,342 SQ. FT.

SECOND FLOOR: 511 SQ. FT.

TOTAL: 1,853 SQ. FT.

BEDROOMS: 3

BATHROOMS: 2

WIDTH: 44' - 0"

DEPTH: 40' - 0"

FOUNDATION: PIER
(SAME AS PILING)

■ Amenities abound in this delightful two-story home. The foyer opens directly into the fantastic grand room, which offers a warming fireplace and two sets of double doors to the rear deck. The dining room also accesses this deck and a second deck shared with Bedroom 2. A convenient kitchen and another bedroom also reside on this level. Upstairs, the master bedroom reigns supreme. Entered through double doors, it pampers with a luxurious bath, walk-in closet, morning kitchen, and private observation deck.

second floor

first floor

grand room
20'-0" x 18'-0"
vault. clg.

fireplace

deck
17'-0" x 9'-0"

dining
12'-8" x 11'-0"
8' clg.

deck

kitchen
11' x 12'

br. 2
12'-0" x 11'-8"
8' clg.

br. 3
12'-0" x 10'-0"
8' clg.

foyer

entry porch

©THE SATER DESIGN COLLECTION, INC.

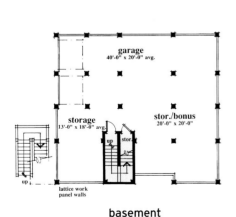

garage
40'-0" x 20'-0" avg.

storage
13'-0" x 18'-0" avg.

stor./bonus
20'-0" x 20'-0"

lattice work
panel walls

basement

PLAN: HPK1300296

STYLE: NORMAN

FIRST FLOOR: 1,932 SQ. FT.

SECOND FLOOR: 1,327 SQ. FT.

TOTAL: 3,259 SQ. FT.

BEDROOMS: 4

BATHROOMS: 3½

WIDTH: 50' - 0"

DEPTH: 51' - 0"

FOUNDATION: FINISHED
WALKOUT BASEMENT, SLAB

■ For sheer comfort and satisfaction of a wide spectrum of needs, this stately two-story home can't be beat. An outstanding grand room and elegant formal dining room will host many enjoyable get-togethers. To the left of the two-story foyer, the library is perfect for cordial conversations with friends or quiet reading time. The rear keeping room, just off the well-equipped kitchen, will draw family members together for informal meals, games, and discussions. A gorgeous master suite is also found on this level, and upstairs, three more bedrooms allow ample sleeping space for family members or guests. A good-size media room and lots of storage space are also on the second floor.

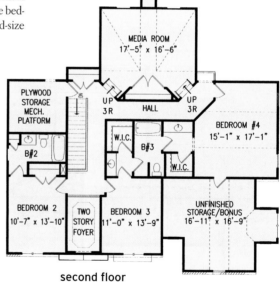

second floor

first floor

PLAN: HPK1300297

STYLE: FLORIDIAN

MAIN LEVEL: 1,677 SQ. FT.

LOWER LEVEL: 40 SQ. FT.

TOTAL: 1,717 SQ. FT.

BEDROOMS: 3

BATHROOMS: 2

WIDTH: 50' - 0"

DEPTH: 39' - 4"

FOUNDATION: UNFINISHED

WALKOUT BASEMENT

■ This elegant home makes the most of the hillside lot by using the lower level for a two-car garage and expandable basement space. A striking stair leads to the entry where another half-flight continues up inside. The vaulted dining room has an open rail that overlooks the entry. A vaulted ceiling in the great room accents the fireplace. A modified galley kitchen provides a snack bar and a breakfast nook. The master suite features a sitting room, compartmented bath, and walk-in closet. Two family bedrooms share a full hall bath.

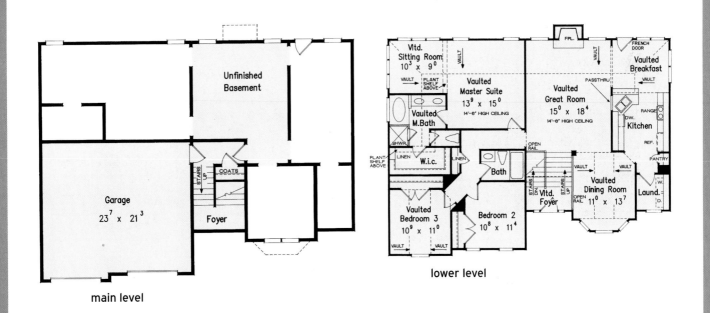

main level

lower level

PLAN: HPK1300298

STYLE: COUNTRY COTTAGE
SQUARE FOOTAGE: 1,884
BEDROOMS: 3
BATHROOMS: $2^1/_2$
WIDTH: 50' - 0"
DEPTH: 55' - 4"
FOUNDATION: SLAB,
CRAWLSPACE, UNFINISHED
WALKOUT BASEMENT

■ Arched openings, decorative columns, and elegant ceiling details throughout highlight this livable floor plan. The country kitchen includes a spacious work area, preparation island, serving bar to the great room, and a breakfast nook with a tray ceiling. Set to the rear for gracious entertaining, the dining room opens to the great room. Note the warming fireplace and French-door access to the backyard in the great room. The master suite is beautifully appointed with a tray ceiling, bay window, compartmented bath, and walk-in closet. Two family bedrooms, a laundry room, and a powder room complete this gracious design.

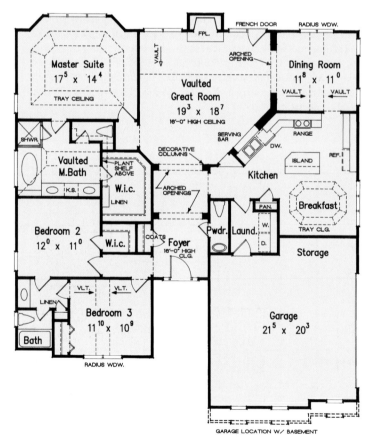

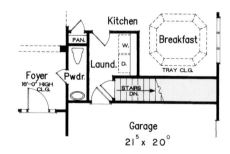

optional layout

PLAN: HPK1300299

STYLE: TRADITIONAL

FIRST FLOOR: 1,796 SQ. FT.

SECOND FLOOR: 1,057 SQ. FT.

TOTAL: 2,853 SQ. FT.

BONUS SPACE: 220 SQ. FT.

BEDROOMS: 4

BATHROOMS: 3½

WIDTH: 50' - 0"

DEPTH: 56' - 0"

FOUNDATION: SLAB

■ This contemporary Mediterranean home features an exterior with an intriguing mix of styles, blending brick and stucco with an upper-floor balustrade and a vibrant octagonal entrance. The interior presents formal living and dining rooms, a gourmet kitchen with adjoining nook and laundry facilities, and a first-floor master suite. A spacious family room abuts the breakfast nook, and features a fireplace flanked by a built-in entertainment center. Upstairs, three family bedrooms, two full baths, and an optional bonus room complete the floor plan.

first floor

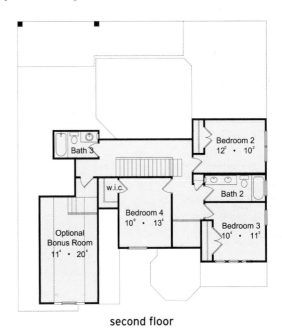

second floor

PLAN: HPK1300300

STYLE: EUROPEAN COTTAGE
FIRST FLOOR: 1,152 SQ. FT.
SECOND FLOOR: 1,434 SQ. FT.
TOTAL: 2,586 SQ. FT.
BEDROOMS: 4
BATHROOMS: 3
WIDTH: 44' - 0"
DEPTH: 44' - 0"
FOUNDATION: UNFINISHED
BASEMENT

■ Tall, robust columns flank the impressive two-story entry of this European-style home. Views can be had in the living room—in the turret—and with the open dining area just steps away, entertaining will be a splendid affair. The kitchen features a breakfast bar and adjoining sun room. Upstairs, the master suite is enhanced by a large sitting area, bumped-out bay window, and a relaxing bath. Three family bedrooms and a full bath complete this level.

first floor

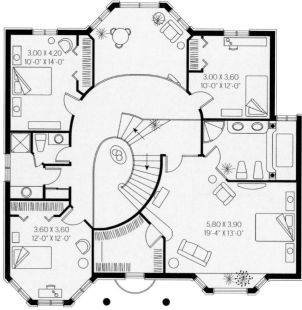

second floor

PLAN: HPK1300301

STYLE: CONTEMPORARY

FIRST FLOOR: 1,554 SQ. FT.

SECOND FLOOR: 1,448 SQ. FT.

TOTAL: 3,002 SQ. FT.

BEDROOMS: 3

BATHROOMS: 2½

WIDTH: 50' - 0"

DEPTH: 43' - 0"

FOUNDATION: UNFINISHED BASEMENT

rear exterior

■ You are sure to be amazed at what lies behind this traditional stone facade. A luxurious floor plan from top to bottom, this home is a dream come true for anyone who loves to entertain or just enjoys the finer things. A living room with a bay window resides on the left, defined by a two-way fireplace that also warms the dining room. The kitchen is wide and inviting with a bumped-out window over the sink. Family areas include a two-story main gathering room—with space for an indoor spa—and a closed off entertainment room. A U-shaped staircase reveals four bedrooms, each with beautiful bay windows. The master suite will pamper and soothe.

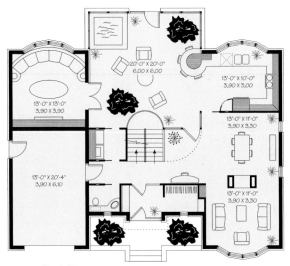

first floor

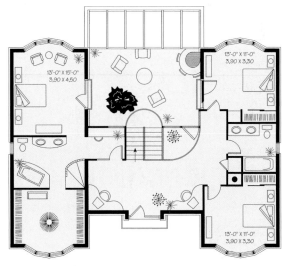

second floor

PLAN: HPK1300302

STYLE: TRADITIONAL
FIRST FLOOR: 2,193 SQ. FT.
SECOND FLOOR: 1,004 SQ. FT.
TOTAL: 3,197 SQ. FT.
BEDROOMS: 4
BATHROOMS: 4½
WIDTH: 67' - 0"
DEPTH: 74' - 4"
FOUNDATION: CRAWLSPACE

■ A dramatic, soaring entryway, steep rooflines, and elegant corner quoins add breathtaking depth and beauty to this home design. Formal spaces flank the foyer, and more casual rooms sit to the rear. An open layout among the family room, breakfast bay, and kitchen encourages interaction. The master suite features a tray ceiling, terrace access, large walk-in closet, and full bath. Three secondary bedrooms enjoy private baths and walk-in closets. A spacious computer and media room will be a favorite gathering spot for family friends.

first floor

second floor

PLAN: HPK1300303

STYLE: EUROPEAN COTTAGE

FIRST FLOOR: 2,216 SQ. FT.

SECOND FLOOR: 947 SQ. FT.

TOTAL: 3,163 SQ. FT.

BONUS SPACE: 409 SQ. FT.

BEDROOMS: 4

BATHROOMS: 3½

WIDTH: 49' - 0"

DEPTH: 89' - 4"

FOUNDATION: CRAWLSPACE

■ A charming portico, unique dormer window, and French shutters accent the front of this home's facade, while four beautiful bay windows make the rear facade appealing as well. Inside, the central gathering room—with a fireplace, built-ins, and access to the outdoors—serves as the heart of the home. The nearby breakfast bay shares a snack bar with the kitchen; a separate dining room is available for formal gatherings. All bedrooms—the first-floor master suite as well as three second-floor family bedrooms—include walk-in closets. A separate studio suite, located above the garage, serves as a retreat for visiting relatives or teenagers who need privacy.

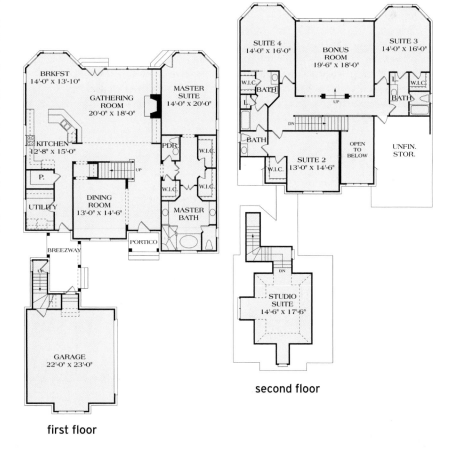

first floor

second floor

PLAN: HPK1300304

STYLE: FRENCH

FIRST FLOOR: 1,724 SQ. FT.

SECOND FLOOR: 700 SQ. FT.

TOTAL: 2,424 SQ. FT.

BEDROOMS: 3

BATHROOMS: 2½

WIDTH: 47' - 10"

DEPTH: 63' - 8"

FOUNDATION: WALKOUT BASEMENT

■ All the charm of gables, stonework, and multilevel rooflines combine to create this home. To the left of the foyer, you will see the dining room highlighted by a tray ceiling. This room and the living room flow together to form one large entertainment area. The gourmet kitchen holds a work island and adjoining octagonal breakfast room. The great room is a fantastic living space, featuring a pass-through wet bar, a fireplace, and bookcases. The master suite enjoys privacy at the rear of the home. An open-rail loft above the foyer leads to two additional bedrooms with walk-in closets, private vanities, and a shared bath.

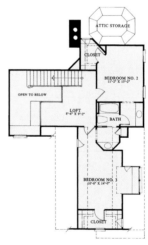

first floor

second floor

PLAN: HPK1300305

PLAN: HPK1300305

STYLE: COUNTRY COTTAGE

FIRST FLOOR: 1,743 SQ. FT.

SECOND FLOOR: 762 SQ. FT.

TOTAL: 2,505 SQ. FT.

BONUS SPACE: 361 SQ. FT.

BEDROOMS: 4

BATHROOMS: 2½

WIDTH: 47' - 0"

DEPTH: 68' - 0"

FOUNDATION: UNFINISHED BASEMENT

■ The graceful sweep of the facade, softened by molding details, sets this home apart from the crowd. Beneath the striking roofline is nestled a columned porch entry with double doors. The floor plan is equally impressive, highlighted by a dramatic bow-windowed, two-story great room with built-in shelves flanking the fireplace. At the right of the plan, the kitchen provides ample counter space plus an island. The adjacent breakfast room features an 18-foot ceiling and flows into the two-story keeping room with a second fireplace, vaulted ceiling, and double doors to the deck. The master bedroom also opens to the deck through double doors and is accented by a tray ceiling and a bath with His and Hers closets, a dual vanity, oversized tub, and separate shower. On the second floor, three additional bedrooms are joined by a balcony overlooking the great room, while a bonus room is available for future development.

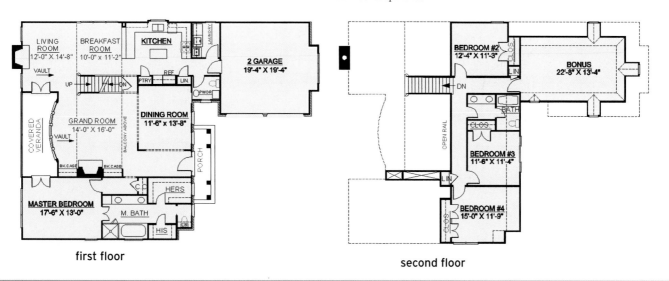

first floor

second floor

PLAN: HPK1300306

STYLE: TRADITIONAL
SQUARE FOOTAGE: 2,366
BEDROOMS: 4
BATHROOMS: 3
WIDTH: 50' - 0"
DEPTH: 86' - 0"
FOUNDATION: SLAB

■ Looking a bit like a French Country manor, this alluring home maintains privacy with a stucco wall that encloses a splendid courtyard. Inside, 14-foot ceilings grace the family living areas. The foyer opens to the dining room on the left or to the brightly lit living room straight ahead. Thoughtful amenities in the living room include French doors to the rear porch, a fireplace, and a built-in entertainment center. The U-shaped kitchen is accentuated by an island and hosts bookshelves and a phone niche. Sleeping quarters begin with a guest room (with a semiprivate bath) and two secondary bedrooms, one of which also makes a perfect study. The master suite is separated for privacy, enhanced by a private bath with a garden tub and dual walk-in closets.

PLAN: HPK1300307

STYLE: EUROPEAN COTTAGE
FIRST FLOOR: 1,884 SQ. FT.
SECOND FLOOR: 1,034 SQ. FT.
TOTAL: 2,918 SQ. FT.
BEDROOMS: 4
BATHROOMS: 3½
WIDTH: 49' - 0"
DEPTH: 79' - 0"
FOUNDATION: SLAB

■ Designed for a narrow lot, this enchanting cottage is perfect for urban in-fill and is "at home" in an established neighborhood. Enter past a side-loading garage that blends beautifully with the home's brick and stucco facade. The foyer leads to a living room that is created for elegant entertaining with a corner fireplace, built in library and entertainment center, and a convenient wet bar; porch access expands the space visually. The kitchen is equipped with an angled serving bar to easily cater to the eating nook and formal dining room. At the rear, the master suite provides porch access and a pampering bath. Up a stylish staircase, three bedrooms are graced with unique appointments: Bedroom 2 is lit by a dormer window and has a private bath; Bedroom 3 enjoys flower-box windows and a built-in desk; and Bedroom 4 has a cozy sitting room.

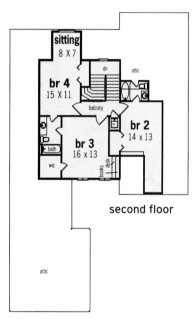

second floor

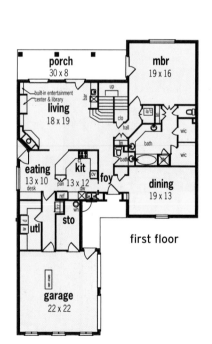

first floor

PLAN: HPK1300310

STYLE: EUROPEAN COTTAGE

FIRST FLOOR: 1,820 SQ. FT.

SECOND FLOOR: 592 SQ. FT.

TOTAL: 2,412 SQ. FT.

BEDROOMS: 2

BATHROOMS: 3

WIDTH: 42' - 0"

DEPTH: 70' - 8"

FOUNDATION: SLAB,
UNFINISHED BASEMENT

■ A stylish angled entry at the front door leads to a well-lit foyer. At right, an optional dining room or den opens to the great room, which features a delightful fireplace. The master bedroom, conveniently located on the first floor, provides a luxury bath with all the trimmings. Differently abled individuals will appreciate the roomy master bath. The kitchen offers bar-style seating and also opens to the great room. The rear porch features an outdoor wood-burning fireplace. The plan offers a slab foundation or a basement foundation with an eight-or nine-foot basement ceiling.

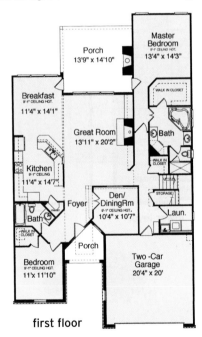

first floor

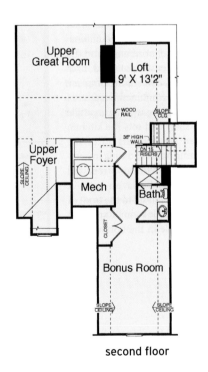

second floor

PLAN: HPK1300311

STYLE: EUROPEAN COTTAGE

FIRST FLOOR: 2,351 SQ. FT.

SECOND FLOOR: 501 SQ. FT.

TOTAL: 2,852 SQ. FT.

BEDROOMS: 3

BATHROOMS: 3

WIDTH: 50' - 0"

DEPTH: 75' - 0"

FOUNDATION: SLAB,

UNFINISHED BASEMENT

■ Attention to detail is the crux of this home's appeal. The pleasing facade gives way to a well-designed floor plan perfect for an empty-nester or small family. The first-floor master suite is a blend of practicality and lavishness. The library adjacent to the master suite is an ideal location for a home office. The family bedroom on this level can serve as a guest suite or accomodations for an in-law. An island snack bar in the spacious kitchen floats between the adjoining breakfast nook and great room. Access to the rear covered porch—equipped with an outdoor fireplace—through sliding doors in the breakfast nook, welcomes alfresco meals and entertaining. With the majority of the living space on the first floor, a bonus room and full bath on the second floor is great for additional guests or visiting children.

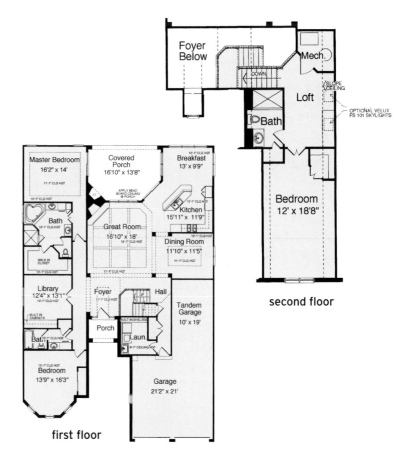

first floor

second floor

PLAN: HPK1300312

STYLE: COUNTRY COTTAGE

FIRST FLOOR: 1,606 SQ. FT.

SECOND FLOOR: 496 SQ. FT.

TOTAL: 2,102 SQ. FT.

BEDROOMS: 2

BATHROOMS: 3

WIDTH: 40' - 0"

DEPTH: 64' - 2"

FOUNDATION: UNFINISHED
BASEMENT, SLAB

■ Owners will love the convenience of a two-car garage and a first-floor master suite. The great room and semi-formal dining room work well with the peninsula-style kitchen, providing a locus for everyday space at the center of the home. Take advantage of the nearby covered porch—complete with wood-burning fireplace—for larger gatherings and outdoor entertaining. On the first floor, an additional bedroom is available to guests. The second floor's bonus space can become a third bedroom, a library or recreation area.

Dining Room
9'-1" CEILING HGT
11'4" x 13'

Porch
13' x 14'3"

Master Bedroom
9'-1" CEILING HGT
13'4" x 14'3"

Great Room
15' x 16'10"

Kitchen
9'-1" CEILING HGT
10'5" x 14'7"

Master Bath

Hall

CLOSET

WALK IN CLOSET

Bath

WALK IN CLOSET

Foyer

Laun.
9'-1" CEILING HGT

UP 15 RISERS

CLOS.

Porch

Bedroom
9'-1" CEILING HGT
11' x 11'10"

Garage
20'4' x 20'

WALK IN CLOSET

first floor

Upper Great Room

PLANT SHELF BELOW

Loft

SLOPE CEILING

36" HIGH WALL

Upper Foyer

Mech

DN 15 RISERS

CLOSET

Bath

Bonus Room

SLOPE CEILING   SLOPE CEILING

second floor

PLAN: HPK1300313

STYLE: EUROPEAN COTTAGE

FIRST FLOOR: 1,832 SQ. FT.

SECOND FLOOR: 651 SQ. FT.

TOTAL: 2,483 SQ. FT.

BEDROOMS: 2

BATHROOMS: 3

WIDTH: 42' - 0"

DEPTH: 75' - 0"

FOUNDATION: UNFINISHED
BASEMENT, SLAB

■ Perfect for empty nesters, this floor design features a sophisticated layout, with unique contours, a first-floor master suite, and rooms for optional uses upstairs. An angled entry harbinges the foyer, offering views to the great room and formal dining area. Segues between rooms provide an effect of spaciousness. The kitchen offers an oven cabinet and snack bar with seating. The master bedroom suite boasts a luxury bath, large walk-in closet, and access to the rear porch.

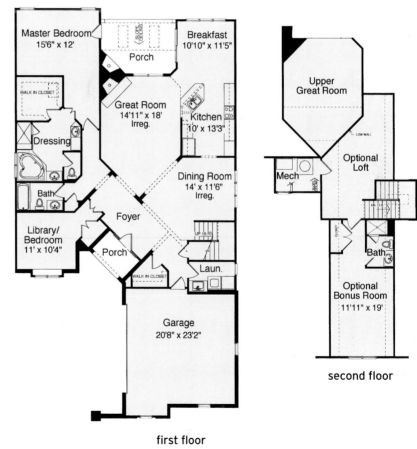

first floor

second floor

PLAN: HPK1300314

STYLE: FRENCH COUNTRY

SQUARE FOOTAGE: 2,640

BEDROOMS: 3

BATHROOMS: 2½

WIDTH: 50' - 0"

DEPTH: 70' - 4"

■ Escape to the French countryside in your private cottage. A hipped dormer anchoring a pitched roof announces this house of distinction. Sunlight graces the entryway, upon which you enter through French doors, and are rewarded with a view to the gathering room with fireplace down the main hallway. A split staircase leads to the combination game/rec room with bar, exercise room, an extra bedroom with attached bath, and plentiful storage space. Bedrooms 2 and 3 are tucked away to the right of the entry on the main floor. Upon touring the kitchen—complete with separate dining and eating areas, and pantry—be sure not to miss the master suite with dual vanity, spa tub, separately compartmented shower and toilet, and two closets.

second floor

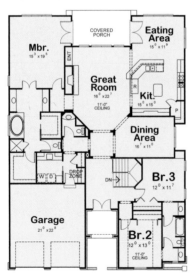

first floor

PLAN: HPK1300315

STYLE: MEDITERRANEAN

FIRST FLOOR: 1,484 SQ. FT.

SECOND FLOOR: 614 SQ. FT.

TOTAL: 2,098 SQ. FT.

BEDROOMS: 3

BATHROOMS: 3

WIDTH: 40' - 0"

DEPTH: 64' - 0"

FOUNDATION: SLAB

■ This charming country design puts its best foot forward by placing the two-car garage up front, thus protecting the living areas from most of the street noise. Inside, the living and dining areas flow together, defined by one simple column, letting the glow of the corner fireplace in the living area enhance any dinner party. The efficient kitchen has easy access to the garage and features a sink island and a pantry. The first-floor master suite offers a private bath and a walk-in closet, while a secondary bedroom accesses a hall bath. Upstairs, another spacious secondary bedroom provides a walk-in closet, private bath, and access to a large study area that over looks the living room below.

first floor

second floor

PLAN: HPK1300316

STYLE: FARMHOUSE
FIRST FLOOR: 1,491 SQ. FT.
SECOND FLOOR: 1,368 SQ. FT.
TOTAL: 2,859 SQ. FT.
BEDROOMS: 4
BATHROOMS: 3
WIDTH: 35' - 0"
DEPTH: 56' - 0"
FOUNDATION: CRAWLSPACE

■ With no shortage of curb appeal, the elaborate front porch rivals the entrance to any home in the neighborhood. The interior reveals an open floor plan with most of the common living areas on the first floor. The exception is a second floor game room, complete with a wet bar and built-in bookshelves. The lavish master suite boasts a spacious walk-in closet and a private fireplace. Two additional bedrooms on the second floor share a full bath. A bedroom on the first floor is ideal for guests or in-laws.

first floor

second floor

PLAN: HPK1300317

STYLE: TRADITIONAL

FIRST FLOOR: 1,383 SQ. FT.

SECOND FLOOR: 1,437 SQ. FT.

TOTAL: 2,820 SQ. FT.

BEDROOMS: 4

BATHROOMS: 3½

WIDTH: 42' - 0"

DEPTH: 53' - 0"

FOUNDATION: CRAWLSPACE

■ Bold lines modernize this home's traditional facade and give it stand-out appeal. An open floor plan facilitates movement between the living room, dining area, and kitchen with accent columns, bumped-out bays, and a butler's pantry. The kitchen combines with an eating nook—with double French doors to the rear—and the two-story great room with fireplace and built-in storage. Upstairs, three large family bedrooms—one with a private bath—and a vaulted master suite provide comfortable family space.

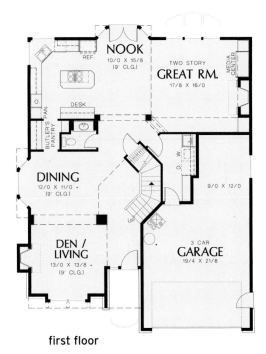

first floor

second floor

PLAN: HPK1300318

STYLE: COUNTRY COTTAGE

FIRST FLOOR: 1,561 SQ. FT.

SECOND FLOOR: 578 SQ. FT.

TOTAL: 2,139 SQ. FT.

BONUS SPACE: 284 SQ. FT.

BEDROOMS: 3

BATHROOMS: 2½

WIDTH: 50' - 0"

DEPTH: 57' - 0"

FOUNDATION: CRAWLSPACE, FINISHED WALKOUT BASEMENT

rear exterior

■ Nostalgic and earthy, this Craftsman design has an attractive floor plan and thoughtful amenties. A column-lined covered porch is the perfect welcome to guests. A large vaulted family room, enhanced by a fireplace, opens to the spacious island kitchen and roomy breakfast area. The private master suite is embellished with a vaulted ceiling, walk-in closet, and vaulted super bath with French-door entry. With family in mind, two secondary bedrooms—each with a walk-in closet—share a computer workstation or loft area. A bonus room can be used as bedroom or home office.

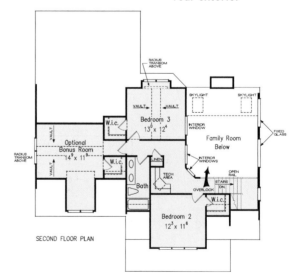

first floor

second floor

PLAN: HPK1300319

STYLE: FARMHOUSE

FIRST FLOOR: 1,725 SQ. FT.

SECOND FLOOR: 1,248 SQ. FT.

TOTAL: 2,973 SQ. FT.

BONUS SPACE: 406 SQ. FT.

BEDROOMS: 4

BATHROOMS: 3½

WIDTH: 46' - 0"

DEPTH: 85' - 0"

FOUNDATION: CRAWLSPACE, SLAB

■ Southern charm can be seen throughout this farmhouse design. A wrapping porch is accessed by the dining room, the kitchen, and through the vaulted foyer. The family room is embellished with a coffered ceiling and fireplace. The kitchen provides a snack bar and breakfast nook. The first-floor master suite accommodates privacy and is outfitted with a full bath with dual-sink vanity and a walk-in closet. Upstairs, three family bedrooms share two full baths and a spacious recreation room. A third floor houses bonus space that can be completed as another bedroom suite.

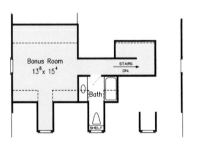

optional layout

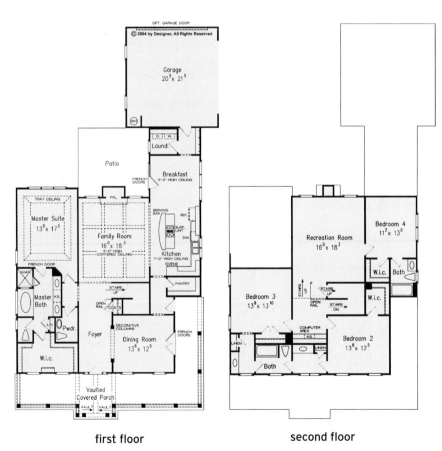

first floor

second floor

PLAN: HPK1300320

STYLE: COLONIAL
FIRST FLOOR: 1,495 SQ. FT.
SECOND FLOOR: 1,600 SQ. FT.
TOTAL: 3,095 SQ. FT.
BEDROOMS: 4
BATHROOMS: 3½
WIDTH: 49' - 0"
DEPTH: 57' - 0"
FOUNDATION: WALKOUT
BASEMENT

■ Complete with widow's walk detailing and a pedimented front entry, this wood-and-stone cottage is a true delight. Formal living and dining rooms dominate the right side of the plan, while more casual gathering and eating areas are found to the rear. The open family room, bayed breakfast area, and island kitchen provide a fantastic layout for gatherings of all kinds. The counter-filled kitchen is truly a gourmet's delight. A double stairway leads to the second floor, which revels in an incredible master suite with a sitting room and an exercise room, in addition to three family bedrooms. Bedroom 4 includes its own private bath and a walk-in closet.

first floor

second floor

PLAN: HPK1300321

STYLE: BUNGALOW

SQUARE FOOTAGE: 2,137

BEDROOMS: 3

BATHROOMS: 2

WIDTH: 44' - 0"

DEPTH: 63' - 0"

FOUNDATION: UNFINISHED
WALKOUT BASEMENT

■ The horizontal lines and straightforward details of this rustic plan borrow freely from the Arts and Crafts style, with a dash of traditional warmth. At the heart of the home, the kitchen and nook bring people together for easy meals and conversation. Clustered sleeping quarters ramble across the right wing and achieve privacy and convenience for the homeowners. The master suite is all decked out with a wall of glass, two walk-in closets, and generous dressing space. On the lower level, a mud area leads in from a covered porch, and the two-car garage leaves plenty of room for bicycles.

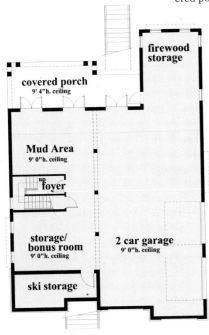

basement

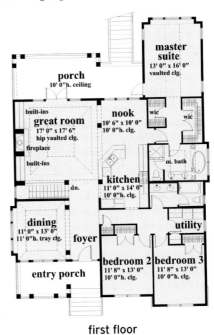

first floor

PLAN: HPK1300322

STYLE: GEORGIAN

FIRST FLOOR: 1,813 SQ. FT.

SECOND FLOOR: 1,441 SQ. FT.

TOTAL: 3,254 SQ. FT.

BEDROOMS: 5

BATHROOMS: 4

WIDTH: 49' - 0"

DEPTH: 59' - 0"

FOUNDATION: UNFINISHED BASEMENT

■ Your future dream home awaits in this Early American Georgian design. Once inside, you are immediately enveloped by a sense of spaciousness. The open layout of the dining room and parlor follows the trend of informality in living areas. A guest room to the left enjoys a private entrance to a full bath. A fireplace in the living room warms the adjacent breakfast nook and island-cooktop kitchen. Upstairs, the master bedroom's intricate design, enhanced by tray ceilings, features a sitting area, a roomy bath, and a large walk-in closet with two entrances. Three additional family bedrooms and two full baths complete the second floor.

first floor

second floor

PLAN: HPK1300344

STYLE: TRANSITIONAL

FIRST FLOOR: 1,036 SQ. FT.

SECOND FLOOR: 861 SQ. FT.

TOTAL: 1,897 SQ. FT.

BEDROOMS: 3

BATHROOMS: 2½

WIDTH: 48' - 0"

DEPTH: 38' - 0"

FOUNDATION: UNFINISHED BASEMENT

■ The refined exterior of this distinctive plan introduces a charming and livable home. Highlights of the floor plan include a furniture alcove in the formal dining room, a high ceiling and French doors topped with arched windows in the great room, a wood rail at the split stairs, a walk-in pantry in the kitchen, and a laundry room that's roomy enough to do a family-size laundry with helpers. The view from the foyer through the great room to the rear yard enhances indoor/outdoor entertaining, while the spacious kitchen and breakfast area encourage relaxed gatherings. The second floor features a window seat at the top of the stairs and a computer desk in the extra-large hallway. The deluxe master suite offers a whirlpool tub, separate vanities, a shower stall, and a spacious walk-in closet.

first floor

second floor

PLAN: HPK1300345

STYLE: FARMHOUSE

FIRST FLOOR: 1,320 SQ. FT.

SECOND FLOOR: 1,268 SQ. FT.

TOTAL: 2,588 SQ. FT.

BONUS SPACE: 389 SQ. FT.

BEDROOMS: 4

BATHROOMS: 2½

WIDTH: 45' - 0"

DEPTH: 64' - 0"

FOUNDATION: SLAB,
UNFINISHED BASEMENT

■ Country farmhouse with a touch of Victorian gingerbread describes this two-story wrap-porch design. The rear garage with the side entry into the breakfast area allows for easy access. Formal elegance is the feeling when entering this foyer with its flanked living and dining rooms. A rear staircase allows access to the room above the garage, making the perfect home office or bonus room for the children with access to their bedrooms. Three bedroom share a hall bath while the master enjoys all the amenities—garden tub, adjoining shower, double sinks, a dressing vanity and an oversized walk-in closet. The family room features a full window wall overlooking the deck that is also accessible from the rear entry of the garage. Corner cabinets house the sink and surface unit, keeping everything within a few steps of each other.

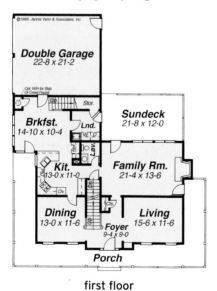

first floor

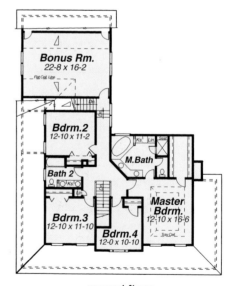

second floor

PLAN: HPK1300346

STYLE: VICTORIAN

FIRST FLOOR: 911 SQ. FT.

SECOND FLOOR: 861 SQ. FT.

TOTAL: 1,772 SQ. FT.

BEDROOMS: 3

BATHROOMS: $2\frac{1}{2}$

WIDTH: 38' - 0"

DEPTH: 52' - 0"

FOUNDATION: UNFINISHED BASEMENT

L

■ Victorian houses are well known for their orientation on narrow building sites. Only 38 feet wide, this home still offers generous style and comfort. Beautiful arched glass panels, skylights, and large double-hung windows allow natural light to fill this home, giving a golden glow to oak and maple hardwood floors and trim. From the covered front porch, the foyer leads to the living and dining rooms, with an extended-hearth fireplace and access to both the veranda and screened porch. Sleeping quarters on the second floor include a master suite and two family bedrooms.

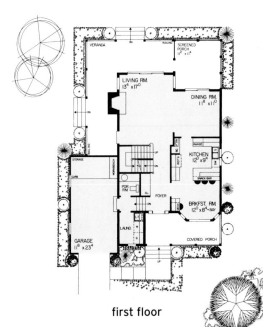

first floor

second floor

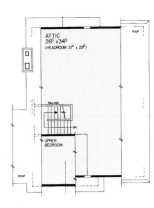

PLAN: HPK1300347

STYLE: TRANSITIONAL
FIRST FLOOR: 1,112 SQ. FT.
SECOND FLOOR: 881 SQ. FT.
TOTAL: 1,993 SQ. FT.
BEDROOMS: 3
BATHROOMS: 2½
WIDTH: 49' - 0"
DEPTH: 54' - 4"
FOUNDATION: UNFINISHED
BASEMENT

This classic American homestead is all dressed up with contemporary character and country spirit. Well-defined rooms, flowing spaces, and the latest amenities blend the best of traditional and modern elements. The spacious gathering room offers terrace access and shares a through-fireplace with a secluded study. The kitchen is set between the dining and breakfast rooms. The second-floor master suite shares a balcony hallway, which overlooks the gathering room, with two family bedrooms. Dual vanities, built-in cabinets and shelves, and triple-window views highlight the master bedroom.

rear exterior

first floor

second floor

PLAN: HPK1300348

STYLE: EUROPEAN COTTAGE

FIRST FLOOR: 1,115 SQ. FT.

SECOND FLOOR: 690 SQ. FT.

TOTAL: 1,805 SQ. FT.

BEDROOMS: 3

BATHROOMS: 2

WIDTH: 43' - 0"

DEPTH: 32' - 0"

FOUNDATION: UNFINISHED BASEMENT

rear exterior

■ This quaint Tudor cottage has an open floor plan that is designed for easy living. The gathering room is accented with a cathedral ceiling and a full Palladian window. The dining room is joined to the efficient kitchen, with extra entertaining space available on the deck. The first-floor master suite has a large compartmented bath and bumped-out windows. Upstairs, a lounge overlooks the gathering room and accesses an outside balcony. Two additional bedrooms and a full hall bath complete the second floor.

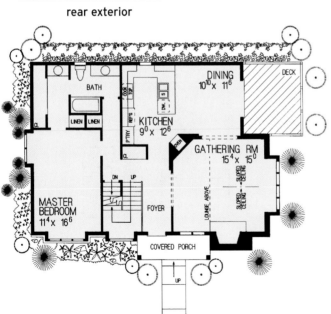

first floor

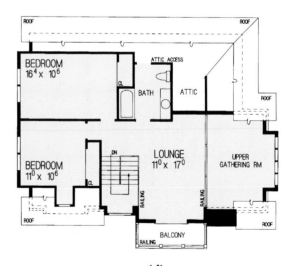

second floor

Affordable Dream Homes

PLAN: HPK1300349

STYLE: FRENCH COUNTRY
FIRST FLOOR: 2,080 SQ. FT.
SECOND FLOOR: 1,362 SQ. FT.
TOTAL: 3,442 SQ. FT.
BEDROOMS: 5
BATHROOMS: 3½
WIDTH: 49' - 0"
DEPTH: 79' - 6"
FOUNDATION: CRAWLSPACE

■ Elegant hipped rooflines, fine brick detailing and arches galore combine to give this home a wonderful touch of French class. Inside, the two-story foyer is flanked by the formal living and dining rooms, while casual living takes place at the rear of the home. Here, a spacious family room features a fireplace, access to a screened porch and an adjacent breakfast area. The C-shaped kitchen offers a cooktop island and a walk-in pantry. Secluded for privacy, the first-floor master suite includes two walk-in closets, a lavish bath and a sitting area. Upstairs, four suites provide walk-in closets and share two full baths.

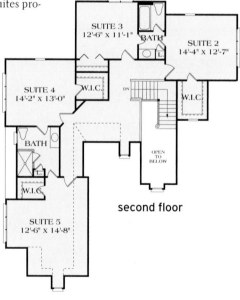

first floor

second floor

PLAN: HPK1300350

STYLE: TRADITIONAL

FIRST FLOOR: 1,748 SQ. FT.

SECOND FLOOR: 1,748 SQ. FT.

THIRD FLOOR: 1,100 SQ. FT.

TOTAL: 4,596 SQ. FT.

BEDROOMS: 4

BATHROOMS: 3½

WIDTH: 50' - 0"

DEPTH: 63' - 0"

FOUNDATION: UNFINISHED BASEMENT

■ This Early American brick exterior serves as a lovely introduction to a thoroughly modern floor plan. The tiled foyer opens through decorative columns to the formal living room, which offers a fireplace framed by built-in cabinetry. The convenient island kitchen offers a snack bar and opens to a conversation room with a bay window and a hearth. Second-floor sleeping quarters offer a master suite with its own fireplace, a bumped-out bay window and a lavish bath with a whirlpool tub. Two family bedrooms share a full bath with a double-bowl vanity. A sumptuous guest suites shares the third floor with a library or playroom.

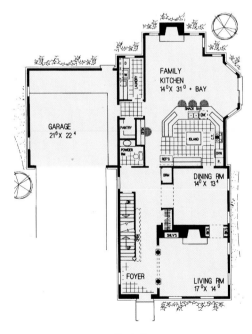

first floor

second floor

third floor

With more than 50 years of experience in the industry and millions of blueprints sold, Hanley Wood is a trusted source of high-quality, high-value pre-drawn home plans.

Using pre-drawn home plans is a **reliable, cost-effective way** to build your dream home, and our vast selection of plans is second-to-none. The nation's finest designers craft these plans that builders know they can trust. Meanwhile, our friendly, knowledgeable customer service representatives can help you every step of the way.

WHAT YOU'LL GET WITH YOUR ORDER

The contents of each designer's blueprint package is unique, but all contain detailed, high-quality working drawings. You can expect to find the following standard elements in most sets of plans:

I. FRONT PERSPECTIVE

This artist's sketch of the exterior of the house gives you an idea of how the house will look when built and landscaped.

2. FOUNDATION AND BASEMENT PLANS

This sheet shows the foundation layout including concrete walls, footings, pads, posts, beams, and bearing walls, and foundation notes. If the home features a basement, the first-floor framing details may also be included on this plan. If your plan features slab construction rather than a basement, the plan shows footings and details for a monolithic slab. This page, or another in the set, may include a sample plot plan for locating your house on a building site. Additional sheets focus on foundation cross-sections and other details.

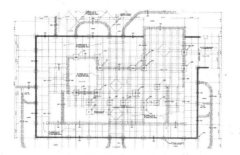

3. DETAILED FLOOR PLANS

These plans show the layout of each floor of the house. Rooms and interior spaces are carefully dimensioned, doors and windows located, and keys are given for cross-section details provided elsewhere in the plans.

4. HOUSE AND DETAIL CROSS-SECTIONS

Large-scale views show sections or cutaways of the foundation, interior walls, exterior walls, floors, stairways, and roof details. Additional cross-sections may show important changes in floor, ceiling, or roof heights, or the relationship of one level to another. These sections show exactly how the various parts of the house fit together and are extremely valuable during construction. Additional sheets may include enlarged wall, floor, and roof construction details.

5. ROOF AND FLOOR STRUCTURAL SUPPORTS

The roof and floor framing plans provide detail for these crucial elements of your home. Each includes floor joist, ceiling joist, rafter and roof joist size, spacing, direction, span, and specifications. Beam and window headers, along with necessary details for framing connections, stairways, skylights, or dormers are also included.

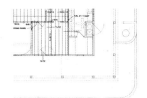

6. ELECTRICAL PLAN

The electrical plan offers a detailed outline of all wiring for your home, with notes for all lighting, outlets, switches, and circuits. A layout is provided for each level, as well as basements, garages, or other structures.

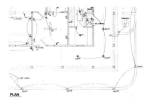

7. EXTERIOR ELEVATIONS

In addition to the front exterior, your blueprint set will include drawings of the rear and sides of your house as well. These drawings give notes on exterior materials and finishes. Particular attention is given to cornice detail, brick and stone accents, or other finish items that make your home unique.

BEFORE YOU CALL

You are making a terrific decision to use a pre-drawn house plan—it is one you can make with confidence, knowing that your blueprints are crafted by national-award-winning certified residential designers and architects, and trusted by builders.

Once you've selected the plan you want—or even if you have questions along the way—our experienced customer service representatives are available 24 hours a day, seven days a week to help you navigate the home-building process. To help them provide you with even better service, please consider the following questions before you call:

■ **Have you chosen or purchased your lot?**
If so, please review the building setback requirements of your local building authority before you call. You don't need to have a lot before ordering plans, but if you own land already, please have the width and depth dimensions handy when you call.

■ **Have you chosen a builder?**
Involving your builder in the plan selection and evaluation process may be beneficial. Luckily, builders know they can have confidence with pre-drawn plans because they've been designed for livability, functionality, and typically are builder-proven at successful home sites across the country.

■ **Do you need a construction loan?**
Construction loans are unique because they involve determining the value of something that is not yet constructed. Several lenders offer convenient contstruction-to-permanent loans. It is important to choose a good lending partner—one who will help guide you through the application and appraisal process. Most will even help you evaluate your contractor to ensure reliability and credit worthiness. Our partnership with IndyMac Bank, a nationwide leader in construction loans, can help you save on your loan, if needed.

■ **How many sets of plans do you need?**
Building a home can typically require a number of sets of blueprints—one for yourself, two or three for the builder and subcontractors, two for the local building department, and one or more for your lender. For this reason, we offer 5- and 8-set plan packages, but your best value is the Reproducible Plan Package. Reproducible plans are accompanied by a license to make modifications and typically up to 12 duplicates of the plan so you have enough copies of the plan for everyone involved in the financing and construction of your home.

■ **Do you want to make any changes to the plan?**
We understand that it is difficult to find blueprints for a home that will meet all of your needs. That is why Hanley Wood is glad to offer plan Customization Services. We will work with you to design the modifications you'd like to see and to adjust your blueprint plans accordingly—anything from changing the foundation; adding square footage, redesigning baths, kitchens, or bedrooms; or most other modifications. This simple, cost-effective service saves you from hiring an outside architect to make alterations. Modifications may only be made to Reproducible Plan Packages that include the license to modify.

■ **Do you have to make any changes to meet local building codes?**
While all of our plans are drawn to meet national building codes at the time they were created, many areas required that plans be stamped by a local engineer to certify that they meet local building codes. Building codes are updated frequently and can vary by state, county, city, or municipality. Contact your local building inspection department, office of planning and zoning, or department of permits to determine how your local codes will affect your construction project. The best way to assure that you can make changes to your plan, if necessary, is to purchase a Reproducible Plan Package.

■ **Has everyone—from family members to contractors—been involved in selecting the plan?**
Building a new home is an exciting process, and using pre-drawn plans is a great way to realize your dreams. Make sure that everyone involved has had an opportunity to review the plan you've selected. While Hanley Wood is the only plans provider with an exchange policy, it's best to be sure all parties agree on your selection before you buy.

CALL TOLL-FREE 1-800-521-6797

Source Key
HPK13

CUSTOMIZE YOUR PLAN –
HANLEY WOOD CUSTOMIZATION SERVICES

Creating custom home plans has never been easier and more directly accessible. Using state-of-the-art technology and top-performing architectural expertise, Hanley Wood delivers on a long-standing customer commitment to provide world-class home-plans and customization services. Our valued customers—professional home builders and individual home owners—appreciate the convenience and accessibility of this interactive, consultative service.

With the Hanley Wood Customization Service you can:
- Save valuable time by avoiding drawn-out and frequently repetitive face-to-face design meetings
- Communicate design and home-plan changes faster and more efficiently
- Speed-up project turn-around time

- Build on a budget without sacrificing quality
- Transform master home plans to suit your design needs and unique personal style

All of our design options and prices are impressively affordable. A detailed quote is available for a $50 consultation fee. Plan modification is an interactive service. Our skilled team of designers will guide you through the customization process from start to finish making recommendations, offering ideas, and determining the feasibility of your changes. This level of service is offered to ensure the final modified plan meets your expectations. If you use our service the $50 fee will be applied to the cost of the modifications.

You may purchase the customization consultation before or after purchasing a plan. In either case, it is necessary to purchase the Reproducible Plan Package and complete the accompanying license to modify the plan before we can begin customization.

Customization Consultation..$50

TOOLS TO WORK WITH YOUR BUILDER

Two Reverse Options For Your Convenience –
Mirror and Right-Reading Reverse (as available)
Mirror reverse plans simply flip the design 180 degrees—keep in mind, the text will also be flipped. For a minimal fee you can have one or all of your plans shipped mirror reverse, although we recommend having at least one regular set handy. Right-reading reverse plans show the design flipped 180 degrees but the text reads normally. When you choose this option, we ship each set of purchased blueprints in this format.

Mirror Reverse Fee (indicate the number of sets when ordering).........$55
Right Reading Reverse Fee (all sets are reversed)..............................$175

A Shopping List Exclusively for Your Home – Materials List
A customized Materials List helps you plan and estimate the cost of your new home, outlining the quantity, type, and size of materials needed to build your house (with the exception of mechanical system items). Included are framing lumber, windows and doors, kitchen and bath cabinetry, rough and finished hardware, and much more.

Materials List...$75 each
Additional Materials Lists (at original time of purchase only).......$20 each

Plan Your Home-
Building Process – Specification Outline
Work with your builder on this step-by-step chronicle of 166 stages or items crucial to the building process. It provides a comprehensive review of the construction process and helps you choose materials.
Specification Outline...$10 each

Get Accurate Cost Estimates for Your Home –
Quote One® Cost Reports
The Summary Cost Report, the first element in the Quote One® package, breaks down the cost of your home into various categories based on building materials, labor, and installation, and includes three grades of construction: Budget, Standard, and Custom. Make even more informed decisions about your project with the second element of our package, the Material Cost Report. The material and installation cost is shown for each of more than 1,000 line items provided in the standard-grade Materials List, which is included with this tool. Additional space is included for estimates from contractors and subcontractors, such as for mechanical materials, which are not included in our packages.

Quote One® Summary Cost Report......................................$35
Quote One® Detailed Material Cost Report..........................$140*
***Detailed material cost report includes the Materials List**

Learn the Basics of Building – Electrical, Plumbing, Mechanical, Construction Detail Sheets
If you want to know more about building techniques—and deal more confidently with your subcontractors—we offer four useful detail sheets. These sheets provide non-plan-specific general information, but are excellent tools that will add to your understanding of Plumbing Details, Electrical Details, Construction Details, and Mechanical Details.

Electrical Detail Sheet...$14.95
Plumbing Detail Sheet...$14.95
Mechanical Detail Sheet..$14.95
Construction Detail Sheet..$14.95
SUPER VALUE SETS:
Buy any 2: $26.95; Buy any 3: $34.95; Buy All 4: $39.95

Best Value

GETTY IMAGES (2)

MAKE YOUR HOME TECH-READY – HOME AUTOMATION UPGRADE

Building a new home provides a unique opportunity to wire it with a plan for future needs. A Home Automation-Ready (HA-Ready) home contains the wiring substructure of tomorrow's connected home. It means that every room—from the front porch to the backyard, and from the attic to the basement—is wired for security, lighting, telecommunications, climate control, home computer networking, whole-house audio, home theater, shade control, video surveillance, entry access control, and yes, video gaming electronic solutions.

Along with the conveniences HA-Ready homes provide, they also have a higher resale value. The Consumer Electronics Association (CEA), in conjunction with the Custom Electronic Design and Installation Association (CEDIA), have developed a TechHome™ Rating system that quantifies the value of HA-Ready homes. The rating system is gaining widespread recognition in the real estate industry.

Developed by CEDIA-certified installers, our Home Automation Upgrade package includes everything you need to work with an installer during the construction of your home. It provides a short explanation of the various subsystems, a wiring floor plan for each level of your home, a detailed materials list with estimated costs, and a list of CEDIA-certified installers in your local area.

Home Automation Upgrade...........................$250

GET YOUR HOME PLANS PAID FOR!

IndyMac Bank, in partnership with Hanley Wood, will reimburse you up to $600 toward the cost of your home plans simply by financing the construction of your new home with IndyMac Bank Home Construction Lending.

IndyMac's construction and permanent loan is a one-time close loan, meaning that one application—and one set of closing fees—provides all the financing you need.

Apply today at www.indymacbank.com, call toll free at 1-866-237-3478, or ask a Hanley Wood customer service representative for details.

DESIGN YOUR HOME – INTERIOR AND EXTERIOR FINISHING TOUCHES

Be Your Own Interior Designer! – Home Furniture Planner

Effectively plan the space in your home using our Hands-On Home Furniture Planner. It's fun and easy—no more moving heavy pieces of furniture to see how the room will go together. The kit includes reusable peel-and-stick furniture templates that fit on a 12"x18" laminated layout board—enough space to lay out every room in your house.

Home Furniture Planning Kit.............................$15.95

Enjoy the Outdoors! – Deck Plans

Many of our homes have a corresponding deck plan, sold separately, which includes a Deck Plan Frontal Sheet, Deck Framing and Floor Plans, Deck Elevations, and a Deck Materials List. A Standard Deck Details Package, also available, provides all the how-to information necessary for building any deck. Get both the Deck Plan and the Standard Deck Details Package for one low price in our Complete Deck Building Package. See the price tier chart below and call for deck plan availability.

Deck Details (only)..$14.95
Deck Building Package........................Plan price + $14.95

Create a Professionally Designed Landscape – Landscape Plans

Many of our homes have a front-yard Landscape Plan that is complementary in design to the house plan. These comprehensive Landscape Blueprint Packages include a Frontal Sheet, Plan View, Regionalized Plant & Materials List, a sheet on Planting and Maintaining Your Landscape, Zone Maps, and a Plant Size and Description Guide. Each set of blueprints is a full 18" x 24" with clear, complete instructions in easy-to-read type. Our Landscape Plans are available with a Plant & Materials List adapted by horticultural experts to eight regions of the country. Please specify your region when ordering your plan—see region map below. Call for more information about landscape plan availability and applicable regions.

LANDSCAPE & DECK PRICE SCHEDULE

PRICE TIERS	1-SET STUDY PACKAGE	5-SET BUILDING PACKAGE	8-SET BUILDING PACKAGE	1-SET REPRODUCIBLE*
P1	$25	$55	$95	$145
P2	$45	$75	$115	$165
P3	$75	$105	$145	$195
P4	$105	$135	$175	$225
P5	$145	$175	$215	$275
P6	$185	$215	$255	$315

TERMS & CONDITIONS
OUR 90-DAY EXCHANGE POLICY

Hanley Wood is committed to ensuring your satisfaction with your blueprint order, which is why we offer a 90-day exchange policy. With the exception of Reproducible Plan Package orders, we will exchange your entire first order for an equal or greater number of blueprints from our plan collection within 90 days of the original order. The entire content of your original order must be returned before an exchange will be processed. Please call our customer service department at 1-888-690-1116 for your return authorization number and shipping instructions. If the returned blueprints look used, redlined, or copied, we will not honor your exchange. Fees for exchanging your blueprints are as follows: 20% of the amount of the original order, plus the difference in cost if exchanging for a design in a higher price bracket or less the difference in cost if exchanging for a design in a lower price bracket. (Because they can be copied, Reproducible blueprints are not exchangeable or refundable.) Please call for current postage and handling prices. Shipping and handling charges are not refundable.

ARCHITECTURAL AND ENGINEERING SEALS

Some cities and states now require that a licensed architect or engineer review and "seal" a blueprint, or officially approve it, prior to construction. Prior to application for a building permit or the start of actual construction, we strongly advise that you consult your local building official who can tell you if such a review is required.

LOCAL BUILDING CODES AND ZONING REQUIREMENTS

Each plan was designed to meet or exceed the requirements of a nationally recognized model building code in effect at the time and place the plan was drawn. Typically plans designed after the year 2000 conform to the International Residential Building Code (IRC 2000 or 2003). The IRC is comprised of portions of the three major codes below. Plans drawn before 2000 conform to one of the three recognized building codes in effect at the time: Building Officials and Code

Administrators (BOCA) International, Inc.; the Southern Building Code Congress International, (SBCCI) Inc.; the International Conference of Building Officials (ICBO); or the Council of American Building Officials (CABO).

Because of the great differences in geography and climate throughout the United States and Canada, each state, county, and municipality has its own building codes, zone requirements, ordinances, and building regulations. Your plan may need to be modified to comply with local requirements. In addition, you may need to obtain permits or inspections from local governments before and in the course of construction. We authorize the use of the blueprints on the express condition that you consult a local licensed architect or engineer of your choice prior to beginning construction and strictly comply with all local building codes, zoning requirements, and other applicable laws, regulations, ordinances, and requirements. Notice: Plans for homes to be built in Nevada must be redrawn by a Nevada-registered professional. Consult your local building official for more information on this subject.

TERMS AND CONDITIONS

These designs are protected under the terms of United States Copyright Law and may not be copied or reproduced in any way, by any

means, unless you have purchased a Reproducible Plan Package and signed the accompanying license to modify and copy the plan, which clearly indicates your right to modify, copy, or reproduce. We authorize the use of your chosen design as an aid in the construction of ONE (1) single- or multifamily home only. You may not use this design to build a second dwelling or multiple dwellings without purchasing another blueprint or blueprints or paying additional design fees. Multi-use fees vary by designer—please call one of experienced sales representatives for a quote.

DISCLAIMER

The designers we work with have put substantial care and effort into the creation of their blueprints. However, because we cannot provide on-site consultation, supervision, and control over actual construction, and because of the great variance in local building requirements, building practices, and soil, seismic, weather, and other conditions, WE MAKE NO WARRANTY OF ANY KIND, EXPRESS OR IMPLIED, WITH RESPECT TO THE CONTENT OR USE OF THE BLUEPRINTS, INCLUDING BUT NOT LIMITED TO ANY WARRANTY OF MERCHANTABILITY OR OF FITNESS FOR A PARTICULAR PURPOSE. ITEMS, PRICES, TERMS, AND CONDITIONS ARE SUBJECT TO CHANGE WITHOUT NOTICE.

CALL TOLL-FREE
1-800-521-6797
OR VISIT EPLANS.COM

IMPORTANT COPYRIGHT NOTICE

From the Council of Publishing Home Designers

Blueprints for residential construction (or working drawings, as they are often called in the industry) are copyrighted intellectual property, protected under the terms of the United States Copyright Law and, therefore, cannot be copied legally for use in building. The following are some guidelines to help you get what you need to build your home, without violating copyright law:

1. HOME PLANS ARE COPYRIGHTED

Just like books, movies, and songs, home plans receive protection under the federal copyright laws. The copyright laws prevent anyone, other than the copyright owner, from reproducing, modifying, or reusing the plans or design without permission of the copyright owner.

2. DO NOT COPY DESIGNS OR FLOOR PLANS FROM ANY PUBLICATION, ELECTRONIC MEDIA, OR EXISTING HOME

It is illegal to copy, change, or redraw home designs found in a plan book, CD-ROM, or on the Internet. The right to modify plans is one of the exclusive rights of copyright. It is also illegal to copy or redraw a constructed home that is protected by copyright, even if you have never seen the plans for the home. If you find a plan or home that you like, you must purchase a set of plans from an authorized source. The plans may not be lent, given away, or sold by the purchaser.

3. DO NOT USE PLANS TO BUILD MORE THAN ONE HOUSE

The original purchaser of house plans is typically licensed to build a single home from the plans. Building more than one home from the plans without permission is an infringement of the home designer's copyright. The purchase of a multiple-set package of plans is for the construction of a single home only. The purchase of additional sets of plans does not grant the right to construct more than one home.

4. HOUSE PLANS IN THE FORM OF BLUEPRINTS OR BLACKLINES CANNOT BE COPIED OR REPRODUCED

Plans, blueprints, or blacklines, unless they are reproducibles, cannot be copied or reproduced without prior written consent of the copyright owner. Copy shops and blueprinters are prohibited from making copies of these plans without the copyright release letter you receive with reproducible plans.

5. HOUSE PLANS IN THE FORM OF BLUEPRINTS OR BLACKLINES CANNOT BE REDRAWN

Plans cannot be modified or redrawn without first obtaining the copyright owner's permission. With your purchase of plans, you are licensed to make non-structural changes by "red-lining" the purchased plans. If you need to make structural changes or need to redraw the plans for any reason, you must purchase a reproducible set of plans (see topic 6) which includes a license to modify the plans. Blueprints do not come with a license to make structural changes or to redraw the plans. You may not reuse or sell the modified design.

6. REPRODUCIBILE HOME PLANS

Reproducible plans (for example sepias, mylars, CAD files, electronic files, and vellums) come with a license to make modifications to the plans. Once modified, the plans can be taken to a local copy shop or blueprinter to make up to 10 or 12 copies of the plans to use in the construction of a single home. Only one home can be constructed from any single purchased set of reproducible plans either in original form or as modified. The license to modify and copy must be completed and returned before the plan will be shipped.

7. MODIFIED DESIGNS CANNOT BE REUSED

Even if you are licensed to make modifications to a copyrighted design, the modified design is not free from the original designer's copyright. The sale or reuse of the modified design is prohibited. Also, be aware that any modification to plans relieves the original designer from liability for design defects and voids all warranties expressed or implied.

8. WHO IS RESPONSIBLE FOR COPYRIGHT INFRINGEMENT?

Any party who participates in a copyright violation may be responsible including the purchaser, designers, architects, engineers, drafters, homeowners, builders, contractors, sub-contractors, copy shops, blueprinters, developers, and real estate agencies. It does not matter whether or not the individual knows that a violation is being committed. Ignorance of the law is not a valid defense.

9. PLEASE RESPECT HOME DESIGN COPYRIGHTS

In the event of any suspected violation of a copyright, or if there is any uncertainty about the plans purchased, the publisher, architect, designer, or the Council of Publishing Home Designers (www.cphd.org) should be contacted before proceeding. Awards are sometimes offered for information about home design copyright infringement.

10. PENALTIES FOR INFRINGEMENT

Penalties for violating a copyright may be severe. The responsible parties are required to pay actual damages caused by the infringement (which may be substantial), plus any profits made by the infringer commissions to include all profits from the sale of any home built from an infringing design. The copyright law also allows for the recovery of statutory damages, which may be as high as $150,000 for each infringement. Finally, the infringer may be required to pay legal fees which often exceed the damages.

BLUEPRINT PRICE SCHEDULE

PRICE TIERS	1-SET STUDY PACKAGE	5-SET BUILDING PACKAGE	8-SET BUILDING PACKAGE	1-SET REPRODUCIBLE*
A1	$450	$500	$555	$675
A2	$490	$545	$595	$735
A3	$540	$605	$665	$820
A4	$590	$660	$725	$895
C1	$640	$715	$775	$950
C2	$690	$760	$820	$1025
C3	$735	$810	$875	$1100
C4	$785	$860	$925	$1175
L1	$895	$990	$1075	$1335
L2	$970	$1065	$1150	$1455
L3	$1075	$1175	$1270	$1600
L4	$1185	$1295	$1385	$1775
SQ1				.40/SQ. FT.
SQ3				.55/SQ. FT.
SQ5				.80/SQ. FT.

PRICES SUBJECT TO CHANGE

* REQUIRES A FAX NUMBER

PLAN #	PRICE TIER	PAGE	MATERIALS LIST	QUOTE ONE	DECK	DECK PRICE	LANDSCAPE	LANDSCAPE PRICE	REGIONS
HPK1300001	A2	8	Y						
HPK1300002	A4	12	Y	Y					
HPK1300003	C1	13							
HPK1300004	C1	14							
HPK1300323	C2	15							
HPK1300005	C1	16							
HPK1300006	C2	17							
HPK1300007	A2	18	Y						
HPK1300008	A4	19							
HPK1300009	A4	20	Y						
HPK1300010	A4	21	Y						
HPK1300011	A4	22	Y						
HPK1300012	A4	23							
HPK1300013	C1	24	Y						
HPK1300014	C1	25	Y						
HPK1300015	C2	26	Y						
HPK1300016	A3	27	Y						
HPK1300017	A2	28	Y						
HPK1300018	A4	29	Y						
HPK1300019	A3	30	Y						
HPK1300020	A3	31	Y						
HPK1300021	C2	32							
HPK1300022	A4	33	Y	Y					
HPK1300023	A4	34							
HPK1300024	C3	35	Y						
HPK1300025	C1	36							
HPK1300026	C2	37	Y						
HPK1300027	C2	38							
HPK1300028	C3	39							
HPK1300029	C3	40							
HPK1300030	C2	41							
HPK1300031	C3	42							
HPK1300032	C2	43							
HPK1300033	C3	44							
HPK1300034	C2	45							
HPK1300035	C1	46							
HPK1300036	C1	47							
HPK1300037	C1	48							
HPK1300038	A2	49	Y						
HPK1300039	A3	50	Y						
HPK1300040	A2	51							
HPK1300041	C2	52							
HPK1300042	C3	53							
HPK1300043	A3	54							
HPK1300044	C2	55	Y						
HPK1300045	A3	56	Y						
HPK1300046	A4	56	Y						
HPK1300047	C3	57	Y						
HPK1300048	C3	58	Y						
HPK1300049	A3	59	Y						
HPK1300050	A3	60	Y						
HPK1300051	C1	61	Y						
HPK1300052	C2	62							
HPK1300053	C1	63	Y						
HPK1300054	C1	64	Y						
HPK1300055	C1	65	Y						
HPK1300056	C2	66	Y						
HPK1300057	C2	67	Y						
HPK1300058	A4	68							
HPK1300059	A4	69							
HPK1300060	C1	70							
HPK1300061	C1	71							
HPK1300062	C1	72							
HPK1300063	C1	73	Y						
HPK1300064	C1	74							
HPK1300065	A4	75							
HPK1300066	A3	76	Y						
HPK1300067	A4	77	Y		ODA016	P2	OLA001	P3	123568
HPK1300068	A3	78	Y						
HPK1300069	A3	79	Y						
HPK1300324	C1	80							
HPK1300071	A4	81							
HPK1300070	A3	81							
HPK1300072	A3	82	Y						
HPK1300073	A4	82	Y						
HPK1300074	A2	83	Y						
HPK1300075	C1	84							
HPK1300076	A2	85	Y						
HPK1300077	A2	86	Y						
HPK1300078	A3	87							
HPK1300079	A3	88	Y						
HPK1300080	A3	89	Y						
HPK1300325	C2	90							
HPK1300081	A2	91	Y						
HPK1300082	A2	92							
HPK1300083	A2	93	Y						
HPK1300084	A4	94	Y						
HPK1300085	A3	95	Y				OLA001	P3	123568
HPK1300086	A3	96	Y						
HPK1300087	C3	97	Y	Y					
HPK1300088	C2	98	Y	Y					
HPK1300089	C2	99	Y						
HPK1300090	A4	100							
HPK1300091	C1	101	Y						
HPK1300092	C1	102	Y						
HPK1300093	C1	105							
HPK1300094	C3	109							
HPK1300095	C1	110	Y						
HPK1300096	A4	111							
HPK1300097	C2	112							
HPK1300098	A3	113	Y						
HPK1300099	A4	114	Y						
HPK1300100	A4	115	Y						
HPK1300101	A4	116	Y						
HPK1300102	C1	117	Y						
HPK1300103	C1	118	Y						
HPK1300104	C1	119	Y						
HPK1300105	C2	120	Y						
HPK1300106	A4	121							
HPK1300107	A4	121							
HPK1300108	C2	122							
HPK1300109	C1	122	Y						
HPK1300110	C2	123							
HPK1300111	C2	124							
HPK1300112	A4	125	Y						
HPK1300113	C1	126	Y						
HPK1300114	C1	127	Y						
HPK1300115	C2	128							
HPK1300116	C1	129							
HPK1300117	C2	130							
HPK1300118	A4	131							
HPK1300119	C1	132							
HPK1300120	C2	133							
HPK1300121	C2	134							
HPK1300326	C2	135							
HPK1300122	C1	136							

ORDER BLUEPRINTS 24 HOURS, 7 DAYS A WEEK 1-800-521-6797 OR EPLANS.COM

Table 1

PLAN #	PRICE TIER	PAGE	MATERIALS LIST	QUOTE ONE*	DECK	DECK PRICE	LANDSCAPE	LANDSCAPE PRICE	REGIONS
HPK1300123	C1	137							
HPK1300124	C1	138	Y						
HPK1300125	C1	139	Y						
HPK1300126	C2	140	Y						
HPK1300127	C1	141	Y						
HPK1300128	C1	142	Y						
HPK1300129	C1	143	Y						
HPK1300130	A4	144	Y						
HPK1300131	A3	145							
HPK1300132	A3	146							
HPK1300133	C1	147	Y						
HPK1300134	A3	148	Y						
HPK1300135	A3	149	Y						
HPK1300136	A4	150	Y						
HPK1300137	A4	151							
HPK1300138	A3	152	Y						
HPK1300139	A4	153	Y						
HPK1300140	A4	154	Y						
HPK1300141	C1	155	Y						
HPK1300142	A4	156							
HPK1300143	A4	157							
HPK1300144	A4	158	Y						
HPK1300327	C1	159							
HPK1300328	C1	160							
HPK1300145	C1	161							
HPK1300146	A3	162	Y						
HPK1300147	A4	163							
HPK1300148	A3	164							
HPK1300149	A4	165							
HPK1300150	C2	166							
HPK1300151	C2	167							
HPK1300152	C3	168							
HPK1300153	C2	169							
HPK1300154	C3	170							
HPK1300155	C1	171							
HPK1300156	C2	172							
HPK1300157	C1	173							
HPK1300158	C2	174	Y						
HPK1300159	C1	175							
HPK1300160	C1	176	Y						
HPK1300161	A4	177							
HPK1300162	A4	178							
HPK1300163	C2	179							
HPK1300164	C2	180							
HPK1300165	C2	181							
HPK1300166	C2	182							
HPK1300167	C1	183	Y						
HPK1300168	C2	184	Y						
HPK1300169	A3	185	Y						
HPK1300170	A3	186	Y						
HPK1300171	C1	187	Y						
HPK1300172	C1	188	Y						
HPK1300173	A4	189	Y						
HPK1300174	A4	190	Y						
HPK1300175	C1	191	Y						
HPK1300177	C1	192							
HPK1300176	C1	192							
HPK1300178	C1	193							
HPK1300179	A4	193	Y						
HPK1300180	C1	194							
HPK1300329	C2	197							
HPK1300181	A3	201	Y						
HPK1300182	C1	202	Y						
HPK1300183	C1	203							
HPK1300184	C1	204	Y						
HPK1300185	A3	205							
HPK1300186	A4	206							
HPK1300187	A4	207							
HPK1300188	A2	208							
HPK1300189	A3	209	Y						
HPK1300190	C1	210							
HPK1300191	C1	211							
HPK1300192	A4	212							
HPK1300193	C1	213							
HPK1300194	A3	214	Y						
HPK1300195	C1	215	Y						

Table 2

PLAN #	PRICE TIER	PAGE	MATERIALS LIST	QUOTE ONE*	DECK	DECK PRICE	LANDSCAPE	LANDSCAPE PRICE	REGIONS
HPK1300196	A3	216							
HPK1300197	C3	217	Y						
HPK1300198	C3	218							
HPK1300199	C3	219	Y						
HPK1300200	C1	220							
HPK1300201	C2	221							
HPK1300202	A3	222	Y						
HPK1300203	A2	223							
HPK1300204	A3	224	Y						
HPK1300205	A4	225	Y						
HPK1300206	A2	226	Y						
HPK1300207	A3	227							
HPK1300208	A3	228							
HPK1300209	A3	229	Y						
HPK1300210	A3	230	Y						
HPK1300211	A4	231							
HPK1300212	A3	232							
HPK1300213	A2	233	Y						
HPK1300214	C1	234							
HPK1300215	C1	235							
HPK1300216	C2	236							
HPK1300217	A4	237	Y						
HPK1300218	A4	238	Y						
HPK1300219	C2	239							
HPK1300220	C2	240							
HPK1300221	A3	241							
HPK1300222	A4	242	Y						
HPK1300223	C2	243							
HPK1300224	A3	244	Y						
HPK1300225	C1	245	Y						
HPK1300226	A2	246	Y						
HPK1300227	A3	247	Y						
HPK1300330	C2	248							
HPK1300228	C1	249							
HPK1300229	C1	250							
HPK1300230	A2	251							
HPK1300231	A3	252	Y						
HPK1300232	A3	253							
HPK1300233	C1	254							
HPK1300234	C1	255							
HPK1300235	A4	256							
HPK1300236	A4	257							
HPK1300237	A4	258							
HPK1300238	C3	259	Y						
HPK1300239	C1	260	Y						
HPK1300240	C3	261	Y						
HPK1300241	C1	262	Y						
HPK1300242	C3	265	Y						
HPK1300243	C1	269							
HPK1300331	C2	270							
HPK1300244	C1	271	Y						
HPK1300245	C1	272							
HPK1300246	C1	273							
HPK1300247	A4	274							
HPK1300332	C2	275							
HPK1300333	C2	276							
HPK1300334	C2	277	Y						
HPK1300335	C2	278	Y						
HPK1300336	C3	279							
HPK1300337	C1	280							
HPK1300338	C2	281							
HPK1300248	A4	282							
HPK1300249	C1	283	Y						
HPK1300339	C3	284							
HPK1300250	L1	285							
HPK1300251	C3	286							
HPK1300252	A3	287							
HPK1300253	A3	288							
HPK1300254	A3	289							
HPK1300255	A3	290	Y						
HPK1300256	C3	291							
HPK1300257	C1	292	Y						
HPK1300258	C1	293							
HPK1300259	C1	294							
HPK1300260	C3	295	Y						
HPK1300261	C3	296							

Table 3

PLAN #	PRICE TIER	PAGE	MATERIALS LIST	QUOTE ONE*	DECK	DECK PRICE	LANDSCAPE	LANDSCAPE PRICE	REGIONS
HPK1300262	A3	297							
HPK1300263	A2	298	Y						
HPK1300340	C2	299							
HPK1300341	C1	300							
HPK1300342	C2	301							
HPK1300264	C1	302							
HPK1300265	C1	303					OLA001	P3	123568
HPK1300266	C3	304	Y						
HPK1300267	C2	305	Y						
HPK1300268	A3	306	Y						
HPK1300269	C2	307	Y						
HPK1300270	A4	308	Y						
HPK1300271	A4	309							
HPK1300272	A3	310	Y	Y					
HPK1300273	C1	311	Y						
HPK1300274	A4	312	Y						
HPK1300275	A4	313	Y						
HPK1300276	A3	314	Y				OLA004	P3	123568
HPK1300277	A3	315	Y						
HPK1300278	C2	316	Y						
HPK1300279	C3	317							
HPK1300280	C3	318	Y						
HPK1300281	C1	319							
HPK1300282	A3	320							
HPK1300343	A3	321							
HPK1300283	C2	324	Y						
HPK1300284	C4	328							
HPK1300285	C4	329							
HPK1300286	C1	330							
HPK1300287	C1	331							
HPK1300288	C3	332							
HPK1300289	C1	333							
HPK1300290	C3	334	Y						
HPK1300291	C3	335	Y						
HPK1300292	A3	336	Y						
HPK1300293	C1	337	Y						
HPK1300294	C3	338							
HPK1300295	C3	339							
HPK1300296	C2	340							
HPK1300297	C1	341							
HPK1300298	C1	342							
HPK1300299	C1	343							
HPK1300300	C1	344	Y						
HPK1300301	C2	345	Y						
HPK1300302	C4	346							
HPK1300303	C3	347							
HPK1300304	C2	348	Y	Y					
HPK1300305	SQ1	349							
HPK1300306	A4	350							
HPK1300307	C1	351	Y						
HPK1300308	A3	352							
HPK1300309	C2	353							
HPK1300310	C1	354	Y						
HPK1300311	C1	355	Y						
HPK1300312	A4	356	Y						
HPK1300313	C1	357	Y						
HPK1300314	C1	358	Y						
HPK1300315	A4	359							
HPK1300316	C1	360	Y						
HPK1300317	C1	361	Y						
HPK1300318	C1	362							
HPK1300319	C4	363							
HPK1300320	C4	364							
HPK1300321	C2	365							
HPK1300322	C2	366							
HPK1300344	A3	367	Y						
HPK1300345	C1	368							
HPK1300346	A4	369	Y	Y			OLA024	P4	123568
HPK1300347	A4	370	Y	Y	ODA017	P2			
HPK1300348	A3	371	Y	Y			OLA004	P3	123568
HPK1300349	C4	372							
HPK1300350	L2	373	Y	Y	ODA009	P2	OLA011	P3	123568

GETAWAY HOMES
ISBN 1-931131-37-6

$11.95 (288 PAGES)

250 Home Plans for Cottages, Bungalows & Capes
This is the perfect volume for anyone looking to create their own relaxing place to escape life's pressures—whether it's a vacation home or primary residence! Also included, tips to create a comfortable, yet beautiful atmosphere in a small space.

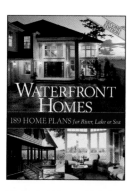

WATERFRONT HOMES
ISBN 1-931131-28-7

$10.95 (208 PAGES)

189 Home Plans for River, Lake or Sea
A beautiful waterfront setting calls for a beautiful home. Whether you are looking for a year-round home or a vacation getaway, this is a fantastic collection of home plans to choose from.

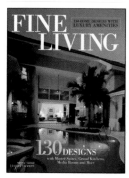

FINE LIVING
ISBN 1-931131-24-4

$17.95 (192 PAGES)

130 Home Designs with Luxury Amenities
The homes in this collection offer lovely exteriors, flowing floor plans and ample interior space, plus a stunning array of amenities that goes above and beyond standard designs. This title features gorgeous full-color photos, tips on furnishing and decorating as well as an extensive reference section packed with inspiring ideas.

Whether you are looking for a quaint cabin in the woods or a luxurious mansion on a rocky bluff, your perfect sanctuary is within reach with these collections from HomePlanners.

HANLEY WOOD CONSUMER GROUP
One Thomas Circle, NW, Suite 600, Washington, DC 20005

NLH1

This home is just 43 feet wide, but its wraparound porch and intelligent layout inside gives it the spacious feel of a much larger design. For details, see page 12.

©ALAN MASCORD DESIGN ASSOCIATES, INC. PHOTO BY BOB GREENSPAN